"GOING THERE BY RIDING YOUR BIKE MAKES YOU FEEL GREAT"

"As simply and naturally as breathing. Riding a bicycle restores your sense of proportion, makes you feel that you're part of the universe, that it and you are both doing your thing the right way.

"You can share in a marvelous freedom, no matter what the sum of your years is. You can do it—no matter how crowded your town's streets are, no matter how long since you dreamed you could fly, no matter how out-of-condition your muscles are or how new they are to bicycling. All it takes is a little wisdom, which other bicyclists are happy to share—that's why this book exists—and a little practice.

"Come, join the fun . . . get yourself onto a bike, out in the air, and *go!*"

BIBS McINTYRE was born in Chicago and is a graduate of the University of Chicago. Formerly in advertising, Mrs. McIntyre is now a free-lance writer living with her husband in New York City. She is a devoted and extremely competant bike-rider who believes that "no matter where or why you're going out, going there by bike makes you feel great."

THE
BIKE BOOK

*Everything You Need to Know
About Owning and Riding a Bike*

●

BIBS McINTYRE

▲

PYRAMID BOOKS　•　NEW YORK

Grateful acknowledgement is made:

For excerpts from AMERICAN YOUTH HOSTELS'
NORTH AMERICAN BICYCLE ATLAS by Warren
Asa, © Copyright 1969 American Youth Hostels, Inc.,
published by American Youth Hostels, Inc., 20 West
17th Street, New York, N.Y. 10011, and THE HOSTEL
GUIDE AND HANDBOOK, published by American
Youth Hostels, Inc. Reprinted by permission.

For the original photographs (excepting of the tricycle)
by Lester Kraus.

To Joyce Portnoy for the photograph of a tricycle appear-
ing on page 16.

To *Gene's Discount Bike Shop*, New York, New York,
and Harry K. Gerstle for the equipment and bicycles
used in the illustrations.

THE BIKE BOOK

A PYRAMID BOOK

Pyramid edition published August 1973

ISBN 0-515-03112-7

Library of Congress Catalogue Card Number 72-76968

Pyramid Books are published by Pyramid Communications, Inc.
Its trademarks, consisting of the word "Pyramid" and the por-
trayal of a pyramid, are registered in the United States Patent
Office.

Pyramid Communications, Inc., 919 Third Avenue, New York,
New York 10022

CONTENTS

The Bike Book

CHAPTER 1

Bicycling Offers the Happiest Promise Anyone Ever Made You

I DON'T REMEMBER how old I was when I got my first bicycle—a balloon-tired Pegasus if there ever was one—but I know for sure that until then I used to dream I could fly, and after that I didn't need to dream it: I *could* fly, on my bicycle. So could my next-younger brother, and we went everywhere our two-wheeled steeds could take us. Birds in the air were hampered, by comparison: they had to forage for insects and berries; all we had to do was be back from the library in time for supper. Or from wherever it was—the swamps of the Skokie, the Harbor Street Beach, the thrilling depths of the ravine that was three long towns away. In prairie-flat Illinois, a hill is worth riding to, even when it's a hill-in-reverse: in a ravine, first you go down, then labor up, and down-and-up we went, over and over, exultant in our freedom.

In 1966, the year of Mike Quill's famous subway strike, I was a grown-up; I had moved to New York and married; and my coaster-brake days were so far behind me I had almost forgotten what it was like to ride a bicycle. When my husband Jim insisted we give bicycles to each other as anniversary presents that cold February, I privately thought, "some present!" But I was wrong

1

and he was right, as we soon discovered. We got a whole new view of the crazy, complicated urban dilemma they call New York, and we did it with delicious, unhampered, unexpected freedom, all because we were riding bicycles.

No transit fares, no timetables, no "musts"—yet we got to places, discovered things we otherwise never would have seen. And had fun doing it. We didn't even get the sunstroke we deserved, walking our bikes across the Brooklyn Bridge to "ride over and see some friends" in Brooklyn Heights, in the blazing noon of the hottest Fourth of July I'll ever remember.

But our new freedom had a funny price. Jim seems to be a natural athlete, while I have been the last-chosen for any team (and its greatest handicap) ever since I started wearing glasses and still not hitting the balls, aged something like six. I'm about as athletic as Webster's English Dictionary. And, when we'd meet you at a party and both listen while Jim told uproarious tales of where we'd been and what we'd seen, I'd have died a couple of inner deaths before I revealed my own secret awful truth: we were doing all this on three-speed bicycles—yes, the only way—*but I was using only my lowest gear*. Anything more made me go faster than I thought I could stop. I was terrified of hills—up or down, little or big—and terrified of trucks, standing or moving. They were all so much bigger than me. And everything else that moved on the street seemed to know what it was doing, while I knew I did not.

Today that's all different, thanks to an innate stubbornness, the help of better bicyclists than me, and God's care when I got in a tight place. All those are available to you, too. Take it from a hundred-and-fifty-pound weakling: what I can do, you can do.

You can learn what to expect from traffic, learn to anticipate problems ranging all the way from the unlooking pedestrians who'll try to walk into you (repeatedly!) to the low-flying newspaper delivery trucks who'll cut you off at any corner, and prefer to do it after coming up from behind you first. Once you know what the problems *are*, you're about two-thirds of the way toward having them solved.

You'll discover for yourself how to use your gears and top your own hills. You may pant a bit at the top—I usually do—but you'll be flushed with triumph, too. And if you've been leading a sit-about life, more passive and less active than it should be, you'll feel for yourself how the exercise and yes, even the panting, are healthy things to do. You'll *feel* your lung capacity stretching and your circulatory system waking up. You'll like the feeling.

You'll discover that cyclists—you, and I, and some seventy-five million others like us in America today—are capable of behaving like responsible vehicles when we get out in that mass of moving traffic, knowing what to expect and what to do so that we can move with freedom like the rest, going farther afield than feet alone could ever take us, seeing and enjoying infinitely more than we would ever do through a car window—and then come safely, sanely, joyously skimming home, cheeks glowing, hair blowing, heart pounding with health and happiness.

That's what nobody can really make clear until it happens to you. No matter where or why you're going out, *going there by riding your bike makes you feel great*. As simply and naturally as breathing. Riding a bicycle restores your sense of proportion, makes you feel that you're a part of the universe, that it and you are both doing your thing the right way.

Simple competence is all too often lacking in our days, and it is a rare delight to do a difficult thing well. Bicycling is a glorious way to achieve that competence and that delight.

If that sounds too lyrical for you, you just don't know what you are missing. I'm as free on my bike today as when I was that child who thought bicycling was flying. Freer, in fact, because I have a better grasp of what it and I can and cannot do, what I must expect and watch out for—and I've got gears to help me do what my muscles once had to do by themselves.

You can share in this marvelous freedom, no matter what the sum of your years is. If you've reached the age of reason, you know enough to learn the rest; if you've been there a while, you're still not past your chance. You can do it—no matter how crowded your town's streets are, no matter how long since you dreamed you could fly, no matter how out-of-condition your muscles are or how new they are to bicycling. All it takes is a little wisdom, which other bicyclists are happy to share—that's why this book exists—and a little practice.

What's greatest about the whole idea is that you'll have fun with it from the very first moment you slip onto a bicycle saddle and discover you *can* balance. Even learning to ride is easier today: we share with you the most painless method ever invented. And as you go on having fun and riding more, you'll be doing good things for both your body and your brain (for doctors' testimonials to that, see page 150.) You'll also be helping decrease the pollution in a world so full of it that every little bit matters more than it ever did. As one ecology slogan puts it, "If you're not part of the solution, you're part of the problem." Come, join the fun, and be part of the solution; get yourself onto a bike, out in the air, and *go*!

You'll never be the same again.

And that's the happiest promise anyone ever made you.

CHAPTER 2

Which Bicycle is Your Best Bet?

WHEN YOU STAND in a big bicycle dealer's shop and look at all those gleaming chromium wonders, it's sure to seem as though there are millions of bicycles to choose from. Surely there are a million variables, when you consider wheel sizes, frame sizes and shapes, different weights, gearing and braking systems, touring or racing handlebars, pedals and saddles—and then count in the modifications most good dealers can supply: different gearing ratios, achieved with new hubs or sprockets; refinements in saddle-heights, carriers, light systems, bells and horns, as well as training wheels and tricycle conversion kits. It all adds up to one thing: you can have an incredibly personal bicycle today—so you need to know what's available, to make the best possible choices.

We still haven't mentioned, except by implication, differences between different manufacturers and different countries-of-origin. They add greatly to the confusion: the so-called "English racer" is currently being made well by the English, the French, the Italians, the Americans, and, lately, the Japanese; most of the bicycles referred to are *never* used or intended for racing. Moral: their names aren't going to be much help to you, even if we get them straight between us.

But surprisingly enough, whatever you buy or borrow

Fig. 1: **The bike most people start on: a coaster brake middleweight. Plump tires, also traditional, make even bumpy roads feel smoother.**

or rent falls into one of six main categories. Let's start with the bike a youngster usually learns on and loves.

1) *Middleweights* come in a multitude of wheel and frame sizes. A rugged ability to withstand punishment is their chief virtue, achieved at the cost of considerable weight (50 to 60 pounds). They usually have large, low-pressure tires, and coaster brakes—the *only* braking system that should be considered for any young beginner. It takes more strength than a youngster has to work handbrakes safely. Coaster brakes usually mean no gears, which is good; gear choices can be confusing and new cyclists who try to learn everything at once can be frustrated and upset.

Some smaller-frame middleweights offer what I call uni-sex styling, achieved oddly but usefully: the bar across the top is removable and replaceable. This is a good choice for several reasons: the bar can be removed *for learning* as well as for gender differences, and in the learning period the learner is a lot safer when he's able to reach the ground easily and directly.

Also, although the initial price may shock you, it's well worth it to buy a good bicycle. Amortized over the number of times it's used, you're getting a lot of value and workmanship for your money; and a good, fairly well cared for bicycle *always* has a trade-in or resale value. The cheaper hunk-of-junk will only fall apart and need replacement, with no benefit to anyone.

Middleweights are built to suit all sizes and all ages; wheel sizes range from 10 inches, 12 inches, and 14 inches, working up by 2 inch increments to the full adult size 26-inch wheel, with frame sizes ranging to match. In the smaller sizes, $20 to $40 is the price range of a well-made bike; larger ones run between $35 and $60.

2) *High risers* are utterly different from middleweights: shorter wheelbase, smaller wheels even on the bigger frame size, flashy high handlebars, and banana

Fig. 2: The high riser bike, which is definitely *not* designed for beginners, makes flashy riding almost dangerously easy.

seats make them instantly identifiable. *They are definitely not for beginners.* Those low, little wheels, the short wheelbase, everything about the design aims to help the rider make quick turns and perform show-off maneuvers. They are designed for "fun"—but what makes them sporty makes them tippy and hard to steer. Serious distance riders consider them adolescent and showy. If you must get one, get it without gears and with a coaster-brake; accident studies agree that gear levers or stick shifts, "sissy" handlebars and other protruberances can cause serious injury if you fall into or over them—and falls are the most frequent form of accident with this bike. High risers come in regular and long-boy frames; a good single-speed one costs between $40 and $100; geared models run higher for the same quality. When buying, make certain the handlebars do not rise above the user's shoulder height in a comfortable sitting position—or else balance will be extremely precarious.

Fig. 3: **The 3-speed lightweight responds beautifully, survives almost any road conditions and asks little in the way of upkeep—three of the many reasons for its worldwide popularity.**

3) *Lightweight three-speed* non-racing bicycles come in an incredible range of sizes and styles, all designed for riders who want speed and easy handling with endurance. They have narrow, higher-pressure tires, touring-style handlebars, and 3-speed in-the-hub gears. Price is fairly low: $50 to $95. Wheel size is usually 26 inches, on an 18-inch, 19½-inch, 21-inch, or 23-inch frame; occasionally you meet one with slightly smaller wheels. At the low end of the price range, you may not find all the frame sizes.

A well-made lightweight three-speed bicycle can come from anywhere, as pointed out before. And the good reason for its universal popularity is that it is a delightful bicycle, reasonably responsive, reasonably carefree, reasonably rugged. Just right for street bicycling anywhere in the world. It is not too delicate for everyday over-the-bumps-and-around-the-broken-glass riding, and it doesn't take half your weekend to oil and adjust just right. The simplicity of the gears alone (which leads to remarkable reliability) endears this bike to a wide spectrum of cyclists.

I am in love with mine, and it was inexpensive; little goes wrong with it, and that little is easily fixed; it stays unstolen when parked and locked, and I value that because I like to get around in the city and go *into* places when I've gotten to them. I believe, quietly but unshakeably, that ten-speed bikes on city streets are status symbols, pure and not-so-simple, for the large majority of their riders, and that for city use they are generally impractical and mechanically over-sophisticated, compared with three-speed models. But let's look at them all before we judge.

4) *Ten-speed derailleurs* (say it de-rail-ers as any dealer will) are the beauties made for racers and long distance cyclists. They are incredibly light; 18 to 23 pounds, as compared with the three-speed lightweight's 35 to 43 pounds, before accessories. To achieve this,

Fig. 4: A good 10-speed derailleur is king of bicycles—lightest, fastest, often best-built, too. Made for and treasured by racers and long-distance cyclists in very different models: This is a standard male frame, stripped of most weight-adding accessories.

the bike is stripped of everything "extra": mudguards and chainguards, plus obvious weight adders like kickstands, lights, and carriers. The gears are carefully arranged to give you ten or fifteen speeds, and are undoubtedly as wonderful going up a long hill as everybody who rides one says.

Some five-speed derailleurs exist, even a few six-speeds, modified from three-speed hubs; both are unusual and almost as expensive as ten-speed models.

Since the ten-speed classification includes racing, touring and city riding models, about which each owner seems to feel that his is the only kind anyone could really want, we need to make some differences clear.

City riding models usually have the most in weight-adding accessories—everything from generator powered lights to rat-trap carriers for attaché cases. Touring model owners tend to remove some accessories. Some say you don't need a kickstand; others clip water bottles and hand pumps to their frame, and save compensating weight by removing fenders and chain guards, then complain when they get spattered by mud or grease. The most experienced long distance pleasure riders say you're silly to do without either mud or chain guards and rat-trap carriers from which to sling saddle-bags. *They* save weight by never taking an unnecessary thing. Road racers are the ones who (to me, at least) go well beyond the normal limits in their concern about weight. Some even go so far as to drill holes in their frames, to make the bike weigh just that competitive little bit less; most dispense with guards, carriers, and often even lights.

True track racers are on an utterly different breed of bike, but belong to this group because, although they have direct drive only—no gears at all and no possibility of free-wheeling or coasting—their direct drive matches the top or tenth gear of a ten-speed bike. (If your gears go out-of-whack, three-speed or ten-speed, what you *always* have left is top gear, since gears are a means of getting more power out of the same pedaling motion by using it more slowly.) Also, track racing bikes, for weight reasons, have no brake. "What do they do when they *have* to stop?" I instantly wanted to know. "What if there's an accident in front of them, a pile-up of people and fallen bikes?" That brought up the story about the only American girl ever to win an Olympic medal for track racing. When she was asked the same question, she explained "It's easy. Since you have to run into something, I look for the biggest, softest looking guy in the pile and run into him. He can probably take it best, and you get hurt a lot less that way."

Good ten-speed derailleurs are being made in America, England, France, Italy and Japan. Price slopes sharply up from around $100; for $150 or so, you can have a basic bicycle adapted quite astonishingly to your personal preference and physique by a good bicycle dealer. The seat can be made much higher or lower; handlebars of your choice, racing or touring, angled as you prefer; for saddle, either the narrow racing sort or the wider sprung one; pedals offer a wide range of choices, usually with toe-clips; you can even have the gear levers moved up. (That's a sensible idea for city riders; if you're bent over your handlebars in the low racer's position, crouched against the wind of your own progress, gears where they are, are okay; if you're sitting up more, looking around for traffic movement and pedestrians, it's a long look down to change gears.) At the upper price levels, you may specify not only style but the makers of the parts you like; made-to-order derailleurs are put together from scratch for you, with the best brazed frames, the best "Campy" gears and hubs (that's for Campagnolo) unless you like Simplex or Huret better, plus your choice of a wide variety of tire weights and tread designs in either clincher (with tubes) or sewn-up (tubeless) tires. Most ultralightweights have 27-inch wheels; frames are often but not always made in the high-bar "male" models; sizes vary sharply with the

Fig. 5: The 10-speed that men or women can ride with equal ease is this "mixte" frame made only by Peugot; city riders and many distance ones would add mudguards and chain guards, lights and accessories to this stripped model of the bike.

maker but tend toward the tall side. One maker's progression is 20½, 21⅝, 22⅞, 24, and 25½ inches; others make only the 22½-inch, or just 21½ and 23½ inches. The smallest frame size is 19 inches, and is not always available. You can, of course, always have even the frame made to order, which runs around $350 before you start adding any other parts. Depending on your choices among all the tempting variables, you pay from $350 to $450 for the best ultralightweights—not including import taxes.

The great frame strength of the male-model high-bar ten-speed or three-speed bicycle was always based on either the diamond-frame design or a triangular variant of it. But often the high-bar has gotten in the rider's way. Now the Peugeot people are making a marvelous crossbreed, a ten-speed derailleur bicycle built on what they call the "mixte" frame, which can be ridden by either sex in safety and comfort. As you see, the triangle is still there, so only a little strength is sacrificed. They make it in two ten-speed versions: one (shown) stripped to minimal weight; the other city-planned model, heavier than a racer only because of its accessories, but much more useful *in cities* because of them. It has strong clincher tires instead of the sewn-up lightweights; touring handlebars instead of the down-curving type racers crouch over; and it's complete with light, rat-trap carrier, mudguards and chainguards. When they come out with a three-speed version, that'll be the one I'll sigh for—for I believe this is the bike of the future, with a frame that's strong enough for anything but shaped so anybody can use it comfortably.

5) *Folding bikes and pull-aparts* offer a solution to the hemmed-in apartment dweller's problem of how to have a bike and live with it in a restricted space. They differ greatly, but most pull-aparts are regular models modified to include some pull-apart and reconnect mechanism built into the framing.

Fig. 6: **This is how a pull-apart bike looks when put together and ready to ride . . .**

Fig. 7: **. . . and this is how it pulls apart for storage in close quarters.**

The majority of fold-ups fold in half; one group with a full-size frame has 18-inch or 20-inch wheels, runs from $40 to $100. The Moulton-type has 16-inch wheels with a low bar and ingeniously folds down into less than

Fig 8: Another close quarters solution, the fold-up bike takes incredibly little storage room but weighs a fair amount, takes a lot of energy to pedal.

half. It's a lot heavier than you expect when you look at it, like most fold-ups(well over 40 pounds), and those little wheels mean you pedal more for every mile you travel. Considerably more. If you want exercise, that's a plus; if you're tired or in a hurry, it's a minus. It runs $80 to $90.

One imported fold-up comes in a lightweight, multi-geared model with standard-size 26-inch wheels. It costs a lot—$110 or more—but seems to make its owners very happy.

All pull-aparts and fold-ups have to have some connecting and locking device in their middles, and this is their weak spot. Here you probably get exactly what you pay for, and the danger of inefficient engineering is that your bike can fold up or come apart while you're riding, usually when you're making a turn. This produces or invites disaster, so investigate carefully any model you're considering. Also investigate how to be *sure* you're properly locked-into-position for riding; it's not always clear. One good foreign model has a generator on the rear wheel; just by turning your lights on, you see (as the front light lights) that all connections are made and all systems are "go."

6) *The adult tricycle:* its current popularity would astonish you. Clever people have made up their own versions, out of various parts, with varying results— others buy them ready made or have them made to order from kits that alter any standard three-speed. All enjoy a steadiness, safety, and ability to carry things that two-wheelers don't offer.

Fig. 9: The adult tricycle is tricky to "corner" but easy to ride otherwise. You can order it whole; convert a 3-speed with a kit; or make up your own.

The easiest to pedal is one made from a conversion kit that adds about $60 to the cost of the three-speed bicycle you choose. There are also at least two pre-built American brands, one sturdy but heavy and slow, the other tippy, unreliable, and alarmingly difficult to steer or stop. Be warned: investigate *thoroughly* anything you plan to buy, with an owner of a similar model or a reliable dealer, before you purchase. Prices for good pre-built tricycles run around $125; some sell as low as $85, some as high as $175.

The seventh and rarest category is the *tandem*, as in the famous song, "The Bicycle Built for Two." It's often a mistake for both of you. Don't ever buy one unless a) you're an experienced rider and so is your partner, b) you tend to think alike about when to press forward, when to hold back, and such decisions, and c) you both *know* you want one. They look easy, but they are very difficult to handle, and the doubled weight factor of two riders gives you a momentum, particularly downhill, that changes small hazards into bigger ones very quickly. Steering a tandem is harder, so is pedaling—the front rider must be really strong and steady. If you do want one, they come in heavy, medium, and lightweights, with only the lightweight suitable for long distance riding. Even that doesn't "pack" as much as two lightweights could, separately. American-made tandems cost between $90 and $120 and weigh a lot; a few ten-speed lightweights from Italy or France are available at costs between $200 and $275.

But if your heart is set on a tandem, don't let me naysay you out of it; there are clubs of people who ride only tandems, and reportedly they have a splendid time of it. Maybe you would too. I seriously doubt that you would if you didn't know exactly what you were getting into and onto, however.

One final rarity that deserves only a mention here is the *unicycle*. Since this is a bicycle book, they're literally outside our province. But you may wish to know they exist, and are ridden with surprising skill and ease by some people. I'm even told there's a whole town where the teenagers snub anyone who rides anything else.

You may also wish to know that falling off of them is considerably more frequent than with a bi- or tri-cycle, and could be more dangerous, since you're generally falling from higher up. The pedals center on the one wheel, and the seat is on a (moveable) vertical directly above the wheel's middle, when properly ridden; there are no handlebars or other steering mechanisms beyond your own balance. I can't imagine this construction would lend itself either to good gearing or easy steering. If a unicycle tempts you, I strongly urge that you learn to ride on a rented or borrowed one, so you can change your mind before making any financial commitment— and I, personally, would up my insurance, perhaps I'm just chicken.

Now: How Do You Choose?

The major elements in the decision are 1) what will you use it for? 2) who will take care of it when something goes wrong? and 3) where will you put it?

What will you use it for? brings to mind my father and his horse—a horse he loved and rode joyously for many years, until she died. Then he had to get a new horse. The stable people looked around, found him a beauty, and got it for him against spirited bidding. But when he started to ride his new horse, the horse had one more gait than Daddy knew; my four-gaited father had to go back to school, unlearn a lot of old habits, and learn afresh how to use his five-gaited horse. He's glad now that he did—but there was a while in there . . .

The transition from his horse to your decision about a bicycle is obvious: do you lead a three-speed life or a ten-speed life? Should you have hand brakes or coaster brakes? What do you want your bike to help you to do? How complicated must it be to give you that help? And if it is complicated, can you give it the care, attention, even the technical understanding and adjustment it needs to perform well? If you haven't the room, the equipment, the time, or the know-how to solve these problems yourself, have you the money to buy your way out of the difficulties ahead? And, when you're making your equation of what's worth what to you, have you any overpowering reason (such as being elderly, which is a good reason to want all the help that multiple gears can give) that would justify extra time, trouble, and expense?

"Racers aren't the only ones who need ten-speeds, Bibs," one rider told me firmly. "I'm only middle-aged, but with my previous bike, I felt like a pokey old lady. A ten-speed is the real secret for those who are not muscularly gifted. Really. If you can walk across the room, you can ride this bike—happily."

She's absolutely right: ten-speeds are very easy to propel. Which brings us back to the root question. Why are you riding, and what can the bike contribute? Are you out just to be in the air? To get somewhere quickly? Are you riding for exercise? Are you building up to long trips you'd like to take on your bicycle?

If you're a Sunday rider, or a daily rider who's willing to push a little more weight around in exchange for more ruggedness and less trouble from your bike, or a newcomer to the world of bicycling, I am sure you'll be happier on a three-speed lightweight for many years and for many reasons. Three-speeds stand up well to the bumps and jars of street riding without constant delicate readjustments. They're easier to learn to operate, and simpler controls give you less to be confused by if you get into a tense traffic situation. Their gears offer you a great deal of help, enough to top most hills when you learn to use them right and get into condition; and, unless you live in a terribly hilly area, they're all you really need. Most ten-speed riders, cycling on city streets, ride in a gear that gives them the same middle speed as the middle or normal speed on a three-speed bicycle. Finally, your initial outlay and your upkeep costs are both usually sharply lower. An additional reason to choose three-speed over ten-speed involves its actual financial value to a thief; if you don't yet own a bike and you're deciding between those two types, by all means read the suggestions, pages 78-79, on how to make your bike less tempting to anyone who might wish to steal it.

If you plan to race, or tour extensively, and still do some street riding in city or suburbs, obviously you go for broke and get the best ten-speed model you can afford and your dealer can service. Because—and don't fool yourself—it'll need a lot of servicing, by you or by him, to stay in good running condition if you ride it a lot on streets as they are today. Also consider getting two sets of wheels for your ten-speed. Sewn-up tires and clincher tires can't be alternated on the same wheel, but you can have a pair of wheels with heavier tires for street conditions, and another with lighter ones for long distance and country riding or sewn-up ones for actual racing, depending on your preference. It's a lot quicker to slip two wheels in and out than to change two tires.

If you are elderly, or not muscularly gifted, by all means follow my friend's advice and consider a street-model ten-speed derailleur; here, ease-of-effort will probably more than repay the greater trouble the bike is likely to have. Or consider adapting a three-speed into a steady-going tricycle.

A crowded apartment, or a plan to take your bike in a car to a jumping-off point and cycle from there, could lead you to choose a fold-up bike. You might do better to investigate simple, home-made or purchased racks that let you put as many as three or four bikes atop a car as little as a Volkswagen; check for information under the Bicycle Institute of America, in the *Where to Learn*

More chapter, page 247.

* * *

Once you know what you're looking for, don't take anybody's word for anything—go rent some somewhere.
If you live in a big city, it should be easy. If your town is small, keep watching until you find someone else who owns the sort you like. Offer some reasonable security and reasonable compensation, and see if he or she won't let you rent it for an afternoon, a day, or a weekend. Just understand that the person who already owns the bike will (a) want to tell you all about it, enthusiastically, while, if they don't know you, they'll be wondering (b) is he a thief, and is this some new con-game? You would, too, with an expensive, covetable bicycle. Act accordingly.

As a matter of fact, if you're undecided about the *type* that suits you best, renting could also help solve your problems. There is only one thing to remember if you rent a bike that is available for public use: it may well be beaten up by the traffic it's borne, and not even adjusted to be as responsive as such a bike, owned by one owner, would be. Don't damn them all because of a single bad experience; if you find defects, check with people who own such a bike.

Once you've made up your mind about type, check into the dealer situation and begin comparing various manufacturers' models available in your town. Here we come to a time-consuming job many of you will want to skip, but it's as important to your final happiness with your bicycle as it would be in the purchase of a car, or any major appliance. More so, probably, since bicycles can be so much more personal in the way they fit *to you*. Makers differ astonishingly in what they splurge on and what they skimp on to sell at similar price levels; models from the same maker can also show surprising differences. Often, for a little less money, you get a lot less bicycle. Alternatively, you may pay a lot for a benefit that you don't particularly value. Ask questions until you understand. But pick a reasonable time for your questioning, when the dealer or his men aren't too busy to answer.

Whatever make and model you pick, remember that *dealerships are local,* and the representative of the manufacturer in your town, or a town nearby, is the man you'll be dealing with for the life of the bike.

While every manufacturer will stand behind his product, it's often difficult or time-consuming to try to reach the manufacturer yourself, so, for all practical purposes, *the manufacturer's guarantee is only as good as your dealer will make it.* Look him over while you're looking the models over. Ask about them, but watch and listen to him. See how he treats customers with complaints. Watch how well he fits a new bicycle to its new owner. The atmosphere of the place will tell you a lot; I don't mean shiny paint or fancy show-windows; I mean, literally, the sounds of the voices you hear. If you hear a lot of arguing, I suggest you shop somewhere else.

One last word about dealers: when they're good, they're very very good. That's why it pays *not* to go to a discount-supermarket-department store sort of quick-sale outlet where you will get "the same bike for ten . . . twenty . . . thirty dollars less than . . ." In the first place, maybe it is the same bike and maybe it isn't; unless you're truly expert, it's easy to be fooled.

Far more important, *buying the correct size frame for you* is a matter for experts, not percentage-happy clerks who expect never to see you again. A good dealer can almost do it by eye. A department store clerk may not even bring out the size you ask for, and while you may know what you need, and have specified the size correctly, if you don't triple-check you may well go home with something else. It's a headache, all around, in those places.

Even the best chart showing frame size in relation to height is only an approximation: you have to check it out with your foot, your knee, your tip-toe's reach. And that's the final, overwhelming reason to buy from a bicycle dealer. There, you can sit on the bike, feel if it fits, watch how it's adjusted until it *does* fit. If you're still growing, he'll know if you need the next size now, or if you're better off getting a longer stem to your saddle and keeping everything manageable on a smaller-frame bike. (Oversized bicycles, in relation to what a youngster can handle easily, contribute largely to accidents that the youngest groups of bike riders have.)

Be aware, ahead of time, that a good dealer may not let you ride the bike around the block — a common request. His refusal may sound unreasonable, until you start figuring (a) how many riders would just vanish with a free new bike? and (b) he would soon have a stockroom full of used bicycles, just from having them all ridden around the block so many times. Which would *you* want to buy—a really-new one, or one that has been around the block a lot? There's his answer, and yours, if he refuses.

But he will not only help you select the bike and fit it to your size and bike-riding plans; he's also certain to adjust things for you if something turns out to need it, within a reasonable period. This alone is worth its weight in money-saving three-day-only offers. But, add to it: when and if something does go wrong, he's there, you take the bike to him, and you and he talk about it, face to face.

If you've bought it at a discount-outlet's sale, they have no bicycle expert staff to help you; the best they can offer is to send it back to the manufacturer and get it fixed. How long do you think that would take? And if the problem's delicate, something you can't put your finger right on, only explain by "it feels strange when I do such-and-such"—how accurately do you suppose it can be diagnosed and treated, after going through all those channels, no matter how good the manufacturer's staff is?

* * *

Before you buy, there's still one more important question: *Where Will You Put It?* There's always somewhere! Axiomatically, the easier it is to get your bike out, the oftener you will use it. Storage possibilities include everything from hanging it on the wall as "pop art" to hanging four, around the walls of a garage, on laundry hooks. Mine sits under the stoop, in the city, behind a locked gate; not optimum, because weather gets at it, but easy to get out. Eight to ten inches will clear most parts of most bikes except the pedal width and the handlebars, if you store it in riding position. If your front-to-back space is small, turning the front wheel at right angles shortens overall length, but then needs greater width.

Cellars, sheds, outbuildings, front halls — all work. Even a bedroom that's near the front or back door. Or, do you have a back porch? Weather protection and thief protection must both be considered. Obviously, if you have a garage, you have it made. But if you don't, perhaps you know someone who does, who'd rent you some garage space? Again, lock–ability becomes important—not just of the garage, but inside it, since your neighbor may leave the garage door open when you don't expect it.

Do remember tires should *not* spend a whole winter sitting on one part of themselves. I strongly recommend hanging from hooks, or at least turning the wheels occasionally. The best suggestion is that you *ride* in good weather, or even half-good. You'd be surprised how it cheers you to go biking in January. Unless you have a good working blizzard or its remnants on the streets, it's usually possible to bike quite safely almost all the year round. Dress in layers, so you can subtract clothing warmth as you warm up, and enjoy!

What About Brand Names? What About Imports?

Personally, in buying a bicycle I believe it's the dealer who is more important to you than the brand name, and that he's likely to have more than one kind or even price-level of bicycle that could make you very happy for many years. In any case *you* will be a better judge *for yourself* of what you like than anyone else could ever be. The brand name offers you one kind of security, if you're in doubt; the dealer, another. Often, you can combine the two. If you can't, trust your instincts about the quality of the object you're being offered, and the honesty of the man offering it. After that, trying it, riding it, feeling it on your street and up your hill makes all the difference. If you're not happy then, go back to the dealer and talk about it; maybe it isn't adjusted right, after all. But my suspicion is, if he's a good dealer, you'll have a good bike, and you won't need to go back. You may even go back *before* anything's really wrong, because you like the man. Bicycling seems to attract the nicest sorts of enthusiasts, and dealers are no exception to this rule.

On the American vs. import question, anything anyone believes seems to be *dis*believed equally strongly by another, equally informed person. I have tried to determine the *logic* of people's choices—*reasons* why one is to be preferred over another. My conclusion is that it's not a choice people make on logic. Anything but, it seems. Identical facts are viewed quite differently by different people, and cited to prove exactly opposing views. One man's must, easily-available replacement parts, is canceled by another's "but then everyone has the same thing you do!"; one person's patriotism, another's snob-appeal, are simply opinions about where the bike was built—not necessarily the maker, the model, or the special design features involved. And true bike buffs enjoy long, happy, and quite fruitless discussions of the merits of a given maker's parts, models, or styling; whatever's said during the talk changes no one's mind, usually —so it's all back to what your opinion is.

The clearest summary of the whole picture came from a dealer who also rents bikes (not too usual a combination): "Why buy American bikes? Lady, they *last*. I can rent out a ten-speed Schwinn and it won't drop dead. A ten-speed Peugeot wouldn't last a week under rental traffic. Renters *murder* a bike." Pause, while we looked at the two in silence. Then he sighed: "But that Peugeot—she's a *beauty*!"

Substitute any good American name or any good foreign one, at will, and there you have just about all the *facts* you'll get. The only possible generalities are that as a rule of thumb, the American model of almost anything will be somewhat heavier, somewhat more durable, and somewhat easier to get parts for.

If You're Buying a Second-Hand Bike

Some of them are among the best buys ever offered, and some are sure lemons. Don't be misled by a bright, shiny appearance. Ask the history, if you're buying from an individual, and the reason for selling. If you're buying from a dealer, ask what sort of guarantee he'll give. Look for signs of misuse—any bent parts, wrinkles in the paint (they mean the metal has been bent, or bent-and-then-unbent, underneath). Look for anything that indicates how it has been treated, or abused: nicks in the paint are normal, but is there rust underneath? Are the brake blocks worn to a nub? Is there much tread left on the tires, or are they new ones? Do the wheels spin easily, when you lift the front or back off the floor (always check both); do the brakes grab, when you squeeze them, if they're hand brakes?

Always have a second-hand bike given "the works"

by a competent mechanic. If you buy it from a dealer, that should be included in his price. If you buy from an individual, the presumably lower price allows for it. *Everything* should be carefully checked out, and *any*thing badly worn should be replaced—rubber parts such as brake blocks, inner tubes and tires are especially likely to need replacement.

Whatever bike you buy, you're buying it for enjoyment, and to that end, *don't take it into traffic until you and it are used to each other.*

If you're using your first bike, check out our easy way to learn in Chapter Ten. If you already know how to ride but haven't ridden in a while, be sure to brush up on the rules of the road also in Chapter Ten. If you're changing from one bicycle type to another, it is particularly important you practice where people and cars can't disturb your new relation to gears you're not accustomed to or brake levers in unfamiliar places. And if you're a two-wheel rider learning to ride a tricycle, the balancing act and cornering are disturbingly different at first, and take time to become automatic reactions.

Learn in peace, get used to each other, and enjoy!

CHAPTER 3

A Guided Tour of Your Pride and Joy— Plus Possible Extras for More Fun, More Safety

THIS TOUR begins with your handlebars and the attachments usually found on them, and works around the bike approximately clockwise. You will find all kinds of information here, so even if you know your bike well, it's worth checking through.

When you start planning what you do and don't want to fix yourself, or what you want a professional to do and you need to know how to describe ailing parts of your bike, check back to this chart for their proper names. In fact, you can use this chart with the close-up ones of adjustments and functioning parts, in Chapter Nine, to know **exactly** where you are and what you are doing.

Bell or **horn** must be audible 100 feet away; sirens or whistles are usually illegal, always to be avoided since they confuse non-riders.

Light: White light for after-dusk riding is legal must; needs to be visible 500 feet in front of you. Battery or generator models available.

Touring handlebars curve up from the head tube.

Brake levers mount just under grips for easy reach on this style bar. (**Racing handlebars** usually turn down from top of head tube, to offer crouched rider several hand positions. Not shown here.)

Gear-control levers come in two styles: above-the-bar, as shown, simpler to operate, or a turn-the-whole-grip kind; each, on three-speed bike, offers three forward gears.

Head tube, or front column of the bike, as it goes down turns into the **front fork,** into which the front wheel fits. The **headset** is the usual description of the total unit —fork bearings and general front of the frame.

Wheel nuts hold wheel **hub** between forks; should be checked periodically for proper tightness. Inside them, at each end of the axles, are the **cones.**

Brakes, front and rear; good three-speed bikes use side-pull caliper brakes; ten-speed derailleurs, which go faster, need center-pull brakes.

Wheel rims are where brakes grip; keep wax and oil away from them at all times. Should be perfect circles, rarely are. If dented or seriously out of true, take at once to a good repairman.

Spokes connect wheel rims to hubs—each should be equally tight to keep wheel perfectly centered. Forty rear-wheel spokes and thirty-two front is good measure for lightweight bike; some ultralightweights have thirty-six front and back. Where wheel is less than 24 inches, twenty-eight spokes apiece is *minimum* for adequate strength.

Tires: vary greatly according to bicycle type. Wide, low-pressure 1⅝-inch tires go with one-speed coaster-brake bikes; three-speed bikes usually have narrower inner-tube style "clincher" tires, pressured between (usually) 40 and 80 pounds per square inch; long distance riders use lighter clincher tires; racers use inner-tubeless "sewn-up" tires, lightest of all, most subject to flats, but quick to change.

Pedals and **pedal cranks** hang from the bottom bracket.

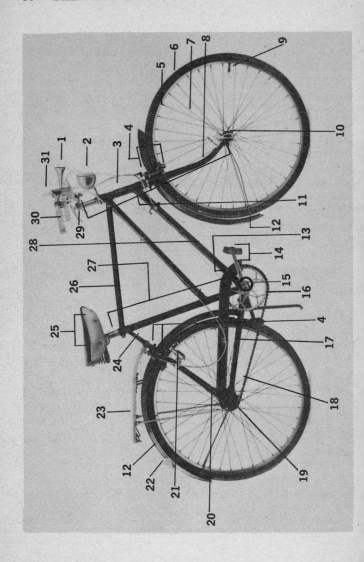

Fig. 10: This is a 3-speed lightweight, but the parts are keyed to match similar parts on most other bicycle models:

1. Bell or Horn
2. Light
3. Head Tube
4. Brakes
5. Wheel-rims
6. Tires
7. Spokes
8. Front Fork
9. Tire Valve
10. Wheel Nuts

11. Headset
12. Fenders (Mudguards)
13. Chain Guard
14. Pedals and Pedal-cranks
15. Bottom Bracket
16. Chain Wheel
17. Chain Stays
18. Chain

19. Rear Wheel-hub
20. Rear Fork
21. Generator
22. Reflector
23. Rat-trap Carrier
24. Seat Stays
25. Saddle
26. Top Tube

27. Seat Tube
28. Down Tube
29. Brake Levers
30. Touring Handlebars
31. Gear Control Levers

They revolve around the large **chain wheel;** its size helps determine the gearing levels of your bike.

Down tube meets **seat tube** at **bottom bracket;** hand pump or water bottles frequently mount here for long distance riding; also brake cables, and generator wires if you have them.

Tire valve: where you put air into tire; correct air pressure usually stamped on tire wall; hand pump does best job. Many tire leaks occur where valve enters tire tube— check here first if your tire goes slowly flat.

Chain: dirtiest part of any bike, but the one without which your energy wouldn't create forward movement. Transfers pedaled power into wheel movement through gears in rear wheel hub or derailleurs. (On a ten-speed derailleur bike, this is where you'll find the rear sprockets and ratchet [the freewheel part of the gearing system that lets you pedal backward without going backward, or not pedal at all and still move forward] plus the intricate system of jockey rollers, tension rollers, and adjusting screws that let you change from one sprocket to another and thus change your gearing ratio; none of this is shown here.)

Chain stays hold back wheel in correct relation to front chain wheel; **chain guard** helps keep some dirt off you, and your clothing out of the chain.

Rear wheel hub houses coaster-brake on one-speed bikes (they stop by backpedaling, need no hand lever); or three-speed gears, freewheel and gearing adjustments on three-speed bikes.

Seat stays, as they go down, often support fenders and carriers, then become **rear fork** to hold sprockets, hub, and rear wheel.

Seat tube supports saddle; with top tube and down tube, forms strong triangle of support to distribute your weight evenly, one-third on the seat, one-third on pedals, one-third on handlebars.

Reflector or **rear light,** usually attaches to rear fender, is always red, must legally be *working* and visible 300 feet behind you.

Rat-trap carrier should *bolt* to frame and rear axle; is best all-around choice for general carrying, because rear-located and most versatile. Should *never* carry a person, however, as handlebars should *never*—bikes (except tandems) can't take it, cyclists can't control it.

Fenders or **mudguards**—useful protection, and a good place to apply reflective tape for night-riding visibility.

Saddle: sprung style for general riding, narrow and un-sprung for racing. See page 102 for how to set to your proper height and arm-reach.

Top tube—the high bar of the usual "male model" bicycle.

WHICH EXTRA EQUIPMENT WOULD YOU REALLY USE?

It's a tough question, because it varies not only from individual to individual, but from time to time with the same individual. Oddly enough, you don't usually get much of a price break for taking a highly-gadgeted bicycle model, as compared with getting the same thing without the gadgets and then adding them later. With one or two major exceptions, which we'll take up first, the soundest advice is, wait, learn your riding habits, and then buy.

Legally, you have to have a red reflector or tail-light on the rear of your bike; if you ride at night, or even at dusk, you have to have a white front light, visible 500 feet in front of you, and, day or night, you have to have a bell or horn that's audible at a distance of 100 feet.

Bells and horns can get about as fancy and as expensive as you wish them to, but that can make them less effective than simpler warning devices. Sirens, whistles, and other such noise-makers are illegal almost anywhere, and are a bad idea, since they confuse both motorists and pedestrians. I like the ordinary bell (cost $1) that *sounds* like a bicycle bell; even in noisy traffic, it is a distinctive and generally audible sound; pedestrians react well to it. I suggest you get that, and save the extra money to spend where it makes more difference.

That may well be for a generator-operated front-and-rear light set. They cost upward of $5; lights mount where you'd expect them to, and, in addition a tiny on-off gadget attaches near the back wheel. You flip it on as you need it, to take power directly from your wheel, as you pedal. This means you're never without a working light if darkness overtakes you—a real advantage. There can be some drag to your riding; most riders consider it to be minor. It also means your initial investment is *it* —no more money for replacement batteries, new lights.

Fig. 11: These parts, plus their connecting wires, generate light any time you need it from your own pedal-power; no batteries to wear out or replace.

If you assume you'll *never* ride at night, consider, for emergencies do arise, installing an inexpensive mounting clip that holds an ordinary flashlight in position on your handlebars. You should always have both hands on the handlebars, so you couldn't *carry* a light, if you needed to go out at night.

* * *

If you're part of a bicycling family, it's important you investigate and get a good child seat if you ever plan to carry a child on your bike. You know, of course, that it's terribly dangerous to carry another person *without* a special seat (unless you're both on a tandem).

1) It *must* have some sort of foot-shield, so the child can't kick an innocent foot—or a tired foot, or an angry foot—into your spokes, injuring his foot and turning you both over.

2) It should be a rear-mount, and bolt to both the frame and the rear axle of the bike; nothing else is so safe for you both.

3) Your dealer must know *before* you purchase your bike that you plan to add such a seat—not all models can take them. It's not only expense that matters here; sometimes it's the costlier lightweights that have no support to bolt to safely.

4) It should be well made and sturdy, and have some sort of hold-in straps. For small babies, you do better using the harness from your baby carriage, but as the child grows, he'll need the straps.

5) IT SHOULD NOT BE USED TO CARRY A CHILD MUCH UNDER TWO OR OVER FIVE. Below two years, most children are unpredictably wriggly, and usually bored by the whole expedition—which makes them wrigglier, and difficult for the rider to cope with. Much over five, the child adds more weight than you can safely put onto one bicyclist's energies or steering capacities; also, he's likely to want to exercise for himself, rather than just sit there.

Good child seats run about $10 to $15; if you bolt one to the rear of your bike, of course, it means you cannot have a rat-trap carrier in the same place, so you'll need to plan carefully how you carry anything else besides the child.

* * *

My rat-trap carrier, and two or three of those elastic French hook-at-each-end sandows, are the joys of my life—and if you're not carrying children about, a good rat-trap carrier which bolts to the rear of your bike is the extra I'd recommend you get right away. Spend enough to get a sturdy one—they're only about $4 to $6, and worth every penny. A rat-trap carrier is infinitely variable in its usefulness.

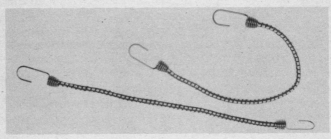

Fig. 12: Stretchy elastic sandows hook almost any size or shape bundle firmly and safely onto your rat-trap carrier: I couldn't bike without mine.

I've carried everything on the back of mine: newspapers, groceries, laundry, live cats in a cat-carrier; even a standard office typewriter, once—using a combination of the rat-trap carrier and sandows. I couldn't live without sandows. You'll soon find you can't, too.

The typewriter was a mistake, because it weighed so much I was easily thrown off balance by any slight swerve I had to make for pavement faults; bringing it home from the repair shop I had learned better, and I sandowed it onto the bike but *walked* the bike home. The funniest thing I ever put on a bike was a ten-foot Christmas tree, and there wasn't room to ride if I'd wanted to try. But, tied to the handlebars and the seat, it made a tidy, well-wheeled bundle and I walked it happily my twenty blocks home, amid much cheery laughter from pedestrians and motorists. I certainly couldn't have carried it, so that was a good way to manage, but it did look odd.

The most dangerous thing I ever carried caused a terrifying ride, and I'll share it with you so you'll know better than I did. I had purchased a special light to grow plants indoors—a four-foot-long fluorescent lampholder, accompanied by two slender, fragile, four-foot special bulbs. I asked the man to wrap it well, and please to give me some extra rope, as I was going to put it on my bike. He used brown paper sparingly, was stingy with the rope, and gave me a very funny look as I carried my bundle out. My plan was to rope it to the carrier and let it stick out behind—I'd even brought a red bandanna. That plan didn't work—the package and the carrier didn't coincide in the right places. And I was three and a half traffic-filled miles from home. So I tied it across my handlebars and prayed. My sense of how wide a space I needed was shot; my balance varied from poor to wretched; with all that weight forward, a slight turn of the handlebars produced a great wobble; I kept expecting, every time a car went by, I'd hear the bulbs break, because the wrapping paper made it hard to see the package, even in full sunlight—and nobody knew I was in trouble but me. Dumb, dumb, dumb. I made it, but I didn't deserve to. Make it your rule, as it now is mine—*if something won't fit securely on your rat-trap carrier, don't take it on your bike*.

My exception to the rule is when I'm carrying light, non-bulky things. I have three canvas "tote" bags, and I use them to carry all sorts of bundles, hung from my handlebars. Balanced weights make steering easier, so I usually balance the tote-bag, on the left, by hanging my purse on the right. *Just don't get things tangled into your brake cables*. We had a cat who used to love to ride that way, even to the vet's: she stood in the tote-bag and viewed the world. Loud, sudden traffic noises made her duck her head into the bag, but it was soon up again, sniffing curiously, watching intently. Not all cats, of course, would take to such a trip, and a leash attached to their collar and your wrist makes the situation less risky. But if you have an animal who hates his carrier . . .

Fig. 13: Open and in working position, this is the sort of hand tire pump that clips onto many bikes. The dark flexible connecting tube simply slips into the end opposite to where it's now attached for storage when not in use.

Two other extras I recommend you own from the beginning are a tire pump you work by hand (unless one comes attached to your bike) and the tire pressure gauge that tells you how much air you've actually pumped into the tire.

Hand pumps range in price and style, from the simple toe-hold ones that cost $3 to $5, to the same kind with a pressure gauge for about $10, to the sort that are made to clip onto a good import ultralightweight, that either cut or add $3 to $6 to the cost of the bike. These can be baffling, when you first unhook one; it should look like Fig. 13 when ready to pump.

The tire-pressure gauge looks rather like an architect's tool, or a special drafting pencil; it's really two metal tubes that work like an expandable curtain rod, one part inside the other extending out as far as the air pressure pushes it. You read the figure, and you know. It only costs about $2 to $3.

*　　*　　*

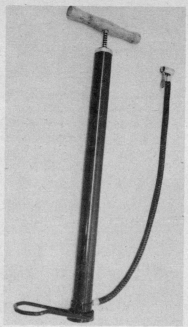

Fig. 14: The home or garage model tire pump is held in position with your foot while pumping. Some of the more expensive models include pressure gauges. It's important to learn to attach either a hand or foot pump to your tire's valve quickly. Doing it slowly lets air escape, makes for extra pumping.

The kind of extra to wait and get later is something like a speedometer. It may look exciting in the store, but in the street, it's hardly worth its weight. Unless you're a real whiz, you're hardly likely to go faster than 15 mph even with a healthy tailwind—and below that, differences aren't likely to matter much. On the other hand, a tiny, inexpensive odometer—a mileage measurer—can tell you things you might really want to know, especially if you plan to use your bike in a regular exercise program. At around $2.50, it's a great add-later item. (It's fault, if it has one, is a tiny, regular click; if you're already a distance cyclist, the click can annoy you, and you've probably got such a good mileage sense you don't need either gadget.)

Fig. 15: A real tire saver, this tire-pressure gauge lets you know tire-pressure accurately: learn to judge it from facts. It may also keep you from blowing tube *and* tire at a gas station air pump.

Front baskets are almost universally chosen by beginning cyclists, who don't realize how putting extra weight high, and in front, complicates your steering; if you want one, make sure it's easily removable; I believe you'll stop using it, once you've a rat-trap carrier in the rear.

SAFETY EXTRAS

The development of day-glow colors and reflective surfaces, and then their application to bicycle safety, has produced a whole new set of relatively inexpensive ways to make night riding much safer than it ever was before. If you ride a lot at night, you really need them; if you think you're only a sunshine rider, you might choose something like the reflective tapes; they're a very inexpensive form of very good insurance.

The most exciting development is the cheapest: simple tape, at about 50¢ a roll, that you attach anywhere you want your bike to reflect a car's headlight. The colors are just what you'd expect—garish—but that's their virtue; they're very easy to see. Bright orange, parrot green, or hot pink—take your choice. The 3M people, who developed them first, have a kit at around a dollar that combines all you'll need for one bike; many bike dealers also carry the colors separately.

When you apply the tape, remember that your front light and your rear reflector are both there to gleam at motorists ahead and behind you—but you've nothing on each side, and that has often proved hazardous; put some tape on the *sides* of your mudguards, or the *sides* of your head tube and seat tube, if you've no mudguard. You know, of course, not to put any on or near your tire-rims, as that would destroy rim-braking effectiveness totally.

The other development I hope will soon become standard equipment is reflective pedals. The front and rear of each pedal have an inset strip that acts as a reflector and makes your pedaling motion itself a moving warning. I strongly urge that if the bike you buy or own does not have these, you get them—at about $3 a pair, they're a splendid idea. (For how to install, see page 128.)

If you go all-out for night riding, you might want to consider safety vests, or a jacket, made in the same day-glow colors, but in fabric instead of tapes. Lightweight and inexpensive ($3 to $9, depending on what you choose), they could prove worth it to you.

Of course, the white or bright colored clothes you *already* own are good protection for daytime riding too. A hunting-red jacket or checked shirt and a non-matching red hat are the device of one trip leader I know. " 'But they don't match' new riders always tell me—and 'That's what made you look at them, isn't it?' I answer. Works every time," he chuckled. "Dr. Paul Dudley White just adds a white hat to whatever he's wearing, and it works too. *Anything* that helps you stand out from the landscape, be easier for a driver to see, makes you that much safer."

* * *

There's only one extra I suggest you avoid at all costs, for city riding—don't even let someone *give* them to you. That's toe-clips. Built into some pedals and added onto others, they form a sort of stirrup-cage for your toes, usually metal, often with the serrated-edge or ridged-edge pedal that racers use, forming a sort of alligator's hungry embrace for your shoes. Racers and long distance cyclists need them and use them, to very real advantage —they help your foot "ankle," as it's called, properly through the 360 degrees of each pedaling circle, so when your foot's not pushing down it can be pulling up, thus giving you a steadier, stronger stroke on each revolution. They are splendid, useful objects for distance cycling—they increase pedaling efficiency by twenty percent or more. But in city traffic they can hold your foot into a pedal's grip when you need it on the ground, to stop short, to balance, or to dismount in a hurry.

CHAPTER 4

Be Safer
Riding the Streets

Know your city's rules of safety

Start with a single, crucial fact: *when you ride your bicycle, you become a vehicle.*

Your vehicular status is a basic fact in every traffic situation you face. You must accept it, and everything that goes with it. It means you're obligated by law to obey *all* the signs, from "STOP" and "SLOW" and "RIGHT TURN NOT ALLOWED" to "SLOW CHILDREN PLAYING" (we laughed at that as children, but it's a meaningful warning)—and, most important and most often violated by cyclists, "ONE WAY ONLY."

If you don't obey, and many bicyclists lack discipline in this respect, you're legally in the wrong if anything happens to you or anyone else; you'll get in real trouble with either party's insurance company, if it comes to that—and you significantly increase your chances of making whatever happens serious.

Take "ONE WAY ONLY," for example. Cars *expect* to come up on moving vehicles going in the same direction they are. They do not expect, and often do not allow a sufficient safety margin, for traffic coming at them.

"But I was brought up to ride *facing* the traffic," I

43

wailed, arguing the point with a most patient man at the Bicycle Institute of America.

"That myth is going to kill some more bicyclists every year," he said, sadly. "And it is a myth. In every single one of the fifty states, a bicycle, legally, is a vehicle, and must therefore move *with* the traffic. Some towns may have a different ordinance for a given stretch, but even that is most unusual now. Every time we try to run down the report of such a law, either the person who told us is remembering wrong (perhaps recalling a pedestrian rule) or else the law's been changed since. Wisely, in our experience.

"Willing to be grisly about it for a minute? Consider what happens if you and an automobile collide. Let's say you're doing 10 miles an hour and the car's doing 30. If you're both moving in the same direction, the force of the impact will be approximately 20 miles per hour times the weight of whoever hits whom; reverse the situation, so you're coming together from opposite directions, and it's 40 miles per hour at impact."

Obviously he's right. Twice as much *pow!* to the crunch. And don't fool yourself—it's going to be un-steel-wrapped you who will bear most of the crunch, no matter who had the right of way.

So "ONE WAY ONLY" is one sign you should be particularly careful to observe, however tempting a momentarily empty looking street may seem.

*　　*　　*

As the operator of a vehicle, you are also legally required to know and obey not only signs and stoplights, but markings on the road itself. This becomes especially important if you're going to teach anyone to ride a bicycle who does not drive a car.

Legally, you are required to give hand signals 100 feet in advance of any turns you make—outside cities and towns, 200 feet ahead. That's about 6 or 12 car lengths, and it's a good idea even when motorists won't believe you know what you mean.

There are also legal requirements about the condition of your bicycle, in most states, even in towns that don't require registration or issue licenses. Your brakes must be good enough to skid your tire on a dry pavement, and, as I mentioned before, you must have a working bell or horn, plus a front light and a rear reflector or working tail-light, visible 5.00 feet away.

*   *   *

An important warning: *Never ride your bike on any city street where parking is forbidden.* There won't usually be signs saying "No Bicycles"—but you still don't belong there. No matter how good a cyclist you think you are, none of us is safe in high-speed auto traffic. That's what no-parking thoroughfarcs are built to carry. Even on Sunday, they are usually full of cars and trucks moving in a hurry, with no room for you (except in the gutter, which is not safe for several reasons) and no mercy even for each other.

Plan your routes to avoid such streets; where you must cross one, do so where there is adequate protection. A stoplight is far more likely to be obeyed by fast-moving cars than a stop sign.

You really won't be giving up much to stick to the streets where cars can park. In fact, you often gain a funny advantage you'll have to watch yourself not to abuse.

Where cars are legally and correctly parked, most cities and towns plan street sizes so you have between three and five feet of space between the parked cars and the moving ones—and it's all yours. Your half-lane is often clear for blocks ahead even on the most congested streets, and you can almost hear the molars grinding as you pedal past stalled and infuriated drivers who have to wait overlong for a light, or for a car or truck ahead to complete some street-blocking maneuver. Often, when you get up to where the trouble is, you can pedal care-fully past or dismount and walk around, then go on your way.

A warning is in order here: *Look out for pedestrians.* When they see traffic stopped, they seem to feel safe walking anywhere—and they enjoy this unusual freedom

Fig. 16: On city streets where cars park legally, there's usually half-a-lane left for you to bike in with reasonable safety—if you watch for double-parkers, door-openers, and paving-faults. Be sure you go in the same direction the cars do, on a one-way street—going the *other* way is about the most dangerous single thing a cyclist can do wrong.

as much as if it were real. It's important *not to increase your speed,* no matter how tempting things look—you must be ready to stop on short notice, to dodge unthinking and unlooking pedestrians.

And a final word of warning, crucial when you ride next to parked cars, is to *watch for people in the cars.* They can represent several dangers to you. We go into this hazard in detail in the next chapter, but if you start out into traffic without getting as far as that chapter, you might not come back.

People in a car may open a door and block your half-a-lane totally—or they may pull out into traffic without warning, cutting you off completely. Always look and listen—learn to spot heads showing movement of any kind inside a parked car. Learn to hear a motor start, or know when it's running in a parked car. Watch for car movement of any kind. A car that's backing up may either be parking or getting ready to come out—give it extra room. You must always be ready to have your half-a-lane cut off, often with little or no previous warning from the person who does it to you.

Use Your Own Rules Of Sense

Surely you already know the following are signs of imminent trouble, which should bring out your best defensive-driving techniques:

1) a drunken driver of anything.

2) any moving ball, because it will shortly be followed by running children.

3) a Sunday and/or incompetent driver who signals one thing and does another, or does anything without signaling.

4) any show-off driver of any vehicle—sometimes on a bicycle, more frequently, alas, driving a high-powered car or motorcycle. If you can be charitable about his antics, you have the disposition of a saint. But if you

neglect to give him extra room when he shaves closer to you than is humanly possible, you may well wind up interviewing the other saints, first-person.

5) any driveway, alleyway, parking lot entrance or side street where your view is blocked. Cars *like* to shoot out, and often they simply do not look—or, seeing no cars, don't see you.

6) sun in your eyes, or sun directly behind you, to blind people coming toward you; glare makes it hard to distinguish objects in motion from objects at rest; a driver simply may not know you're there, so you have to *know* that he may not know.

* * *

Maybe you haven't thought about it, but you have one incredible advantage on your side in the war between you and all those other traffic-congesting buzzards:

YOU CAN BECOME A PEDESTRIAN AT WILL, BY DISMOUNTING, AND THEN TURN BACK INTO A VEHICLE AGAIN BY REMOUNTING.

It doesn't sound like much, but it's quite a weapon. Neither an auto driver nor a pedestrian has such a choice. You may be *legally* a vehicle, but cars won't treat you as one, no matter how important you look to yourself— and pedestrians will rarely break stride for anything smaller than a bus. You can assume both of those as operating maxims. But the laws of most towns and urban areas protect pedestrians to the hilt. Those are the rules, and you've got to abide by them. When in doubt or danger, just turn the laws to your advantage. You, walking your bike, qualify for that extra protection, and the motorist *must* stop. You'll know, and he'll know, it's a bluffing game still—but at least you've upped your odds. And that's really the only safe way to cross certain difficult intersections, or crowded ones. Often it's the only possible way to make certain left turns, at some really clotted corners or multiple-street intersections you find in both big and little cities.

Special Hazards
and How to Handle Them

PART ONE: PHYSICAL HAZARDS

Loaded Question Number One: Do You Know Which Paving Hazards Are Most Dangerous?

Anything you can fall into can send you flying head-long over the handlebars if you're proceeding incautiously fast when you hit it.

So my list starts with those storm sewers with long openings just that much wider than your bicycle tire. There's a movement afoot to have them turned, so the openings aren't parallel with the curb, to protect cyclists —but women with baby carriages will probably then catch those wheels in them, so don't expect much.

You're particularly likely to meet such drain openings when you're turning right at a busy corner, with a stream of motor traffic turning too, leaving you little room between moving cars and moving pedestrians. When your attention is fully occupied with what cars and people are doing, you may be forced into one of these grim traps unless you know to look ahead for them. If one appears, dismount and walk around it, or carefully over it, and you're in no danger at all. I rank them highest on the list of paving hazards because *until you're on a bicycle they do not look, and are not, dangerous.*

Fig. 17: To a bike rider the worst paving hazards are those he can fall into—and this, to me, is the worst of them all, because only a bike can fall into it. Until you're on a bike, it doesn't even look like a danger.

Everybody knows about potholes, which are next worst. Although you can spot paving differences from fairly far back, depending on the light-or-dark conditions and your own acuity, often you cannot see *up* from *down* accurately, or judge how deep a depression is until you're right on top of it. Re-paved patches in the road are especially hard to pre-judge. And what a car does, going over it, offers only a clue. If you see a car slowing down for a hole, then rolling slowly into and through it, that's only proof you've seen (a) a terrific hole and (b) at the same moment, a good driver. Respect them both.

Metal inserts of any sort in any road offer a series of hazards to a bicycle, hazards that motorists do not face. Even if rain is not actually falling—if it's just misty or

Fig. 18: Judging the depth of a pothole before you're in it, for a cyclist, is both almost impossible and absolutely necessary for continued survival. What awaits our rider at the end of the white line? Can you tell?

Fig. 19: When you don't know for sure, slow down. She's heading for real problems. Here a steep drop and skid-provoking loose gravel combine with a steel straightedge that cuts maneuvering room. Sadly, this picture is quite typical of today's streets.

foggy—metal chills faster and condenses moisture out of the air and onto its surface. The already-smooth metal becomes even slicker than before, much slicker than the road, and may well start you on a skid, whether you're braking or not.

Wet or dry, if square or straight-edged they can literally direct your forward progress in a straight line, when some defensive-driving maneuver may make you wish to turn or go at an angle instead. Some of the square ones are set into the pavement in such a way that they're diagonals, as you approach—point towards you. That point can be quite a hazard for an old, or overinflated tire. Intersections being the connecting points for sub-road piping or wiring as well as for streets themselves, the *corners,* where you're most likely to need smooth pavement, are also exactly the places you're most likely to meet these metal interruptions or intrusions in the paving—square, round, big plates or little inserts. *And any sudden change in level—bump up or bump down— is hard on tires, tubes and rims, may even bow or dent a wheel,* if taken too hard and/or fast.

With cities and towns in the financial troubles they're in, you can expect potholes, lumps, and bumps to get worse, not better. You can expect new ones, even in beautifully paved, newly resurfaced streets, after a winter with alternating freeze-and-then-thaw periods—hardest weather for any pavement to survive. You can expect big bad lumps and potholes anywhere a building of reasonable size is being torn down or built anew, because heavily loaded trucks applying air-pressure brakes actually push the paving around. And where telephone, electric, gas, or water supply people have had to make holes in the streets, you can expect the filled-in places to turn into real roller coasters. Some heave up, some heave up-and-down, some just sink. With successive repaving jobs. I have seen manhole covers and other metal-surface things like that as much as six inches above

Fig. 20: Here's a glorious choice of hazards for you: notice how these metal ones are set both square and point-toward-you; some are straightedged, some even raised, all terribly slippery at certain times . . .

here up-and-down twice combines metal and paving-fault . . .

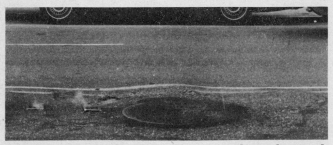

and here's a motley array of square and round, up-and-down, metal- and paving-fault ones together.

or below the *quote* surface level *unquote* of the road or street. Generally, if you complain politely to whatever city agency copes in your town, they're very nice and surprisingly quick—but the first time you meet such a lulu can be quite an experience.

So road watching is as full-time an occupation for the cyclist who plans to live to ride another day as traffic watching. You've got to keep one eye on what the traffic's doing, but you've got to keep the other on what the pavement's going to do to you. Unlike the cars, which can ride over almost anything and usually do, cyclists can be thrown, or caught-and-held, or dangerously deflected off course by almost any inequity in the road's surface. Pieces of glass, you expect to avoid; but since you've no shock absorbers to distribute the blow, any bump you hit you hit twice, in effect—once with the front wheel, once with the back—and any steep up-or-down bump hit too hard can blow a tire or weaken one to the point where it'll blow next time you're in a stress situation.

Fig. 21: Now that you're an expert pavement-watcher, can you say for sure what's up and where's down, in this stretch? Remember, your life may depend on the correctness of your answer—and you haven't long to judge.

So I'll say it again, another way. *It's crucial that you watch the paving as though your life depends on it—because it often does.*

Loaded Question Number Two: What Do You Know About Bicycling in the Rain?

You must know *rain drives all pedestrians crazy.* Unpredictably crazy. Even normally sensible ones, who should know better. Age and gender make no difference —they seem to fear they'll dissolve if they get wet enough, so young and old, wise and foolish, they all skitter in front of you without any sense of traffic rules. Often, in fact usually, they do this without looking, as though that adds to their sense of immunity. Cars stopping to let one out or pick one up often catch this rain virus, too.

But, at the same time, *you can bicycle quite safely in the rain*—even in shallow and still-falling snow, *if you can see adequately,* and if you *know* the *wet pavement tends to change your stopping power to skidding power.* The same rules hold true even on a dry pavement if there are many large puddles after a rain, or wet leaves lying about. Coaster brakes hold better than hand brakes, and center-pull hand brakes hold slightly better than side-pull ones—but each can skid.

The best remedy for the skid problem is to avoid it, and there are two good ways. The first is to slow down enough so you won't have to stop suddenly—slow enough so you can coast to a stop, slow enough so you can put your foot down as an extra brake (which you *cannot* and *must not* do at higher speed). The second is to flutter or pump your brakes, well before you need to stop. This on-off-on-off action, done lightly, either flips the wet off your wheel-rim or dries it by friction. With a dry wheel-rim, your braking power is as it was before. But don't clutch or freeze onto the brake—then you're sure to skid.

If you've neglected those steps, or tried them too late,

and you start to go into a skid, *let it happen.* Sit back, as relaxed as you can make yourself, and ride it out. *Don't attempt to leave the bike* (unless it's headed over a cliff, and maybe not even then); the odds are you'll get tangled up and hurt by the bicycle itself. The better reason not to get off is that if you stay on, *you can often ride the skid out,* steering in the direction you're skidding in and *not touching* the brakes. It's too late to brake; in fact, accelerating can sometimes help—but often, normal traction will reassert itself and your wheels will start to turn as usual if you just stay in charge and keep steering. You will be shaken, but safe, in almost every case—and usually, safer than if you'd abandoned ship.

It sounds like a contradiction in terms, but this learning to *relax alertly* can save you from serious injury, exactly as it would if you started to fall down stairs. If you go down, you're not all tight and tensed, so you're less likely to break bones or pull muscles unduly—and, by staying in charge, you may well save yourself from going down at all.

Most riding in the rain won't involve you in skids, especially now that you know what to do to avoid them. And, if you're dressed so that you either don't get too wet or don't mind getting wet, it can be a delightful experience. You don't want to go overboard on the subject, and November's different from July, but there's something marvelously basic about meeting some rain, deciding you don't mind, going on anyway, and getting thoroughly, totally, happily wet. Like children, engineering puddles. Even soaked to the skin, we are each and all of us washable—and most clothing survives pretty well.

If you know it's going to rain, you can rainproof yourself in advance, or dress in old clothes that won't be hurt; either way, you can proceed quite comfortably, if not very fast, through a sizeable shower. Turn your lights on, to be extra-visible to motorists and pedestrians.

In any really heavy downpour, I suggest you pull over into shelter, (remembering that trees-and-lightning can be real dangers in thunderstorms). Even *with* your lights, motorists won't be able to see you accurately through the water streaming on their windshields and the flick of the wipers.

But don't let a simple shower stop you, if you'd like to bicycle through it, or a weather report that hints at rain. *Just keep your speed minimal, watch your traction on the road, and watch out for people acting crazy.* You'll probably find them!

Loaded Question Number Three: Did You Know You Can Bicycle In Snow and Cold?

Riding in the winter can be delightful—if you know when and how to do it. With no snow on the ground, you can dress warmly enough to be comfortable in anything above about 10°. Below that, no matter what you wear, you'll get too cold. Always wear gloves, and always dress in layers, so you can add or subtract warmth as needed. If you can normally bike all day, in cold weather you can probably bike most of the day—but plan more rest stops. If you're not a distance cyclist, plan your shorter trips the same way—a bit shorter than usual, with more rest stops.

If there is more than 2½ inches of snow on the ground, stay home. If there is less, listen to the weather forecast, and stay home if they predict temperatures over 30°— you'll wind up riding in wet, cold, slippery, dirty slush, otherwise, and you'll hate every minute. Stay home, also, if they predict drizzle; keeping dry, in cold weather, is about half the battle. That's why, when you go indoors for your rest, you must shake the snow off you carefully; what you leave on will melt, and then get you wet, and you can wind up really chilled.

Between 10° and 30°, if your tires are good, snow is very rideable if it is dry. Plan extra rest stops, to warm your feet up—they're going to be the coldest part of you. A good way to warm them is to walk for a few minutes, flexing your toes to stimulate circulation. If you plan to bike in winter a lot, or commute, maybe it would be worth the $10 or so it costs to invest in battery-operated electric socks. Or buy a pair of boots two sizes too big, and wear cotton socks, then wool ones, inside. Trapped air is needed to keep the warmth in, and if you crowd your feet or socks, you don't achieve the warmth even with the double socks. Also plan to bike on streets that have not been salted, if possible; salt residue is very corrosive, and if you bike in it, you must clean your bike *thoroughly* afterward.

Loaded Question Number Four: What Should A Bicyclist Do When A Dog Approaches?

This one has about as many answers as there are cyclists—probably because when the situation gets out of hand, it can get very bad indeed. There seems to be something about the twinkling spokes and the pedaling motions that turns man's official best friend into a snarling, overprotective and utterly dangerous attack system. Maybe it's the territorial imperative, maybe the dog doesn't like bikes—whatever the reasons, he can be a danger.

Veteran riders have all sorts of solutions: one group carries special equipment, another uses speed or psychology. Follow the advice you think fits the dog you meet, but go warily.

The no-equipment camp suggests you (a) speed up and outdistance the dog; (b) dismount and walk your bike past him, keeping your bike between the two of you; (c) talk soothingly to the dog; (d) yell loudly and commandingly, telling him to go home, or stop, or lie down (this sometimes produces his owner, whose command will work where yours may not). The ultimate no-equipment expedient is to kick at the dog, but I don't trust this one—it offers him a handy hunk of you to bite, and he might.

The be-prepared, carry-equipment camp suggests you (a) carry a switch or tree-branch, to shoo away the dog; (b) swing your tire pump, the same way; (c) carry dog biscuits, either stopping to feed them to the dog or tossing them as a distractant; (d) carry a chemical repellent like the ones postmen carry (designed to stop but not hurt the dog; cost, about $3); or (e) carry a plastic squeeze bottle filled with something you think will work as a repellent: household ammonia is one suggestion, lemon juice another, rubbing alcohol a third—best of the home-made bunch, I'd say, because it's least likely to hurt the dog but produces an instant-cold effect which should stop but not anger him.

As you've surely noticed, much of this advice is contradictory, and all of it has disadvantages, some serious. Swinging a tire pump, for example, can so seriously move your center of gravity if you try to do it while riding that you can lose your balance and fall, hurting yourself perhaps more than the dog would have. A repellent takes time to reach for and use, and may only further irritate the dog, if he thinks he's doing his job, keeping you away from where you don't belong. And you have to be pretty sure of your charm to go the dog-biscuit route.

I'm in favor of the dismount method. It takes no equipment, often makes the dog lose interest in you, and most important, gives you the best control of your bike and yourself. Also, if he brushes or rushes into your front wheel, you're not stopped or made to fall.

All experts agree the problem becomes first-priority serious if anyone is bitten. All dog bites should be treated by a doctor, as soon as possible, and the attacking dog identified, to be checked for rabies. If possible, locate his home and owner; otherwise, memorize his build, his markings and coloration, even the sound of his bark, if you can, and the place of the attack, so the dog warden or police can identify him later. The law will be on your side, as a dog dangerous enough to bite should be under restraint—but if you can't find the dog, all the legal rights in the world won't help you.

PART TWO
HAZARDS YOU WOULDN'T EXPECT

It may sound hard to believe, but *the greatest potential danger to you on a traffic-filled street comes not from any other vehicle in motion, but from people in parked cars or trucks.*

Consider for a moment: you're proceeding on a busy street with traffic moving along beside you; you've checked carefully and you not only have the lights, but your half-a-lane, next to the parked cars, looks clear for blocks ahead. But the instant any car occupant (driver or passenger, depending on the side of the street you're on) opens his door without looking, he's thrown a steel barrier across your total right-of-way. He then compounds his felony by stepping out, putting an unpredictably-moving person in your path.

What choices do you have? Can you go around him in time? Is there room enough left in the parking lane? Usually not. Will the cars moving next to you see the problem and move over? Again, usually not. If all other options fail, can you stop in time? And if you can, do you still hurtle forward, into him, his door, or your own bike, and get hurt?

Any way you answer the question, it's a deadly trap, and it is usually created by someone who has literally no idea that his gesture is any threat to anyone. So don't waste time expecting him to worry about it, to premeditate his gesture and look for you, or to stop doing it. Most cities require people to get out on the *curb* side, for their own protection. But they still seem never to look, always to leap into traffic unexpectedly, right where you want to be riding. Which is why *watching for movement*

Fig. 22: **The greatest potential danger you face on a traffic-filled street: the car door opener. He throws a steel barrier across your half-a-lane without any idea he's making trouble; can you stop without harm to him or yourself? The answer can be deadly if you are going too fast.**

of any sort in a parked car is a primary rule of bicycle safety on city, town or village streets. You should *expect* to watch what other vehicles in motion are doing; you know they can be dangerous. You have to *train* yourself to watch for the person in the parked car, or you won't last long as a cyclist.

Unfortunately, you'll meet this problem in big and little cities, in crowded downtown streets and quiet suburban streets. If it isn't a woman with an armload of groceries it's the driver of a pickup truck, or any beverage deliverer, unloading. You should also know it's somewhat more likely from the casual types who pull the car up in a double-parked position, even when there's room at the curb—and it's absolutely predictable from any double-parked truck.

Wherever you meet it, you must be ready. Watch out for it. It is not merely hazardous—it can be lethal.

You must also expect to watch for parked cars to pull out of the parking lane and into traffic without *careful* checking behind them; if they look at all, they often look only for cars, and can cut you off totally without ever seeing you. Clues to watch for: exhaust fumes, sounds from running motors, drivers' heads turning.

* * *

The next most hazardous thing you wouldn't expect is your own reactive temperament when exposed to really bad driving. It'll betray you, every time. The surer you are you're in the right—the more you're absolutely, legally, properly, just where you should be and not one inch over — the more the dunderheads trap you, the more they infuriate by idiocy, complacency, selfishness, and plain old uncaring, unthinking, I'm-going-ahead-whatever-happens driving actions that should be, and usually are, prohibited by law.

When I see "Hertz" or "Avis" or "U-Haul" on a truck, I tend (honestly) to pull over to one side and wait. Or look for a side street to duck into. Anything to get out of the way. It seems that the world's worst-trained drivers run these desperate vehicles on their tortured paths to oblivion. They consistently over-load, over-rate their own abilities, and over-pace the traffic around them. There isn't a rule in the book I haven't seen them break —repeatedly. Why? Because they have the total freedom of anonymity. You don't know who they are—and do they ever interpret that as full diplomatic immunity. Suppose one knocks you flat; whether he's hurt you or not, he's gone before you get his vehicle's license number. So all you can say is, "It was a big blue (or yellow, or whatever) truck rented from ...." You're about as likely to be able to trace such a driver down and sue him successfully as you are the driver of a U.S. Mail truck—who enjoys federal protection from suit, but who drives like a St. Christopher Medallist by comparison. Mail trucks are considered dangerous enough by other motorists—because they don't give ground to anyone, and will race on the slightest provocation; because they enjoy speeding up and then stopping instantly and shudderingly, moments later, no matter what other traffic is doing. Without a signal, usually. But, since you expect them to drive dangerously (word like that gets around) they don't startle and therefore infuriate you so much.

The danger to you is that when some motorist's flagrant disobedience of road rules infuriates you, your human tendency is to react by driving badly yourself. Anger rarely improves one's judgment. No matter how wronged you were by one motorist, you're not justified in taking it out on the next one. That makes you as bad as the person you're condemning. It also puts you in far greater personal jeopardy, since you're driving a bike—a bare, unprotected, unthreatening bike — not the armored tank that seems, some days, more appropriate to the skirmishes and joustings taking place on our streets and highways under the name of transportation.

The most calamity-causing breakdown of law and order today is located inside the heads of people who drive. Big cars, little cars, trucks and taxis, buses and omnibuses—each one seems to be in such a tearing hurry to get somewhere that he's stopped obeying rules, the very rules that should make our overcrowded roads bearable and safe at all for anyone. Each one, cheating only a little, "fudging" a light, moving ahead on the yellow when he knows the red will catch him, thinks his act is unimportant. But the totality of these acts is turning rules-of-the-road into rules-of-the-jungle. And then the jungle question gets asked: who is bigger than whom?

If any motorist is ever out to prove he's bigger than you are, let him. He is. Even the smallest Volkswagen outweighs you and your bike together by some 1900 pounds. *They are all bigger.* The fact that there is any doubt in their minds should demonstrate the probable stupidity and predictable recklessness of anyone who needs to put the question to any sort of road test. Stay as far away as possible.

*   *   *

The final thing about motorists you'll have to remember is that they tend to think they're moving in two dimensions only, left-or-right being one, forward-but-never-back being the other. Hills they recognize but can disregard, as you and I cannot, unless they're so heavily overloaded they don't belong on the road in the first place. But the major point is that even axlebusting potholes seem to offer no threat, and they therefore do not understand or expect that you will steer *around* things, since they do not.

This sounds minor but it can be important, since what a driver expects you to do influences how much room he leaves you to operate in.

PART THREE: AN OUNCE OF PREVENTION

If I've sobered your approach to bicycling by talk of accident possibilities, that's good. You'll be a better bicyclist. Everybody knows what nobody remembers: that you're taking your life into your hands whenever you step into a street, or climb onto your bike, or step into a car or truck or bus, as driver or rider. If we all remembered to take our actions seriously, if we respected our vehicular codes, we'd all have a better safety record.

But I don't want to make you nervous when you shouldn't be.

You're probably safer on your bike than in your bathtub, if you believe in statistics. And nobody has measured the miles you and I bicycle *safely*, any more than they've counted the hundreds upon hundreds of baths we take safely.

Statistically, in fact, bicycling is more than reasonably safe. Recent studies have shown that the likeliest bike-car accident occurs on a Saturday afternoon, in clear weather; the bicyclist is usually male and under fifteen years old, and the responsibility divides about fifty-fifty between young bicyclists who ignored traffic lights or signs and motorists who did approximately the same thing. One-way signs ignored by cyclists counted high in the toll. So did bikes that were too big for their young owners' to handle adequately (that last, in one study, upped the chance of accident *five times*). On learning these facts, many communities are starting or increasing bike-safety programs, teaching the rules of the road to anyone who can be expected to need them. These lessons are expected to reduce accident figures markedly, since ignorance, or innocence, about the rules seems repeatedly to be a contributing factor.

The 1971 edition of *Accident Facts,* a yearly publication of the National Safety Council, reports that in 1970 there were 820 deaths from auto-bicycle collisions reported to them. That's a 3% rise over 1969. When you consider the stunning (and accurate) predictions the National Safety Council makes before each of our big holiday weekends, when well over five or six hundred people are killed in a single three or four day span, eight hundred and twenty in a year's time isn't a lot. Except that if you knew even one of them, or care about any of them, it's always too many; that's why everyone's awareness of traffic rules, and obedience to them, is so crucial.

But don't let anyone scare you out of riding your bicycle. There's absolutely no need. What you need is to know where the dangers lie, to know what you're doing, to learn to do it well, and then to reach the plateau where you can relax and enjoy all but the tiniest maddening fraction that comes when your path crosses that of a fool.

A most effective way to improve your chance of safe cycling is to know the road you're riding.

Are there places you go regularly—a daily ride to a school, a market, an office? A once- or twice-a-week ride to a park, a library, a friend's house, a doctor's office? Even a once-a-month *repeated* ride merits your taking the time to ride the route first, on an inspection trip, then plan according to what you find. (If you're a parent with a youngster who bikes to school, ride the trip with him, the same way, and discuss what you find together.)

Go in full daylight; give yourself plenty of time to explore alternative routes or parts of the route, and *watch for everything.*

Where are the potholes? How deep? How sharp are the edges? What margin does the traffic give you to get around? Do cars have trouble with the holes? Are there any of those deadly storm-sewer openings?

Where are the bottlenecks, where drivers are likeliest to be angry and unthinking?

Where are there double-parkers and general congestion?

Where do the one-ways work to your advantage? If you use one, what's your homecoming route?

Where are there difficulties that crop up at a given hour every day, or a given time and place—like schools that let out at three, but are peace itself at 2:30 and 3:30?

Where will there be difficulties you can *predict* on otherwise usually peaceful streets? You know a church parking lot's not empty on Sunday, and expect a crowd of right- or left-turners into it. But can you foresee a Saturday afternoon high school football crowd? If you learn when the game starts, when it's likely to let out, you can avoid the tie-ups. And that principle is true for every day in every season. If you can spot causes of traffic congestion ahead of time, you can alter your usual route, or your timing, to very great advantage.

Another ounce-of-prevention piece of advice: on a one-way street, where you may legally ride next to the cars parked to the right or left of the street, *always pick the left. You are safer anywhere the motorist can see you sooner, and that's on his side of the vehicle he's driving.*

Often, too, the right-hand lane is a bus lane, with big, lumbering, fume-belching behemoths nosing along one behind the other, offering you the choice of passing on their left—a very dangerous prospect if they start to move suddenly, and they always do—or the unpleasant alternative of breathing in their noxious exhaust while you wait behind for them to discharge and collect their passengers.

You already know enough to expect unsignaled turns from motorists going off your one-way: giving them the whole road doesn't seem to improve their aim at any given turn-off. Often it's simply that they realize too late, "That's it!" and they turn in wild circles that get them off somehow but leave everybody else's insides churned up. Since they do not seem to handle the syndrome visibly better on either side of the street, you might as well *choose the safer side for yourself.*

* * *

That's really your clue to safe bicycling, as it is to safe motoring or safe walking across a busy street. You choose where to be and when to be there, in terms of hazards you know exist, and can predict.

You know what's likely to happen, what to do if it does, and, where possible, some ways to avoid being caught by surprise and forced into letting something dangerous happen.

That knowledge is what gives you true safety, and the only *real* freedom of the road. Without it, you could be a sitting duck. With it, you and your bicycle can fly pretty securely through almost anything—and come out safe and happy on the other side.

CHAPTER 6

The View From the Other Seat, or, What a Motorist Doesn't Know About Bicycling Can Kill You

HAVING CAST all motorists into one universal and undifferentiated lot as the villains of the road, let us now reverse the process and take a long, hard look at bicyclists from the motorist's point of view. You and I know there are degrees of skill and experience in bicycling; maybe you can spot a learner before he's ridden into you in the park, and maybe you can't—but I can almost guarantee you, a motorist can't tell him from you or me.

To start with, he probably lumps all bicycles, scooters, motorized bikes and motorcycles in one class: things not as big or as careful as he is, on the road, likely to confuse things and cause him trouble.

Not accurate? Perhaps. A commuting, careful, defensive-driving trained bicyclist is more like a good, experienced, road-ripened taxi or truck driver, or even a big-crane operator—an expert who does something he loves every day using a machine he loves.

But the show-off antics of a spoiled-brat youngster on a bike, who ignores traffic rules after his parents have told him, "The cars've gotta stop for you, Junior," are dreadfully similar to those of the same spoiled show-off when he's old enough to be stunting about in black leather on a motorcycle or gunning a mufflerless sports car down a quiet street to prove he's Somebody. Surely you'd agree with any good driver who condemned all such actions as reckless—up to the point where he's wrong to lump you into such company.

Next, he assumes (usually from ignorance and innocence) that all bicyclists, at all times and in all places, are in perfect control of their bikes, and if they do something odd or erratic, it's because they meant to (if he takes this as provocation on your part, things go very wrong very fast).

If you were walking and you limped, how many people who don't know you would notice and go slow? Bicycles, when limping, still look owner-directed. How many people who don't bike would recognize the symptoms? And if your trouble is so severe you pull over, they'll just think you're resting, even with your tools spread out.

He is disconcerted by your simple presence.

He's accurate enough, depending on how bicyclists have behaved in his presence. If he's seen them be erratic, unpredictable, breaking laws and lacking in good judgment, he's totally right. How would you like risking your life to avoid hitting someone who isn't observing road rules? And what do you suppose the chances are that either an on-coming car or one behind would *also* see the cyclist and understand the problem the motorist is trying to avoid?

If he's a good driver, he may know that studies of auto-bicycle collisions show that more than three-quarters of them occur in daylight, in good weather, and on residential streets. He may even know that over half of them occur after somebody fails to stop for a traffic sign or signal—and, also more than half the time, it isn't the motorist who is at fault.

In other words, your motorist may not have had much

exposure to responsible bicycle riders. With irresponsible cyclists, he is quite correct to assume that anything can happen.

Is the way you handle your bicycle on the road going to change his opinions, or reinforce them?

He will expect you to ride, as he does, over everything the road offers.

Naturally. If he's a lane-hopper, he thinks he does it just to get around slow cars. If he's good about staying inside lane lines (and that's getting so rare as to be non-existent, in cities, anyway) he expects that if you're any good you'll do the same. Drive in a straight line, that is. And if he ignores lane lines entirely, he's not likely *ever* to understand anybody else's traffic problems. In short, none of the three types will understand why you don't do it his way, although each of the three fails to understand for a different reason.

He will also expect you to have perfect control (i.e., fully functioning brakes) even on wet pavements.

All bicyclists don't even yet know to expect braking problems on a wet pavement. Why should he know, when he (if, as we're assuming, he's a good driver) isn't likely to skid on anything short of glare ice or unsalted snow?

Also, with the rain driving pedestrians crazy around him, and slowing all the cars, he's probably already taking longer to get somewhere than he planned—so he has even less time than usual to be courteous to, or careful of, you.

If anything goes wrong, or is wrong, on the road you're both on, he'll assume you are helping make it worse.

If you really do disconcert him, to some measure he's right. Anything that distracts any driver of any vehicle slows everybody down, as you know. Have you heard those weekend highway congestion reports that locate where an accident just took place and then report "rubbernecking delays"?

He will never know you're in trouble if something you're carrying is causing you steering or balancing difficulties.

He's probably right to assume you shouldn't be carrying something that will give you trouble. I happen to believe women are going to move the world, one grocery bagful at a time, and that it's going to be better for our doing so, so I'm often overoptimistic about what my bike can carry. Ecologically, it's good to carry things on a bike instead of a car; but vehicularly, I'm wrong to overload the bike. When that happens, I get off and walk the loaded bike home. It's really the only safe solution.

If he's one of those lethal door-opening types, he will get angry at you.

It happens. Telling him that what he did was illegal and unsafe for everybody only makes him angrier. Try asking him if he would have preferred you to have been driving a two-ton truck when he pulled his unthinking play for glory. He won't then be less angry, but he just may be, later, and maybe—just barely maybe—he won't do it again.

BUT, then we come to:

If you're both stopped at the same light, he'll talk to you—especially if you're on his left on a one-way street.

A rare few will be abusive, intrusive, or suggestive, but the overwhelming majority will be admiring of you, your bike, and your enterprising attitude. And the quotes you collect are worth the price of admission. Some of my favorites are:

"Have to hand it to ya, lady, ya got *nerve*. You wouldn't catch *me* on a bike in New York City!"

"That's the only way to get around, these days. Bet you can even beat me, cross-town!" (I usually can, but not up- or downtown, and we both know it.)

"Getting your exercise? Nice day for it. But what do you do when your squirrel gets tired?"

And, nicest of all:

He, or she, will smile at you. Simple, uncomplicated communication. Rare in these days of verbal assault, floating anxiety, and misdirected angers.

CHAPTER 7

Keep Your Bicycle
From Being
the Stolen One

Part One: Know Your Enemy

Start with one idea firmly in mind: the thief (or thieves) you're up against want your bike as much as you do.

Maybe more.

If you're negligent and the thief is quick, he gets your bike—*free*. If you're even normally careful and he's quick, his greatest risk is that some passerby will ask, "Why are you fooling around with that bike?" He'll be ready; if he can plausibly suggest it's his bicycle, he just forgot his key . . . shortly it *becomes* his bicycle.

Occupancy, in bike-riding, is about 99 and 44/100ths percent of ownership.

Busy policemen don't usually have time to stop suspicious looking bike riders to ask for proof they own the bike. Even if they did it regularly, most innocent cyclists couldn't prove ownership, either.

Quick, now, without looking, what's the brand name of your bike? Model number? *Serial* number? Can you even describe it accurately?

That last may sound like a dumb question, but in the city of New York, in the last year, an inordinately high

74

percentage of the bicycles reported stolen were *totally* described by their owners as "black with some chrome trim."

Start your defenses by writing out the maker's name, the model number, and the *serial* number of your bike, and carrying it in your wallet; memorize them, if you live or bike in chancy neighborhoods where you don't always carry a wallet. Take the bike and your description, complete with serial number, to your local police station, and ask if they have a registration service. An increasing number do, and it's often your only hope of proof-of-ownership if your bike *is* stolen. A good, all-inclusive color photo is in order here too—especially if yours is made-to-order in any way the photo can show.

As a matter of fact, do you know where to look for your serial number? Unhappily (and unintelligently on the part of the bicycle industry), they're all over the lot. To start, ask the man who's selling it to you, if you're buying a new one; if you've had it a while, and can still reach him, it'll save you a lot of time. Otherwise, you'll

Fig. 23: The three places to look for your serial number are directly under the seat; on the bottom of the pedal-crank housing; and on the left side of the back fork, *opposite* the chain. It will probably be small and will certainly be dirty, hard-to-read.

have to look in three places: at the top of the seat tube, directly under the seat; at the bottom of the same tube, on the underside of the pedal crank housing; or at the rear of the bike, where the axle goes through the back left fork. (Left as you're riding, remember.) Expect the numbers to be small and difficult to read, especially if they're dirty.

For further protection, take your bicycle to your neighborhood locksmith, on a day he isn't too busy. He has punches he uses to mark keys, and they usually include the alphabet plus numbers. Even if he hasn't got all of your name, any of it you can get him to pound into some integral part of the frame (*not* the handlebars, nothing that comes off easily) would be a vast help proving the bicycle belongs to you. Be careful, though, and check that his pounding can be done without bending or weakening your frame. It can, if he's good—just remember to discuss it with him first.

* * *

Now that you're armed, the next step is to decide that it's going to be a war of wits between you and the bicycle thieves; sharpen your wits and prepare to take other steps accordingly. This is the time to consider: *Who else would want your bike?* What is the "profile" of a bicycle thief? Unfortunately, not enough of them have been caught and described to give us an official picture. This is true even though bicycles costing anything from $150 to $250 are common on the streets today, and tempting targets for thieves—and the theft of such a bike, in most states, is considered grand larceny. Penalties, for our purposes, don't matter as much as prevention, so here you must consider what tempts him, and figure out possible answers to that all-important question: *Who else would want your bicycle?*

Is he a drug addict who's going to sell or pawn it for next to nothing to support a costly habit? Such people exist, they often steal, and they're more numerous in cities, so it's a possibility you must not dismiss lightly.

Is he a man operating or working for a "hot bike" ring, like the steal-to-order automobile thieves, who steal a car, repaint it, restamp or obscure its motor number, forge its papers and change its plates, to sell to some unsuspecting car buyer? It undoubtedly happens, and, sadly, is on the increase.

Let's look at what the Bicycle Institute of America reported recently in an article on bicycle thievery, by J. J. Hayes:

> "Organized rings of thieves, equipped with bolt-cutters and panel trucks are reported operating—particularly in college towns—all across the country. Such rings may steal 20 or 30 bikes at a time, drive them to another city, and sell them for half their approximate retail value.
>
> "In Eugene, Oregon, an ad was placed on the bulletin board of the University of Oregon Student Union. The ad said '10-speed bikes available . . . call between 5:30 and 6:00 p.m.' The telephone, detectives found, was that of a campus phone booth. At 5:30 that evening a young man turned up and took orders for a large number of bikes.
>
> " 'We learned that he was going to steal local bicycles to fill the orders he had taken' said Eugene detective Glynn Michael, who works with the department's Community Affairs Detail."

I believe you're far more likely to be waging your war against someone who isn't normally a thief.

He wants the bike for reasons exactly similar to yours: he wants to ride around in style and look down on those slow, foot-bound pedestrians. He is most likely to be an adolescent male, and the more beautiful and gadget-covered your bicycle is, when it becomes his, the more he'll be able to feed his ego with his friends' admiration of him and his new possession—whether or not they know it to be stolen. In some of our subcultures, that would add to its lustre and his daring. With the shoplift-for-kicks craze today found even among the wealthy, your bicycle could literally tempt anyone big enough to ride it.

So now the problem becomes, can you make your bike less tempting? That's where my

SIMPLE PRECAUTION WHEN BUYING

comes in. *For simple city and suburban riding, buy a girl's model bicycle.* Yes. Whatever your gender. Because any pre-thief, given his choice of your girl's model and an equally-accessible boy's model, will almost certainly take the latter. Because that thief in Eugene, Oregon, probably took more orders for boys' bikes than for girls' bikes.

As a matter of fact, you'll find very little difference when riding on pavements and in traffic. As men's coats get longer, as trousers get floppier, as you step off and over with ease, you'll find some unsuspected advantages, too.

As a further matter of fact, in three large, very populous parts of the globe, there is nothing else offered you: China, India, and Africa. That's a huge chunk of the world. And the uni-sex bicycle is in steady demand there.

Your estimate of the potential thief's character will also, if you can stand it, lead to pre-purchase step number two (far more difficult):

Avoid lovely, lively colors, lots of shiny chrome, expensive and decorative built-in gadgets, and pick the plain black quiet job that looks as though it were built for a nun.

It isn't easy—but it's a lot easier than buying the brave beauty, owning it for a short delicious while, and then mourning its expensive loss.

Maybe you'll feel (pre-purchase) the way my husband did one morning when he'd cycled to work and was parking and locking his bike to the tree handiest to his building. He was locking up a girl's bike—exactly the quiet, beat-up, seen-better-days black-and-rusty-too, Frog Prince number suggested above, and he was locking it to a tree to which someone had already chained a golden-yellow deep luster enamel Italian model, chromed and brilliant in the morning sun. His chain wasn't even as rich, fat and heavy as the Other Fellow's opulent Protective Device. You can imagine exactly how he slunk into his building, hurrying to avoid glances that could identify him as the owner of that ratty-tatty thing that passed for a bicycle.

But you can also imagine his feelings that noontime, when he went back, found his own bike safe, sound, and still chained to the tree, below which lay only the Expensive Protective Device, mute witness that the thief preferred the Other Bike enough to saw patiently through 3/8″ chain to get it, and had done so, successfully, between 9 a.m. and noon on New York's busy Third Avenue within home-run distance of Grand Central—literally under the eyes of hundreds and hundreds of people walking past.

Part Two: Keep Your Bike From Being Stolen Out From Under You—Literally!

That shouldn't be a problem, but it often is, especially for the muscularly ungifted—either youngsters or oldsters. It can and does happen to all ages. When someone bigger or stronger, or a group of them, demand either the bike outright, or a ride on it (predictably, neither the bike nor the rider usually returns your way again), you've got real trouble in the air. Sometimes, if you know the path ahead, and you know your own speed and strength, you can spurt up instead of stopping, and make it past or through them. Sometimes you do well to give up the bike and be glad that's all that's asked of you these violence-prone days. Certainly, if a gang of toughs attack a lone rider, giving up the bike can be the least of many evils.

Things to avoid, and to teach a youngster to avoid

especially, are (1) empty areas in almost any city park; (2) rough neighborhoods where he'll be the stranger, alone among many, looking rich whatever the facts are, on a tempting bicycle; (3) unknown terrain in general when he's riding alone—even two or three youngsters riding together can be jumped by a youth-pack if they're foolish about where they go, but it gets less likely as the number of riders increases; and finally, (4) riding after dark or dusk falls, again especially if riding alone.

If you're an adult, you have pretty much the same rules to protect yourself and your bike while riding, but at least you may have a better chance if you take the spurt-of-speed route. Training, experience, bigger muscles, and good condition (if you've got them) can give you a safety margin of extra stamina that may carry you through successfully. Watch out for sticks-in-spokes, though.

My favorite stealing-from-a-rider story concerns the *Time-Life* staff member who was riding in New York's notorious but beautiful Central Park. A gang of big, tough youths stopped him and demanded his bicycle. He shrugged, grinned, and said, "You've got the wrong guy, fellas—I just stole this bike a few minutes ago," so convincingly that the gang let him ride on, *with* his bike.

Part Three: Locking the Barn Door

Once your bicycle has been stolen, what do you do? The article quoted earlier has some interesting answers.

"Recovery rates vary from as low as 20% to as high as 90%.

"Proper identification and speed of reporting the theft seem to be the twin keys to quick recovery, according to Inspector Thomas M. Roselli, Commanding Officer of the Philadelphia, Pa., Juvenile Division.

" 'Once a bicycle is gone,' Roselli warned bicycle owners in a recent newspaper article, 'you'd better report it immediately. Unless the thief has a truck, he can't get very far with a bike, so sometimes an officer can drive the victim around the neighborhood, and if he's lucky, he might just spot his bike.

" 'However, after a few hours, it becomes nearly hopeless. The thief repaints the bike, or reassembles it with parts from other stolen bikes and this makes it tricky to identify.' "

Part Four:
A Summary of Precautionary and Lock-Up Steps
Precautions:

1) Record your bicycle, with serial number, description, and photo, if possible, with your local police department. When you record your serial number, be certain you've not mistaken it for the model number. (Serial number is located in one of three places, remember: stamped into the metal on the underside of the pedal-crank housing; at the bottom of the left rear fork near the rear axle; or on the front of the seat tube, just under the seat.)

2) List your bike, with serial number, full description, photo, and police registration number if you have one, on the personal-property floater of your home-owner's insurance policy. (This usually has a $50-deductible clause, but if your bike's worth more and gets stolen, insurance money will help replace the bike.)

3) Also consider the surprisingly inexpensive Bicycle Theft Insurance sold by independent local bicycle dealers, members of the National Bicycle Dealers' Association. The insuring company is Lumberman's Mutual—a respected firm. If you use your dealer's form which establishes the bike's worth correctly, the bike's full value is insurable with *no* deductions. If you can't find a NBDA dealer near you (he's surely there, but you may not spot the sign) write to Tom Saylor, Dept. PNL, 29025 Euclid Avenue, Wickliffe, Ohio, 44092, and ask

for the name of the nearest NBDA dealer who can sell you such insurance .

Lock-up Techniques:

1) *Always lock your bike out in the open,* where attempted theft may be seen. Don't leave it locked *anywhere* out of doors *overnight.*

2) *Always lock to a heavy, stationary object.* The safest chains are the costly, heavy-duty, case-hardened ones, and if your lock's shackles are thinner than your chain-link's proper ⅜-inch thick, you're wasting your time. Any metal protection less than ⅜-inch thick will barely slow down a competent thief, if he has time to operate.

3) *Always run your chain through both wheels and the frame before circling your stationary object;* if you've got quick-release hubs, release the front wheel, put it next to the rear wheel and run the chain through both at once. Or take the front wheel with you; it makes your bike a lot less tempting, in the row.

Fig. 24: **The sort of lock you need if you leave your bike for any length of time, and a bolt-cutter—the reason you need it. Always run your chain through both wheels and the frame, then lock securely to a stationary object, or your precautions are in vain.**

4) If you go to one place repeatedly (school or office, usually) and carrying a heavy chain seems a drag, consider always leaving your chain at the bike-rack or where you park. When you arrive, you unlock your empty chain, insert your bike properly as outlined above, lock up, and leave. When you go home, unlock as usual, re-lock the empty chain to the rack, and leave.

Fig. 25: The short-time lockup, with two lightweight locks —when you're going to be in-and-out of several places and don't want to carry your heavy lock and chain. But you must lock to a stationary street object, and go through frame and wheel with *each* lock. And it never hurts to keep your eye on the bike—locks like these are not heavy protection, and are not adequate for long periods.

5) Another satisfactory system for *short* lock-up periods, as on a several-stop shopping tour, is my personal favorite. I buy two of the lighter, plastic-covered chains with key locks *that have identical keys*. This takes patience; the key's got a number stamped on it, and you have to stand in the bicycle shop, searching among the locks-with-keys-in-them until you find two with the same number, then check that they *do* unlock each other.

But now you're set to lock to a tree, a metal fence, or any permanent street sign, the special McIntyre way: one lock through front wheel, frame, then around signpost and lock; second lock through back wheel, frame, first lock, then around signpost and lock. When you come out, one key unlocks everything quickly. They're also light enough to ride easily, twisted into a circle, on your handlebars. Sometimes you have only a big, thick tree or heavy lamppost to lock to; shorter locks won't go round them and through both wheels plus frame, your locking minimum. But your two locks, joined together, circle almost anything with room to spare.

6) Final word-of-warning: locking your bike to itself —wheels to frame— or to a moveable object like a litter basket or a short, portable street sign, is worthless, and offers no protection at all.

CHAPTER 8

Running and Safety Tips From the Men Who Mend the Disasters—How to Keep Repair Costs at a Minimum

EVER SINCE I realized I was born into a family of good talkers, I've been a good listener. And ever since I first got a bike, when I decided if I couldn't do it right I wouldn't do it, I've been asking experts questions about bikes and biking. If every one of us bicycle owners could have a long, unhurried chat with these men who put the pieces back together, and the others who have ridden many hundreds of miles, we would surely learn which things are worth doing, and not doing, to make our biking days easier, help us keep our bikes in better condition, with less work, less fuss, and often, lots less money—to make our whole bicycling experience happier all around.

"Bike people," as they style themselves, are almost universally willing to share what they know, tell what they enjoyed that they think you'll enjoy, and sometimes tell about what they did wrong and the troubles it led them into, so you can learn from their disasters how to avoid some you'd otherwise have too. Both the professional "bike person" (be he dealer or mechanic) and the dedicated bicycle enthusiast are full of wisdom all bicyclists can learn from.

This chapter is a distillation of some of these chats, in dialogue form so that you, too, can hear the blunt, practical, experience-honed wisdom coming up from the page, and benefit from it, as I have.

Me: "What can somebody like me—you know, no mechanical genius—what can I do to make sure my bike is okay to ride? Or is that a dumb question?"

Him: "No question is a dumb question if you need the answer.

"About your bike—just look for any nut or bolt that's loose. Tighten everything that needs it, then, to be sure, pick the bike up and shake it. The whole bike. Use your ears. If anything rattles, that's where it needs more tightening."

ON SAFETY CHECKS: "Another thing you should always do, especially if you don't ride every day, is check your brakes and your tires.

"That's just as important on a little shopping trip as it is every morning of a long trip.

"You should get in the habit of checking your brakes whenever you start out—every time—*before* you need them. Then you've always got stopping power.

"About your tires: you'll get so you see right away when they're down. Or feel it, when you mount. A seasoned cyclist can tell how much air he needs by pinching the tire. It should hold its shape, pretty much, but give just a bit under your thumb's pressure. Until you get the hang of it, when you see your tire's down, use your pressure gauge. It takes a minute, but that minute's worth it."

ON TIRE PRESSURE: "Your bike'll respond better, track better, with the right amount of air in your tires. It's stamped right there on the side of most tires, what it *should* be. Much less, and she drags—takes too much effort to push. If it gets really low and you didn't notice, one of those overnight leaks, *don't ride on it when it's flat*. Either fix it right there, or walk it to somebody who can. If you ride on it, you risk ruining your tube, your tire—though both may be shot already—but most important, your rim or your whole wheel. All you need is to hit some bump, with no air in that tire, and kerplowie!"

ON TIRE-PRESSURE NUTS: "Don't get to be a tire-pressure nut, though. It's better to be a little bit under than little bit over. Specially in hot weather. Some people go a little crazy on the subject. With a real tire-pressure bug, everything's gotta be perfect, so he over-inflates for our road conditions" [eloquent gesture at the potholed, glass-strewn road conditions outside] "and he winds up blowing tube and tire both."

ON GAS STATION AIR PUMPS: "That's why I say you shouldn't use a gas station pump unless you have a hand gauge. Even then, you've gotta go slow. Auto tires are big, by comparison—they can take a lot of air. Bicycle tires don't hold that much. You can blow one, almost before you know it. With your hand pump, you're a lot less likely to overdo, and you can check as you go along."

Me: "What else am I likely to overdo?"

Him: "Mmmmmm—maybe oil. A *little* oil is good for a bike, especially in damp weather—but too much can ruin your tires. You know, when it oozes down, gets on the tire, that's very bad. And it's murder on a brake-shoe. You're better off to oil it too little than too much.

"And you know about vegetable oils? They *attract* dust. Forget your 3-in-one oil—save it for your sewing machine. Stick to the regular motor kind you get at a gas station, tell him you want it for your bike, he'll give you S.A.E. Number 20, or lighter. Or buy some from a bike dealer. Sturmey-Archer, Schwinn, they each make one special—you can't get righter than that."

ON TOOLS WE NEED: "You know, you've probably got everything you need already? Your husband got one of those Raleigh wrenches with his bike, right? That, your hand pump, your pressure gauge, and a small adjustable wrench, — they'll handle almost anything you *should* be doing to your bike.

"You know *not to use pliers on a nut* unless you're stuck out in the middle of the countryside and you haven't anything else, don't you? They'll round it's hex sides until you'll never be able to tighten—or loosen—it again. If you do that to a nut, *write down somewhere*— even on the corner of your map— 'Get a new nut for ....' and write in whatever it is—rear wheel, under the saddle, wherever—and when you get home, replace it. If you don't, you'll have nothing but trouble."

ON SPECIAL TOOLS: "You'll laugh, but the most dangerous, maddening and expensive tool to buy is a spoke wrench. It doesn't cost more than a dollar or two but every time I sell one, I know I'm really gonna be making money. That poor guy's gonna be back so quick, for more spokes or to have us balance a really bent wheel . . . It's not that you can't learn, you can, *anyone* can. But balancing a wheel is an art. And you break a lot of spokes, learning the art. That's what you pay a good mechanic for — the things he's broken, and learned from."

ON BIKE THIEVES: "My advice? Just don't leave your bike alone for any length of time. That 'I was only gone a minute' business makes me sick. You know it had to be *some* minute. A thief has to stalk your bike, circle it, just like any animal in the jungle circles his prey. Once he knows it's safe, he won't be interrupted, *then* he'll attack. Well, that stalking's gotta take time. It's your business to get back before he attacks.

"And you know about chains. A pretty good, solid one is important. It's that matter of time again—you've gotta slow down that thief. Anything that helps is important."

Me: "I know—but Jim got one of those good heavy ones, and it's so heavy he hates to take his bike out now.

He says it's a drag, but without it, he knows he's not safe. What do you do then?"

Him: "He carries it in the back, right? I thought so. Tell him to wrap it, and the lock too, around the seat post just below the saddle. He won't feel the weight nearly as much, that way."

ON WHO STEALS: "Oh, come on, now; some kid leaves his bike lying around, *anybody'd* steal it. You go in for a newspaper, you don't lock up—same thing. Who wouldn't? It could be a nice looking guy in a suit, or a guy spends three days in that hole in the street there— his kid needs a new bike; he sees the other kid's careless, or you are; next thing you know, the bike rides home with him.

"You know what gets stolen from Con Ed (Consolidated Edison) and Phone Company trucks the most? Bolt cutters. And that's not teen-age thievery, believe me. People who steal bolt cutters aren't after just one bike. No one can say where people who steal bikes come from, where they go—they're everywhere."

ON DANGERS TO RIDERS: "Would you believe a little thing like a patch of sand or gravel, at the bottom of a hill? It's nearly always a curve, and believe me, it's *dangerous*. Can be responsible for some pretty busted-up bikes; I've seen 'em. If a rider gets going too fast down-hill—and that's awfully easy to do if you don't watch it —then the traffic pushes him into a patch like that, he's in trouble if he doesn't know how to handle a skid. [If you don't, see page 57.] Bike riding's like everything else—you've got to allow room for the unexpected; if you don't, that's just what will happen.

ON HOW TO AVOID UNNECESSARY REPAIRS: "How could people avoid unnecessary repairs? Stay away from curbs. Kids never listen when I tell them. They ride on and off 'em to prove something, I guess. It'll kill even good tires in no time—and worse. Know what happens, every year, the week or so after Christmas? We get four, five, maybe more kids, coming back with a bike we know was bought here—and the front wheel's bent so they can't wheel it in the door. 'How'd you do it?' I ask 'em. 'Oh, I was just riding around, and it bent.' Wind can't bend steel you know— they've gotta have hit something. Some nuts try to tell me it was that way when they got it, and then I get mad. 'Every bike we sell gets *wheeled* out of here,' I tell 'em. Sometimes we can fix it, sometimes we have to sell 'em a new wheel.

"Grown-ups are a little better, but even they could save a bundle if they learned to ride around things, instead of over them. Glass on the road is supposed to be pretty bad, and there sure is a lot, but it doesn't cause as many flats as simple carelessness. If you get the glass out in time, it's often stayed in the tread without doing too much damage. Curbs and bumps, taken too fast, are far worse in my opinion."

ON PREVENTIVE MAINTENANCE: "Another thing that helps, and I'm not pushing my own business, you can go to anybody good. But a bike ought to be looked over, cleaned and greased and checked over, at least once every year. Just like you'd take your body to a doctor, your car to an auto mechanic—your bike needs looking at, the same way, by somebody who can stop little troubles before they've gone so far they're unsafe. It's health insurance for your bike.

"Remember how good your bike felt when we got done with it, that last time? That's how it ought to feel, all the time."

ON HOW TO KNOW A GOOD REPAIR SHOP: "Ask other people. Ask around in the neighborhood, ask other bike owners. 'How'd this guy treat you?' If you don't like what you hear, don't go there. There's such a bike boom today, lots of fly-by-night fellows are setting themselves up as experts. We *need* more good mechanics —lots more—but we don't need those guys. You'll generally be able to tell just by looking in. Look for a responsible adult in charge. Many teenagers are surprisingly good bike mechanics, but they shouldn't be *in charge*. Find out how long the guy's been in business, and who'll do the work, if you can. Look around, see who's doing it on other people's bikes."

ON HOW TO CHECK THEIR WORK: "Then, you see how they do. Check your bike out right away yourself, when you get it back. How's it feel? How does it run? That'll tell you more than I can. Don't worry, you'll *know*.

"And, if it isn't right, go back and yell like hell until he fixes it right. Be polite — okay — but yell like hell politely. He should be as interested in having it turn out right as you are, you know. It's only your bike, but it's his reputation, his *living*.

"Any bike dealer—any man who sells and services anything—as soon as he stops pleasing his customers, he's *dead*, whether or not he knows it."

CHAPTER 9

Even a Wench Can Wield a Wrench— Keep Your Bike at its Best

BEFORE WE DISCUSS what you can do to and for your bike, and what you cannot and must not do to it, we'd better get a little sheep-from-goat sorting done. A little honesty here can save you a great deal of trouble, unnecessary anger, and some real expense.

I hate to drag my father in again, but he's the best illustration I know for exactly the problems we face here. He and me together, that is. He's a brilliant man and an accomplished writer, highly original and effective in all his dealings with the world. He loves tools of all descriptions, and shared with us early his conviction that a hardware store is a kind of earthly heaven. He goes there because he loves what they have to offer; he understands, and showed us, why the best-made tool you can buy often costs more in the beginning but saves you most in the end.

This is the same gentleman who was attacking a stopped-up sink in the kitchen, one morning in my childhood. First from above, then from below, as I remember it. What my mother did was to leave the room and go call the plumber. "I can't stop him," she said, "so you'll have to hurry." She loved my father dearly but she knew at that moment what he'd forgotten—that he couldn't fix plumbing.

Daddy and I—and probably you—can do most simple things. Bolt tightening, putting on of bells and carriers, and even some innocent trouble-spotting: "It must be in that gismo there." But we should all keep our hands off the gismo, because one time out of three we'll fix it, but two times out of three we'll break it.

If you are the sort for whom gismos purr, come apart without "Liquid Wrench" and great trauma, open up to show meekly what the ailment is, then lie still for treatment without shooting springs through the air, never to be found again—you know it. You don't need my warning.

But if you're the other sort, like me and my father, you don't always want to know or admit it. And it's spotty—you can do some things but not the others. The key to the problem lies in knowing what you can't yet do—and in not getting your honor involved. Learn now, if you don't know it already—*the first time you hit any problem is the hardest*—and there, fixing a bike is just like puppy love; you know everything's wrong, but you don't know what the symptoms add up to. That's why *there's no dishonor in going to an expert to find out what's the matter.* In fact, that's when it's costliest *not* to.

Chances are, eight times out of ten, if you ask him right, he'll be happy to tell you what's wrong, and, because he already has lots of bikes that need fixing, he'll be just as happy as you if it's something he can tell you or show you how to fix yourself. For those two out of ten times when you almost certainly need an expert job of fixing, you'll spare your bike from your own ignorance and then anger, and spare your budget the cost of the extra fixing you might not have needed if you hadn't meddled in the first place.

Believe me, in the short run you'll think you're spending recklessly, but in the long run, you'll save a small fortune.

Don't say you haven't been warned. *Know* what you

can do and what you can't. And if you think "it's a little tricky," pay the man, but ask him questions; then, maybe you can do it next time.

Here we go, in list form—first:

Things Anyone Can Do:

Check and tighten loose bolts, nuts, and screws.

Oil, sparingly, as needed.

Inflate tires and check for proper pressure.

Adjust saddle height and tilt for comfortable, more effective riding.

Adjust handlebar height, tilt, and position (front to back) for your arm length.

Learn to listen and look, to identify troubles enough to describe them to your expert.

Things Anyone Can Learn to Do:

Fix a flat tire the right way.

Adjust brakes and replace worn shoes.

Spot brake-cable trouble before a disaster.

Adjust your cones, if a wheel is too tight or too loose.

Adjust three-speed Sturmey-Archer gear at the hub.

Clean chain and check for proper adjustment.

Put new reflective safety pedals on an older bike.

Things Often Worth Paying Someone Else to Do, and How Little They Cost:

Wheel alignment—Usually $3 to $6, depending on what's wrong. And remember — that 50¢ or $1 spoke wrench was the 'most expensive tool anyone can buy,' as my experts reported it—because of troubles it gets you into.

Three-speed gear adjustment—From 50¢ up. If very little is wrong, it really will be 50¢—maybe even free. 99% of the time, "up" tops out at about $4 to $5. But if the trouble is inside the hub, you mustn't touch it and it has to cost more—it must be repaired by someone who knows exactly what he is doing, and will take some time.

Ten-speed gear adjustment (derailleurs)—I say do very little and watch a lot, if they'll let you. Cost depends on what's wrong. If your bike is new, or new to you, most minor adjustments come under the original guarantee—not just the manufacturer's, but the bike shop's. But if you shifted improperly, hurt teeth on chain wheel or sprocket, it can be costly to replace.

Your first flat tire—$2 to $6, depending on what did it and what damage, whether you need new tube and/or tire, or simple patching job. BUT LEARN FROM IT.

Replacement of brake cables—Some people say you can do your own. Certainly you can check for fraying. My mother's phrase about spoiled food is your guide, here: "If there's *any* doubt, there's no doubt." If you don't *know* you can replace it right, pay the man. Brake failure can cost a limb or a life—and the work's not likely to cost more than $5 or so.

Yearly lubrication and general check-up—This one can be time consuming, depending on the dirt in your streets and your care between times. Two hours of a good man's time will run between $10-$15. My suspicion is that for most busy, apartment-based people, that's more than worth it, there being no time or place to do the job right.

Determining question: If you knew you could get down into the bearings successfully and replace them correctly afterwards, *would you know how to tell if they need replacement?* If you don't know, don't do it.

Things you should NEVER do:

Don't attempt any structural repairs; you haven't the

place or the equipment. And it's unsafe—critically unsafe—to do a halfway right job.

Don't let anybody offer to weld a broken joint or broken tube, or to bend a bent tube back and "fix it good as new." It never will be. Any metal part that's bent much out of alignment has been seriously weakened, will be further weakened by the bending-back process; it's next to impossible to repair safely. Get a new piece or part, even if it means getting a whole new frame; as life insurance, it's still cheap.

Don't mess with a bent crank, either. You'll just make things worse. If the crank is loose, the man in the shop has the tools to fix it easily—or to replace it easily; without them, it's a nightmare, and can be a disaster causer.

Don't repaint your own bike frame—unless you're able to take off every single non-frame part and replace it correctly, and unless you have the place to strip off the old paint totally. Touch-ups are okay (remember to sand down first to bare metal and remove rust) but a new paint job must be done from clean bare metal, and can't be done on an assembled bike.

Don't take apart three-speed or coaster-brake rear-wheel hubs. Parts fly all over the place, and unless you *know* how they went together before, you won't get them back right. With Sturmey-Archer, Bendix or other such hubs, a monthly *light* oiling is all that's usually needed.

Ten-speed hubs and their gears are even worse; parts are more complicated, adjustments even more delicate; things can be bent out-of-true without even really leaning on them with your screwdriver. Don't touch them if you can help it—even adjusting them is usually a matter for experts. (If you want to learn, buy an old, beat up junk ten-speed from your dealer and practice 'til you know — *then* work on your good bike. But not before.)

On principle leave bearings alone. They usually need expert handling. Also, you need to know which need grease and which need oil; most non-mechanics get all mixed up on this.

Don't take your chain apart with a chain rivet tool unless you've got an expert who'll stand at your elbow, telling you exactly how far to push and when to stop. It's a highly delicate operation, and if you do it wrong and the chain breaks later on when you're in motion, you'll deeply regret every penny you saved.

If you've ignored our spoke-wrench warnings and tried to tighten or loosen spokes, and discover even one or two out of your set are frozen into their spoke-nipples, stop right there and take the whole wheel to your expert. It's overdue for real maintenance, and you're not equipped to cope with what you face.

Don't ever throw a part away, even if it's broken beyond repair, until you know the replacement part you've gotten fits exactly and *works*. Don't go to a bike shop and ask by model number for the part you need; either take the whole bike and point, take the broken part, or take what it fitted into or onto or around, if it got lost on the road somewhere.

Bike parts are anything but standard, and what fits one won't usually fit the next one; that's true of anything from spokes to chains, from big chainwheels to little nuts, screws, and those zingy, elusive little springs. Chase after them, even in a dirty dusty road; it's worth it to find them, because then you get a true replacement. Even one tiny mis-sized part can do terribly odd things to the workings of a bicycle.

Do not use a chlorine-fortified cleanser on your white-wall bike tires, if that's what you have, without wiping it carefully off of everything else it touches, particularly wheel-rims and spokes. Like street salt, in the presence of dampness it can be highly corrosive.

Finally, Raleigh and other good makers tell you, and we repeat it here, don't use metal polish on any part of your bike. Soap and water, well rinsed (detergent if you must, but then you must re-oil extra-carefully), or kerosene, well wiped-off, will clean the metal parts of your bike best. Rub them dry after any cleaning, with a soft, clean, lint-free cloth, paper-towel, or those non-woven Handi-Wipes. Cleaner waxes, for the painted parts of your bike, must also be carefully handled, kept away from any rubber parts (tires, brake shoes, handle-grips, etc.) and carefully polished off again when you're through.

NOW Down To the Specifics: Things Anyone Can Do

1) Check and tighten loose bolts, nuts, and screws

Learn the long-distance group rider's *Fastcheck*—it's done on every bike in the group, every morning, doesn't take long, averts all sorts of troubles.

1) Check for loose nuts and bolts on fenders and carrier; put a wrench to the axle nuts, handlebar nuts, saddle bolt nut. Then grab the unloaded bike by the saddle and shake vigorously. Investigate and discover cause of any rattle or unusual noise; fix.

2) Clamp front brake on and push the bike forward against the brake to check for play in the headset (fork bearings and general front of frame) and/or unworking brakes.

3) Check rear brake, rear fork similarly.

4) Pick up bike by handlebars (be sure they're tight)

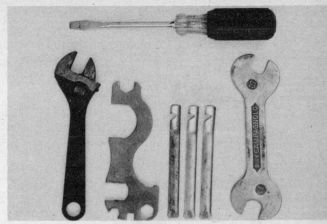

Fig. 26: **A typical set of useful tools for a cyclist: from left, a 6 inch adjustable wrench; a Raleigh wrench; three tire irons; and a Campagnolo wrench to fit cones and pedals (note those useful numberings, stamped in); finally, a good quality, medium size screwdriver, not worn down at the edges.**

so front wheel is off the ground; check tire for hardness by pinching; check wheel for side-to-side shake, and free spin. Any dents in wheel-rim?

5) Give rear wheel same check; hold by carrier or saddle; watch for shake, check free spin, check that tire is pumped up firm, wheel is true.

6) On three-speed bikes, check gear shift lever in each position and see that each gear works; push pedal forward; if everything's okay it will catch in each of the gear settings. Be sure to backpedal before you shift from high to a lower gear (so you won't hurt gears).

2) Oil, sparingly, as needed

Mostly that'll be once-a-month or so, depending on use and weather conditions. REMEMBER, GREASE

AND OIL DON'T MIX. Most *grease* points are jobs for your semi-yearly checkups: wheel bearings, bottom bracket, headset (front fork and connections to frame), and rear fork. They come packed with grease which should last a good six months, unless you ride on the beach or in a sandstorm. *Don't ever oil them.*

You never need more than a light amount of oil—a drop on each of the brake triggers' inside ends, another at the grabbing end where cable moves calipers against pivot blocks, (BUT DON'T GET ANY OIL ON THE BRAKE SHOES); a drop on each end of conventional

Fig. 27: **The arrows indicate the places you're likely to need a little regular oiling on a typical 3-speed lightweight bike. Whatever sort your bike is, the same kinds of places will need the same light oiling—moving parts that are *not* grease-packed bearings.**

pedals (rat-trap styles use grease); plus about half a teaspoonful squirted into rear three-speed hub, if it has an oil fitting. (Oil fittings look like a grommet with a hinged plastic lid, about a quarter inch up from wheel.)

Use only a good bicycle oil, or a light motor oil. *Never*

use 3-in-one oil, because its vegetable oil residue attracts and holds dust.

People once used to oil chains—one drop to each roller, then wipe off with oily rag. Now Lubriplate is considered better, longer lasting, less dirt-attracting. Cleaner to work with, too. Buy it at your bike shop or write Fiske Bros. Refining Co., Newark, New Jersey 07105. During wet weather, double-check things like chain to be sure it's protected against rust, and wipe clean of road gook, which tends to collect. If your bike is brand new, be sure to check out with dealer whether or not lubrication is sufficient—it can dry out on way to dealer and you.

3) Inflate Tires and Check for Proper Pressure

Don't do this with a gas-station air pump unless you *must*. They go too fast for the amount of air bike tires hold. Hand pumps require more effort from you, but are far safer.

Unscrew dust cap, put the valve-connector on and flip the guard down *quickly* (air rushes out if you don't hurry) and start pumping. When tire feels hard, with only a little yielding to your thumb's pressure, check with your hand gauge. Pump more, or let some out, as needed —a little less is better than too much, especially in hot weather. Put dust cap back and do other tire.

Most foot pumps are stay-at-home numbers; most clamp-on-the-bike types unfold in some tricky way. When buying, make sure pump fits your valves (the import tires have different ones, sometimes), then make sure the dealer shows you how to work the pump—or you won't know how when you need to.

For more mileage, easier riding, and lighter steering, keep tires inflated hard; a soft tire is a danger to wheel and rim—but an overinflated tire is likely to blow—so keeping tire pressure right is worth your care.

TIRE PRESSURE CHART

TIRE SIZE	APPROX. WEIGHT OF RIDER				
	Under 100 lbs.	125 lbs.	150 lbs.	175 lbs.	200 lbs.
12″ x 1⅜″	30-40 psi minimum*				
16″ x 1⅜″	30-40 psi minimum*				
18″ x 1⅜″	35-45 psi minimum*				
20″ x 1⅜″	40 psi	43 psi	50 psi	55 psi	60 psi
24″ x 2.125″	35-45 psi minimum*				
26″ x 1¼″	42 psi	45 psi	54 psi	60 psi	65 psi
26″ x 1⅜″	40 psi	43 psi	50 psi	55 psi	60 psi
26″ x 1¾″	30 psi	33 psi	40 psi	55 psi	50 psi
26″ x 2.125″	35-45 psi minimum*				
27″ x 1¼″	60 psi	65 psi	70 psi	75 psi	80 psi

*Add approximately 5 psi per 25 pounds of rider.

All figures indicate pounds of pressure per square inch; most tires have a minimum stamped on their sidewalls. If tire bulges when filled as full as chart indicates and you mount, you are too heavy for pressure used. At best, tire should not bulge, or bulge only a little bit, when ridden. And if it sags before you mount, you need air *urgently*—do not ride, *walk* to the nearest air pump.

4) Adjust saddle height and tilt for comfortable, more effective riding

In theory, it's easy; in practice, it's the subject of much controversy. ONE SURE THING; FOR SOLIDITY'S SAKE, A MINIMUM OF 2½ TO 3 INCHES OF SEAT POST *MUST* REMAIN INSIDE THE SEAT TUBE, NO MATTER WHERE YOU WANT THE SADDLE. If you need a high saddle, you can buy an extra-long seat post; if you need a lower one, get a lowering clamp, which cuts about 3 inches from the normal saddle height, to lowest point possible atop seat tube of your frame.

To move the saddle up or down, loosen the nut (with a wrench, *not pliers*) where the frame meets the seat post, and pull the saddle on its post up or push down, as you need to. (If it's stuck, or rusted into place, a little Liquid Wrench, given a minute to work, does wonders.) Then retighten the nut securely.

To tilt the saddle, or to move it forward or back in relation to the seat post, there are two seat nuts directly under the saddle; loosen one, change saddle as desired, then retighten. Some people like their saddle dead-level; most prefer a slight tilt upward in the fore-part. And the most comfortable front-to-back adjustment depends on your arm length; usually, it is achieved if the nose of the saddle is between two and three inches behind a line that extends directly up (a true vertical, not a tilt) from the center of the bottom bracket and chainwheel.

The controversy rages over a figure developed after research with racing cyclists in England: it stated that most saddles were set too low for efficient riding. They measured and came up with a figure of 109% of your inseam length—the distance in inches from your crotch to your heel, when you stand straight without shoes on. They reported that cyclists who set their saddles that distance (above the norm, usually) did better, with less effort. The distance is measured from the top of the seat to the pedal spindle when it's in a direct line with the seat tube—i.e., on the diagonal along the seat tube.

Until then, the rule of thumb was that you put your *heel* on the pedal and adjusted saddle height until your leg was straight; then, when pedaling with the *ball* of your foot and ankling properly, you get only a slight bend at the knee.

Wherever you set yours, be sure you can still reach ground with your tip-toes while seated; if you can't, stopping and dismounting can be tippy.

5) Adjust handlebar height, tilt, and distance for your arm length

This can involve front-to-back adjustment and tilt as well as up-and-down; each is important to your comfort. To start, raise the bars until the top bar is level with the nose of the saddle. (AGAIN, YOU *MUST* LEAVE 2½ TO 3 INCHES OF STEM INSIDE THE FRONT

TUBE FOR SOLIDITY AND SAFETY; IF YOU CAN'T, YOU NEED A LONGER STEM.) If you have drop or racing-type bars, you may tilt them as you prefer. Touring bars are generally almost level, or if anything, the grip ends raised a tiny bit (they rise from their stem connection naturally).

Front-to-back adjustment can mean purchasing a new stem (they come in front-to-back sizes from 1¾ inches to 4 inches, so considerable adjustment is possible) or moving the saddle forward, if your arms are short. The first is expensive ($5.50 to $7.50); the second, poor for proper ankling techniques you'll want to use as you cycle farther and more expertly. If you are buying a new bike, see if you can get your dealer to let you sit on a bike with an adjustable stem (the $7.50 number) and move it until you know what your arms need when your saddle's where it should be, for real comfort—then buy that size stem for your bike. The usual rough measure is that the distance from the saddle's forward peak to the handlebar should measure about the same as the distance between the tip of your elbow and the tips of your fingers.

6) Learn to listen and look, to identify troubles enough to describe them to your expert.

It sounds so simple. It's not. Any odd noise should be investigated at once. And any funny feeling should be checked out similarly. My bike felt odd, recently—like my sewing machine with a thread caught in it, it could run but *something* was holding me back. I looked and looked, listened and listened, blamed a totally innocent mechanic for a poor lubricating job. It took a *good* mechanic to notice my rear fender had an old bolt where a rear reflector had been that was dragging against the tire—inside the fender, where I hadn't even thought to look. Noises, feeling, smells—the look of the tires when you walk toward the bike, or mount—they all repay constant vigilance on your part. If you give it, you'll be rewarded by a purring, pleasure-to-ride machine, so it's worth your trouble.

THINGS ANYONE CAN LEARN TO DO

1. Fix a flat tire the right way

(We're dealing here only with wired-on "clincher" tires, which have inner tubes.)

1) If you know what caused the flat, you can often skip straight to the end of step #4, because instead of removing the wheel or whole tire, you only need to pull out the part of the inner tube that needs patching, and cope properly with it. Or cope with the valve.

To check the valve (highly suspect if your tire goes flat overnight) pump a little air into the tire, then, with your finger, put soapy water, plain water, or spit, on top of the valve. If bubbles form, your valve stem is loose, or needs replacing. If no bubbles, repeat the same check around the base of the valve; if bubbles form there, you probably need a new tube, may only need to tighten the nut that holds the valve in place.

2) If you know the tire's really flat but not why, start by removing the wheel. (Unless, of course, you can dip wheel and tire and all into a puddle or bucket, to locate the leak that way—then go back to step one and proceed to fix.) If you're on the road, lay the bike gently down, well out of traffic's way. If you're at home and can hang it up, so much the easier. Front wheels are easier to take off than back wheels. You loosen the nuts at each end of the axle where it runs between the front fork ends. Two wrenches make it easier, because each end of the axle's nut turns counterclockwise to come off, but that's in two different directions when you stand looking at the bike from one side. Confusing, but true. When the nuts are loose, gather up any washers that fall out, plus both

nuts, put them on a clean, dry rag or paper, in a paper cup—on your map, if you must—in the order they came off. Anything so you don't dirty or mislay them.

Your wheel should now come out almost by itself. If it doesn't, *with your fingers only,* spread the front fork ever-so-slightly, push the axle down and out, aiming forward.

3) Rear wheels are trickier. If the wheel has hand-brakes, they can be in your way. If it's at all possible to let the air entirely out of the tire (remember you'll have to be able to pump it up again later), do so, and wiggle the wheel out after releasing the wheel nuts as with the front-wheel directions. The maneuver out of the fork is identical, but you'll also have to lift the chain off the

Fig. 28: Here's how you spread the front fork with your fingers, very gently, after the axle-nuts are off, to get your front wheel out. Notice that the bike is sitting on saddle and handle-bars while you work— it's cleaner and easier this way. And remember not to put any parts down in the dirty road, You won't be able to find them.

sprocket teeth as you go. Do all this without bumping your brake-shoes around, or you'll have to reset them later.

If the wheel won't come off without releasing the brakes, I say go find a bicycle shop and carry the bike there—I don't think either you or I should mess about with anything so life-saving as good working brakes. But if your wheel did come out, you're ready for step #4.

4) Now you're ready to cope with tire and tube. Start by prying one side of the tire up from the rim, so you can get at the inner tube. Start by removing the valve-core, valve-cap and lock-nut; then get out your tire-irons. Sold specially and quite inexpensively at almost all bike shops

Fig. 29: The beaded edge of the tire is just beginning to come out of its bed in the wheel-rim; if your prying action isn't gentle, you'll rip that beaded edge, so watch it. You have enough problems now.

for this one job—removing a tire without ruining it or your rims. *Don't* use a screwdriver, or two screwdrivers, or a pen-knife, or anything else, if you can help it— they'll hurt your rim, probably your tire, and possibly you, if they slip—which is likely.

It's a little like prying a jar-lid, or a rubber canning-ring—once you get it going a little, the rest is easy. Don't force anything about a tire, ever. Push in under the rim, lever up, move over 2 to 4 to 6 inches, and just keep going until you've got one side fully out of the rim. LEAVE THE OTHER SIDE IN. Lift out the inner tube and look for what went wrong.

5) If you can't *see* the problem, inflate the tube a little, and either hold it to your ear and listen for a soft hiss of

Fig. 30: Your bead's out now, either all the way or enough to get at the problem, so you can examine and then patch the tube, and, if it needs it, your tire as well.

escaping air or put it in a puddle or bucket and look for bubbles. When you've found the problem (it may be one puncture or several — be sure to check all the way around), hang onto it or them while it dries and then mark the part(s) to be mended with whatever you have handy—chalk, adhesive tape, magic marker—anything you can see.

6) Patch kits come with instructions which are generally about the same; if yours varies, follow it. Usual rules are to use sandpaper or a metal scratcher to rough up the rubber surface so patch will hold; apply rubber cement so it covers a spot at least an inch or more in diameter, centered on the puncture (more, if its shape is funny); blow on the rubber cement, or wait till it gets

Fig. 31: **You're almost finished, but it's exasperatingly slow going now. Notice how your body's weight helps hold the tire down, how you push against your fingers with your thumbs, pinching the tire sides together, so you can make that tire-bead circle just big enough to fit over and then into the rim again, where it came from.**

tacky (three to five endless minutes, if you're in a hurry), pull the paper backing off a little part of the size patch you need for covering your rubber-cemented area. The best way to do this is pull about half off, holding always on the paper-covered part, position the patch in the rubber cement, then lift to pull off all the paper, out from under, so all the patch takes hold. That way, you don't get gummy fingers or spoil the seal by removing stickum from the patch. Now press all the patch down firmly, but be sure you don't do it so firmly you cement the other side of the inner tube to the inside of your patch.

7) While tube and patch dry, check the *tire,* inside and out, to see if you can tell what caused your flat.

Some common causes of bicycle tube and tire damage are illustrated on page 111.

You may find glass, nails, pieces of metal or sharp stone embedded in your tire, and if you don't pry them out, you're simply asking for another flat. Or you might find wear and tear on the tire you didn't suspect, or couldn't see—breaks in the sidewalls can sometimes be mended; breaks in the bead usually mean you're better off with a new tire.

Another common cause of trouble is from the inside of the wheel, under a strip of rubber—lift it and look to see if any spoke is not flush with its spoke-nipple; file down, as needed, and replace the rubber strip on the inside of the tire.

8) If you had to take the whole tire off the wheel to put on a new one, start by putting one side back first. If it doesn't fit, **you've got the wrong size tires. Never use anything but your hands to get a tire onto a wheel.**

9) Now, new tire or old, you've got one beaded edge of the tire into the wheel, and you've a patched tube, deflated, ready to insert. Tuck the tube carefully into the tire, all the way around, starting by putting the valve through the valve-hole in the rim. Now, still using only your bare hands, start tucking the second bead of the

COMMON TIRE AND TUBE DAMAGE

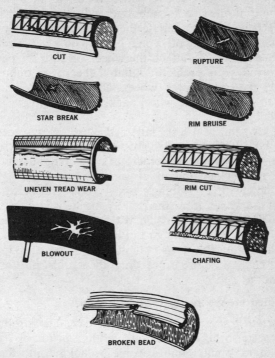

CUT

RUPTURE

STAR BREAK

RIM BRUISE

UNEVEN TREAD WEAR

RIM CUT

BLOWOUT

CHAFING

BROKEN BEAD

tire in, beginning on both sides of the valve and working your way around until all but 8 to 10 inches are in. If this is your first flat, you'll think you'll never make it, but you will. Don't resort to those tire irons—they can pinch your tube and you will be in worse trouble than when you started.

Now that things are tight, instead of pushing the second bead just under the rim, push it flatter, toward the other side and between a half-an-inch or a little more below the top of the rim. The effect is to enlarge the circle of your tire in relation to the fixed circle of your rim, and you can usually pop it in much more easily and be all done at once. If not, pause to cuss a bit, then go back to it; if one side fits, the other will.

10) If you had to deflate the tire to get it past your hand-brakes, coming off, you'll have to do it again going on—but before you attach the wheel, be sure the patch has solved your problem; inflate, check for bubbles, deflate, *then* attach the wheel. Otherwise you'll hate yourself if you put the wheel back, then find you've still got trouble.

11) Now, the acid test: inflate the tire enough to see if she holds. If not, you've got to go through the whole process of locating the other leak, undoing the tube, fixing, re-checking and all, again.

12) Finally, if everything's okay, you're ready to re-mount the wheel, reversing exactly the steps you took to get it off. Tighten the nuts hand-tight (clockwise at each end of the axle, remember) but be sure they don't make the wheel bind. If it starts to bind, read through section 4 of this chapter before proceeding, then adjust nuts and/or cones as needed .

2) Adjust brakes and replace worn shoes

Coaster-brakes: If you feel you have any problem with coaster-brakes, matters are serious (or can be) and you shouldn't make things worse by poking into them. You have two easy choices: take the whole bike to the shop, explain the problem, and let them fix it or advise you what you're doing wrong (both are possibilities); or, if you're *certain* the problem is within the brake itself, take the rear wheel off (most coaster-brake mechanisms are inside rear wheel-hubs) and then take the whole wheel to the man, to be fixed.

I strongly recommend you take the whole bike in, partly because it's easier, and partly because I would want my own diagnosis checked. If you don't, the wheel-alone method will save you only a small amount of money, and will cost you some time.

Hand-brakes are utterly different from coaster brakes. Three-speed bikes tend to have side-pull brakes and ten-speed bikes tend to have center-pull ones, but both act approximately the same way; tightening your grip on the brake lever pulls the brake-shoes in to grip the wheel-rim and bring the bike slowly to a stop, through friction. In either, your "slow-down" message is transmitted through the brake cables to the brake mechanisms.

The most usual adjustment needed is when one shoe is closer to the wheel-rim than the other, so you get grabby braking, with a resulting pull of the whole bike to one side, or a drag, because one shoe is braking even when you don't touch your brake-lever. I've pulled brake-lever arms with my fingers—it's a dirty way, but

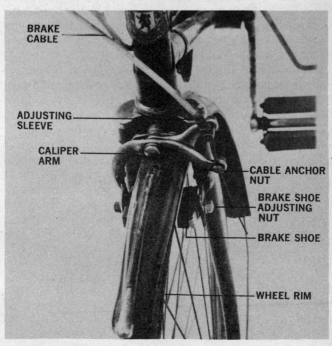

safer for all parts concerned, and necessary when you're jounced into the situation by a bump, as can happen, and without tools. If it happens to you on the road, pull the closer-in brake-arm out by hand, being careful not to bend or exert too much pressure. If *both* arms grab (it can happen) you need a screwdriver or wrench to loosen the caliper part of the arm from the center and give each side a wider swing before it takes hold. When you reach home, fix things properly before you ride again, if road conditions didn't let you do a good job.

If you're "tuning" your brakes in the comfort of your home or workshop, matters are entirely different. Brake cables stretch with age, and can need tightening. You'll spot this when your squeeze on the brake makes the lever travel much more than 2 inches, which is optimum; much more of a distance gives you too slow and perhaps inadequate braking; much less, too quick or grabby braking.

Look for an adjusting sleeve (it can be at either end of the brake-cable and is identifiable by the double-ring look of it interrupting the spaghetti; I believe it is more usual at the wheel-end) and start your operations there. Loosen the lock-ring or nut and turn the adjusting sleeve counterclockwise to tighten the cable the amount you think it needs; retighten the lock-ring and check things out. You may need more slack taken up than the adjusting sleeve can cope with; if so, find where the cable-end comes out of the caliper connection, loosen the lock-nut and/or cable anchor nut and bolt bit, pull the cable through, retighten, and test again until it's right. WHENEVER OPERATING WITH BRAKE-CABLES, DON'T CUT ANYTHING OFF THE ENDS UNTIL YOU ARE CERTAIN-SURE-POSITIVE YOU WON'T NEED TO READJUST TO A LOOSER POSITION.

If everything's as it should be, the hand-lever will now move about 2 inches to put your brakes full "on," and in the "off" position, the brake-shoes will be about ⅛ inch away from the wheel-rim. If your actions have changed that, or knocked the brake-shoes out of alignment, it's important you straighten things out.

Fig. 32: This bike's adjusting sleeve is at the wheel end of the brake-cable, and loosens upward. After you adjust the cable's length, tighten the sleeve back down firmly. Good and firmly—a loose brake-cable is an invitation to disaster.

So we come to *adjusting brake-shoes*. This will sound more complicated than it is. Ideally, a brake-shoe toes in slightly at the front, in a God's-eye view; it will give better rain-traction, for example, if it does, since it then tends to knock water off the wheel-rim; but, equally ideally, the whole brake-shoe should be involved in the grabbing process that stops the wheel, so toeing in too much would make that impossible. Seek a happy medium. One single nut usually holds the brake-shoe to the brake-arm; however you set your shoes, that nut is one you want to be certain stays *tight*.

Some brake-shoes are attached to the arm in such a way that up-and-down is also adjustable; be *certain* that your shoe does all its grabbing on the wheel-rim and none on the tire, or you'll wear both shoe and tire unmercifully, perhaps dangerously. Rims can take it; tire-edges can't, and shouldn't be asked to.

New brake-shoes come either as bare blocks of rubber or in an appropriate metal holder. It's well worth the small financial difference to get the in-the-holder ones, since adjusting and readjusting wears threads, and this way you start fresh and need not worry about old or worn threads stripping on you. Again, be certain that the new part you're putting on exactly matches the old one you're taking off, or there can be trouble.

Fig. 33: Here you have the adjusting sleeve tightened back down as it should be, and the brake shoes set, metal part forward, just that bit of distance from the wheel-rim, not too close at either end.

To replace, use a small adjustable wrench to loosen the nut that holds the shoe to the arm; look carefully before you remove the old shoe and notice how the closed metal end of the old brake-shoe faces forward; BE CERTAIN THE NEW BRAKE-SHOE GOES IN THE SAME WAY, CLOSED METAL END TOWARD THE *FRONT* OF THE BIKE, OR YOUR OWN PRESSURE ON THE BRAKE CAN PUSH THE BRAKE-SHOE PAD RIGHT OUT OF THE HOLDER AND LEAVE YOU WITH NO BRAKING POWER.

When the new shoes are in and adjusted to toe in slightly, grab only the wheel-rim, and rest about ⅛ inch away from the rim when you don't touch the brake, tighten everything firmly (but don't strip those delicate threads) and ride around the block until you're sure it feels right, works right, brakes right.

Your life depends too often on your brakes to ignore such a simple safety check.

3) Spot brake-cable trouble before a disaster

This means you look for fraying and any other weakening in the cable's length and at either end, on each brake cable. This means if you see that the spaghetti-tube that covers your cable has broken or worn thin someplace, you investigate fully to find out (a) why and (b) whether the cable underneath that break has also been damaged. This means that if something "feels funny"—if your braking power isn't as it was, and you can't see any visible reason—you *hasten* to check the whole bike out with an expert who'll know more than you. If it's all in your imagination (highly unlikely) you will at least calm your imagination; if it's real, you may well have added years to your own and your bike's useful life.

Small statement of the obvious: if you even *think* there's anything wrong with your brakes, and you ride

Fig. 34: Why is there a funny kink in that cable? Is the spaghetti tubing just frayed, or broken? If it has broken, is the cable inside frayed and/or broken, too? A regular visual check of your brake-cables sounds like a little thing, but it can save your life. Always check when you take a bike out after winter storage; always check when you're readying your bike for a long trip; and learn to check regularly when you bike regularly.

the bike to the bike-shop man, ride extra-slowly and extra-cautiously, so if foot-dragging is needed for braking, it's safe and possible. Nobody's going to know you haven't adequate brakes except you.

As for cable replacement, this one I leave to the professionals. You can save some money by doing it yourself, but I don't think brake systems are a wise place for penny-pinching, and it takes a fair amount of time, skill, and knowledge to adjust both ends correctly, let alone know the right-length cable to start out with.

4) Adjust Your Cones, if a Wheel's Too Tight or Too Loose

If a wheel binds (you'll discover this either in a fast-check or in riding, then verify it by lifting the wheel off the ground and spinning it) it is probably because your cones are too close to the bearings that ride on them—and you will have to have a shop loosen them or do it yourself. If the reverse is true, and the wheel wobbles even when the axle-nuts are not loose (with a wrench, remember—*no pliers*) then you'll either have to tighten the cones yourself or have someone do it. If you have quick-release hubs, I suggest you take them to a shop. You must work from *both* ends of the axle to move either cone, and it's both maddening and confusing. Of the two,

Fig. 35: Use both hands at once to loosen or tighten your cones—one hand to hold the wrench on your axle-nut (the mechanic's left hand), after you've loosened it just enough so your other hand can slip the cone-wrench around the slots of the cone's end (the mechanic's right hand). Hold the axle-nut in place while you adjust the cone looser or tighter, as needed. After you're done, keep the cone-wrench on your cone as long as there's room for it, so your adjustment doesn't slip in the process of tightening your axle-nuts back.

loose cones are the more dangerous and much more urgent. The life of your bearings and the straightness with which you can ride are both at stake.

To do it, you'll need a thin, offset cone-wrench—often it's just 50¢ or a dollar. Equally often, it's the other end of the thin wrench you'll want to use to keep your pedal lock-nuts tight, so it's a thrifty investment. But it *must* fit the cones on your bike—sizes can be different. Buy carefully.

Each axle contains two cones—one at each end, and they are what the bearings roll on, BUT YOU ONLY WORK AT ONE END.

Stand to the left (left as you're riding) of the bike. Loosen the big axle-nut at that end of the axle (counterclockwise) or the big wing-nut, whichever you have—but DO NOT REMOVE IT. THAT'S IMPORTANT. YOU DON'T NEED TO REMOVE IT TO DO THE JOB RIGHT. And if by some mischance you remove it *and* the cone, you could wind up chasing ball bearings all over the place. A sad fate. And an unnecessary one— while the wheel is in place is the *only* time you can adjust cones—that's why you left the right-end axle nut alone— to hold the wheel in place while you work on the left end. So if the axle-nut comes off accidentally, put it back, loosely, before you proceed.

Fig. 36: So you understand what you're coping with, this is a bare axle with cones and nuts in place. If you begin to see the sloping-down of the cones, as here, you've gone too far and are in trouble. Normally, of course, you'd have a wheel-hub and either front or back forks around all this. Look back at Fig. 33, if you need to compare; there the front axle, hubs, and cone assembly show quite clearly how they normally look.

Before you insert your cone wrench, look at the picture to see what a cone really looks like. You won't see the end that gave it its name—curvey or pointed, where the bearings roll—but you will see an oddly-slotted gismo, inside the wing-nut or axle-nut and the end of the fork (occasionally, there are two axle-nuts—one outside the fork, one inside it) and that's what you want to put your wrench around. The cone's slots and your wrench are made for each other.

Once in place, move the cone wrench clockwise to tighten, counter-clockwise to loosen. The best tightening system is to tighten things hand-tight, then back your wrench off a half or quarter-turn. Maybe even an eighth-of-a-turn. It should be both tight and free moving. When you think you've got it right, spin the wheel—that's your test. When it is right—moving freely without either bind or side-play, tighten your lock-nut (clockwise) with your other wrench while you hold the cone wrench in proper position. Then pull the cone wrench out and finish the job. Check it again, so you're sure.

Remember that cones and bearings are usually grease-packed, so don't mess things up with oil.

5) Adjust three-speed Sturmey-Archer gear

You don't normally need to do this unless your gears suddenly start slipping or you discover a new "neutral" you never had before, where the pedals go around, the wheels go forward, but the gears don't make them connect. Both can happen, both feel terrifying under you, and neither present great difficulties unless your indicator spindle is broken. (That can happen on long trips, or after hard wear, but it is not usual.)

Start by comparing your bike with the illustration nearby so you know we're working on the right side as you face the front of the bike, and we're dealing with an adjuster-ring on the end of the gear-cable and a funny little gismo inside a housing, into which the chain-link end of the gear-cable disappears. When you kneel down behind the right rear corner of the bike and look closely, you discover the housing has a tiny "window" in it, and your goal is to set the gear-cable's length so it pulls the little gismo inside the housing out just exactly as far as it should go, and no farther.

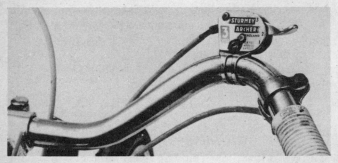

Fig. 37: Here's your middle speed, set on the usual 3-speed Sturmey-Archer gear control. Don't fiddle with this end of your gears; in most cases, you won't need to, and it usually isn't where you'll find the trouble.

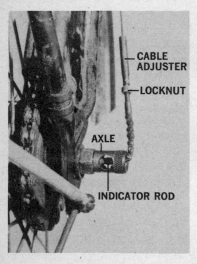

CABLE ADJUSTER

LOCKNUT

AXLE

INDICATOR ROD

Fig. 38: Where the gear-cable enters the rear hub, on the chain side of your wheel, this "window" lets you see both the end of your axle and the end of your indicator spindle. (The gear-cable connects to the spindle by those flat chain-links). In your normal or middle gear, spindle end and axle end should line up approximately as shown; if not, the adjusting sleeve and lock-nut, just above the "window," are what you adjust to shorten or lengthen the cable.

Next, put your bike's gear-control lever into the middle position. Unscrew the lock-nut (it will move down and loosen as you turn it clockwise) so the cable-adjuster is free to move. Kneel behind the rear quarter of the bike until you can see through the circular "window" that the last link of the chain that connects the cable to the spindle is just free of the axle (look inside the window); then adjust, slowly, carefully, upward and downward with the cable-adjuster, *until the end of the indicator-rod is exactly level with the outside end of the axle*, inside the "window." When it's right where it should be, tighten the lock-nut upward to keep everything where you set it. Now, all three of your gears should be correctly adjusted.

Replacing an indicator-spindle is a much more complex undertaking, especially if the spindle's broken off inside the housing. Take it to an expert, or, if you're on a group trip, find someone who's done it before. The indicator spindle is extremely delicate, and in this case, a small amount of messing-up on your part can do costly damage to the whole wheel-hub-gear arrangement, if you're not aware *exactly* of what can and will go wrong.

In The Dark 3-Speed Adjustment

We can also reveal to you, for the first time in print, the Bill Nelson, throughly-road-tested, "works-even-in-the-dark" system for adjusting the 3-speed gear under difficult conditions. It works, as you'd assume, by feel and is suggested for when you haven't got daylight, or a pal to hold a light, or maybe even a light.

You stand on the left of the bike—left as you ride, remember. You reach down with your left hand and back pedal a bit to loosen the indicator-spindle-gear-cable mechanism. Then, with your right hand, pull the chain-end of the gear-cable and the indicator spindle as far out of the housing as you can (without breaking them, of course—it's no tug of war, because you're stronger and should know it), then reach up to your gear control lever and set it to your lowest speed. Then, using the same principles of moving the locknut described above, you adjust the slack in your gear cable to a smoothly-operating minimum. (Easily said, but after the first few times you'll know the right feel. No looseness, no bind.)

Then, check your gears out. Lift the rear wheel or get someone to lift it for you and hold it up. Back-pedal between gear changes so you don't hurt a sprocket-tooth or your chain. Each gear *should* work perfectly. Even when adjusted in the dark.

Remember, that if something happens to your 3-speed gearing, what you'll have left, with direct-drive, is the top speed, and although starts will be tough going, you can probably get back home or to a bike shop in relative safety.

6) Clean Chain and Check for Proper Adjustment

This is messy, and can be as total a job as you want to do, but will *always* get you dirty. Plan on it. Get some mechanic's grease-dissolving hand-cleaner; some clean rags; an old toothbrush, or a wire suede-shoe brush you'll never use again on shoes, a couple of toothpicks or pipe cleaners, and a good supply of newspapers. Wear old clothes, perhaps even ones you plan to throw out later. Put the newspapers down as protection for whatever surface you use and value.

If you're timid, turn your bike upside down on the newspaper bed and start brushing, poking, and wiping off as much dirt as you can, first off the chain-wheel and then off the chain itself. (A dustpan and brush will help keep you from kneeling in your own litter and getting dirtier.) You'll find more dirt than you expect; you'll wind up poking bits of toothpick or brush or something to get lumps of solidified junk out from between rollers, and you'll keep wiping the chainwheel, then turning it, then finding it dirty again from what you still haven't gotten out of the chain. Anything you get out by these means is all to the good for the bike—but it's only a halfway measure, and someday you'll wind up deciding you really need to do a total job, or to have an expert do one.

That usually means removing a wheel; it certainly means removing the chain from the bike, and purchasing kerosene from your hardware store or bike shop. (Don't use gasoline; don't use cleaning fluid. And don't work near an open flame, even with kerosene—which means a gas stove's pilot as well as your best friend's dropping by and lighting a cigarette.) You'll also need a pan big enough to put the chain and kerosene into, at least two inches deep, and Lubriplate with which to lubricate after you've gotten things clean, as well as the rags and stuff listed above.

Start by loosening or removing the rear wheel enough to get the chain off the sprockets of it, and then off the chainwheel (the axle-nuts loosen counterclockwise, remember, and that's different at each end of the axle, if you stand over the bike). Put the chain into kerosene deep enough to cover it and then some, and let it stand a while. Go have a beer, or admire yourself for the neat way you remembered to use a *wrench* on the wheel-nuts and didn't round or damage them by using a pliers. After it's been soaking as long as you can stand (overnight is great, but who has that much patience?) come back and attack the gunk and junk with the toothbrush, shoe-brush, toothpick, rub and slosh method—i.e., you poke and push gunk away from a part of the chain, then you slosh the whole thing in the kerosene and dissolve away another layer, then you poke and push some more. If your kerosene looks as though it's dirtying things more than cleaning them, dump it down the toilet and start again with clean kerosene. Use a rag dipped in the kerosene to clean the chainwheel and sprockets, and check about for nicked, beat-up teeth, and chain links that don't move as easily as they should. (That's what you'd pay an expert to do, so don't ignore it—if you find and solve problems at this stage, it's one more thing that won't go wrong for you out on the road and in traffic.)

Really beat-up or bent or broken teeth on a chain-wheel or sprocket (you probably won't find this except on a secondhand bike, unless you're a real gear-clasher on on the road) mean *instant* replacement, which would lead you to the bike-shop at this point. So would any damaged rollers or links on the chain.

For simplicity, let's assume your chain is fine and so is your chainwheel and your sprocket—now all clean, wiped free of all gunk, dirt, and kerosene, and with no pieces of rag or brush caught in them to create new troubles.

You start your lubrication with Lubriplate wiped *lightly* along the entire chain length—the more you use, the more dirt you'll have to remove next time, the less you use, the more chance you'll have to polish away rust with a bit of steel wool, next time; steer between. Put it around the chainwheel, then lift back over the rear wheel hub and sprocket, if you've just loosened them, or

Fig. 39: See the half-inch you can push a well-adjusted chain out of true? If yours can be pushed much more, it's too slack; much less, and it's too tight. This is a light-push test, remember, not a tug-o'-war, so don't overdo the push-ing and adjusting. Usually you don't need to adjust your chain very often.

reassemble the whole rear wheel, if you had to take it out to get the chain off, *but don't tighten anything yet.* Pull the wheel back far enough so spinning the chainwheel by the pedals makes everything move—be sure it's right, clean, smooth, and easy-moving—no clutch at one gear-tooth, no clunk over a missing or bent tooth; this is your double-check stage.

When everything's as smooth as French custard, you're ready to set the rear wheel into position and pull the chain's slack up to the exact half-inch of extra play that gives you the most efficient movement of your energy through the power-train of pedal, chainwheel, chain, and gears. Push or pull the rear wheel into the correct position *with your fingers only;* start the right axle-nut first, when the wheel is placed correctly front-to-back; then carefully adjust so the wheel is centered properly, side to side, equidistant from the chain-stays. (When you sight from the rear of a three-speed bike, both rims will line up straight through the bike-frame's axis.) Then start the left axle-nut, then tighten both carefully, hand-tight with the wrench, not so tight as to bind, not so loose as to give you side-play.

There are some don'ts about chains to remember: don't put a really rusty chain back on your bike, no matter how clean of dirt you've gotten it; spend the money for a new one, and take better care of it when you've installed it. Regular cleaning and wiping with Lubriplate on a clean rag—even regular oiling, if you haven't any Lubriplate, though any hardware or bike shop can sell it to you—and an extra wipe-clean when you come in out of the rain or off salted, snowy streets, will keep your chain new-feeling longer.

Don't let your chain go slacker than the 1/2 inch of play that's recommended; it'll wear the teeth off your sprockets; and don't let it get tighter, or set it tighter than that, because, oddly, it'll also wear the teeth off your sprockets. Either way it's off-kilter, you lose.

If you get a pants-leg caught in it, or some other

Fig. 40: A new, reflective pedal has been put onto the right pedal-crank and you are set to tighten the lock-nut, turning it clockwise. Be sure, whenever you work on a pedal, to get it back on tight.

piece of clothing, go very gently as you pull it out, or you can bend chainwheel teeth or sprocket-teeth, or pull one or more chain links out of true. Generally, the cloth will go only a part of a revolution before it bunches enough to stop the bike; removal involves a slow rotation of the chain-wheel backward with the rear wheel off the ground. You may need a second person to help.

And if your chain squeaks, it's desperately trying to tell you it needs lubrication—it may already be too late. Don't ignore the warning.

7) Put New Reflective Pedals On An Old Bike For Extra Safety

Pedals are like your hands: they look like each other until you look closely, when you realize they are mirror-image likenesses, not true ones. Pedals, therefore, come in pairs, marked L or R for Left or Right. The crucial thing to hang onto is which pedal you're working with at any given moment, because everything that works one way for one pedal works the opposite way for the other.

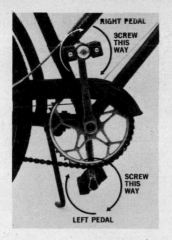

Fig. 41: Arrows tell the story here: both pedals do the same things, but because you work on them from different sides of the bike, they look like opposites. The right pedal loosens going counterclockwise, tightens clockwise. The left pedal loosens going clockwise, tightens counterclockwise. If they bind at the start, try a drop of Liquid Wrench—but don't overdo it—too much makes for trouble tightening later.

I don't believe either you or I should mess with the insides of pedals, but switching one for another is a simple matter of tightening it into the pedal crank by the spindle-end, and that I believe we both can do. It's a lot easier if, when you're buying the reflective pedals that fit your bike, you also spend a big 50¢ or so extra and buy a thin pedal wrench—the lock-nut you'll need to loosen is only a fraction wider than 1/8 inch thick, and most wrenches won't fit between the spinning pedal and the pedal crank.

Start with the *right pedal;* on it, the lock-nut will loosen counterclockwise, tighten clockwise. Loosen the nut, slip out the pedal, slip in the new one after checking for the R that shows you haven't mixed them up, then tighten the lock-nut, turning clockwise, as the picture shows.

Reverse everything for the left pedal: loosen the nut by turning it clockwise, as you face it; slip out the old pedal, insert the new reflective one (and don't be ashamed to look for the L, to be certain you didn't goof, earlier, or someone in a shipping-department didn't goof), and then tighten by turning the lock-nut counter-clockwise.

Both should wind up good and tight, or they will be so loose they allow side-play. However you achieve it, be careful to check—and check after your next ride—that it *stays* tight.

Depending on the pedals you purchased, you may elect to put a drop of oil at each end when you're through and everything's checked out, or a *light* bit of Lubriplate; but if your dealer, or the manufacturer's instructions, say not to, don't add a thing.

The Incredibly-Easy Way to Learn to Ride; The Easy Way to More Effective Cycling; How to Teach Someone Else Without Chills or Spills; and, Finally, a Review of the Rules of the Road for All

Teaching Yourself is Easy—If You Don't Already Know

If you have never ridden a bike before, probably you feel foolish about the whole idea. You don't need to. There are two easy tricks to make teaching yourself almost painless, and you may even keep your learning process a secret.

First, rent or borrow a girl's model bike that's at least two sizes too small for you—a 19½-inch frame three-speed bike is just right for most adults, and you won't need it long. You should be able to sit on the seat and yet put both feet *easily* onto the ground at the same time. Take the bike off by yourself, where people won't get in your way, and where the ground is reasonably level, if at all possible. Many sorts of places like that exist—a park path, a school or supermarket parking lot when they're empty, even a grassy area, if it isn't too damp out (that makes things slippery)—levelness and un-interruptedness are your two prime requirements.

Second, put those feet down on the ground and push yourself along. What you discover first is that you *can* balance a bicycle—in fact, the bicycle almost balances for you, *when you keep it going forward*. Next you find that you can steer, and the bicycle goes where you want it to, still in balance. If you feel yourself starting to fall, turn your handlebars toward the direction you felt yourself falling, and the bike will right itself if you keep going, and you *won't* fall at all. After a short while of this—say ten minutes of just pushing, then twenty-to-thirty of pushing-and-steering—you're ready to raise the saddle, little by little, to a height closer to the one you'd normally bike at, and begin pedaling practice. (For your final best saddle-height, see page 102, but don't move it up by jumps much bigger than ½-inch at first, until you really get the feel of things.)

Once you've got the principle—that the bike itself generally tends to stay up by itself if you just keep it going forward—you're over the worst of the learning period and into the fun. But you'd better practice stopping, using whatever brakes your practice bike has, just so you know how; slow ahead of time if you've got sufficient warning of trouble ahead, then back-pedal, with coaster brakes, or squeeze, with hand-brakes. To slow, with hand brakes, squeeze-release, squeeze-release is best —a fluttering movement. The trick here is to be ready to dismount when the bike stops (which is easier on a girl's model). Because a stopped bicycle tends instantly to lean toward one side or the other, if you want to stay seated put a foot out to one side when your speed is slow enough so it's safe, and lean to that side. All it takes is practice, although in words it may sound complicated; when your feet and your body weight start cooperating with your bike's natural reflexes, the results are just naturally safe, sound, and sensible and you can forget your supply of Band-Aids.

Then you can switch up, as gradually as you find

comfortable, to the size bicycle you really ought to be riding.

This method is kinder both to your posterior and your dignity than having a friend run along behind and push —the old-time way of learning. You don't wobble nearly as much (his sense of where you were going, and yours, almost never coincided, which is what produced those worrisome wobbles); but, far more important, you develop a sense of security about your balance that is the heart and soul of the whole bicycling experience. Practice where pedestrians and traffic don't threaten you too soon, and, literally, you're off to a flying start. Soon you'll think that you *always* knew how, only you just hadn't put your instincts to the road test.

Don't forget, if you're a person who does not drive, once you've got control over your bike, and your reflexes and its reflexes match, you're responsible for obeying not only signs and stoplights; with your new-found skill, you need to know *all* the rules of the road, all the things traffic expects of you. Review them, carefully, at the end of this chapter; they are truly important.

The Easy Way to More Effective Cycling for Anyone from Post-beginner to Novice Olympic Star—Teaching Yourself is a Matter of Practice.

It's not easy and it's not hard; it's a matter of putting your mind on the process and repeating it, correctly, over and over and over and over, until the right techniques are automatic to you. If you've learned other techniques, it's going to take some time to unlearn them before the new ones become natural to you— but you'll be well rewarded by the new efficiency you'll find in your cycling. You'll also enjoy the easy, not effortless but effort-well-directed sense you get when your body and your bike work well together, this better way.

Ankling is the first thing you should learn, after balance, steering, and stopping are natural to you, if you're new to cycling. As a beginner, you have an enormous advantage—you'll learn the correct way the first time, have no bad habits to forget first. For nonbeginners it's much harder, because you have to keep remembering to break your old habits—but it's really not all that difficult.

Assume your pedals are each moving like clock hands: start with your right foot and right pedal in the top, or 12 o'clock position. Place the ball of your foot (*not* the

Fig. 42: Ankling practice begins with the right pedal at the top of a stroke (twelve o'clock) and the ball of your foot centered on the pedal. The clock's in your head, of course, and is what you'd see from the right side of the bike as you rode, not the left, as shown here. Remember, always practice either ankling or cadence counting away from traffic until you've got the hang of it—it's tricky, trying to watch everything at once, as the author's slightly grim expression betrays.

Fig. 43: Right foot's pushing down, past three and towards four o'clock, and the heel begins rising. (The left foot, being on the up stroke, almost coasts—as if you'd lifted the pedal with it, if you could.)

Fig. 44: Right foot's almost to six o'clock, left one's ready to start on the down as it passes twelve o'clock.

toes and *not* the arch—the ball is halfway between those two, and if it doesn't do your pushing, in the ankling technique or any other, your muscles will soon report the sad difference) on the pedal with the heel slightly down and the toes pointing slightly up—and start pushing down.

By the time you've moved the foot from 12 to 3 o'clock, your toes will have pushed down a little and your heel moved up a little; by the time you get to 6 o'clock, still pushing down with the ball, your heel will be about 45° in the air.

Then, when your right foot's at the bottom of its revolution, your left one's at the top, ready to start down; it is poised as the right one was, toes slightly up, to push down with the ball of the foot through the down-part of the cycle.

At the same moment the left starts to push down, your right foot starts to move up. Keep the *ball* of your foot on the pedal and press lightly as you lower the heel

Fig. 45: There you go, you've got it! Your down-moving foot pushes and its heel lifts almost automatically; your up-moving foot coasts or almost-lifts, and its heel moves into position for the next down-stroke's push. That's all there is to ankling.

on the rise of the pedal until, when it reaches 12 o'clock again, you're in position for the next downstroke.

If you were wearing racing shoes and your pedals had toe-clips, you'd be held by them so the movement would become automatic: you could actually *lift* with the one foot on the upstroke while the other foot made the downstroke—a benefit all racers learn to use, or lose the race. But toe-clips for city cycling are a nuisance, and you don't need them to get the idea.

While one foot pushes down, *hard*, with the ball of the foot, the other rides the opposite pedal so lightly it's almost lifting it, but moving from a heel-up position to a heel-down, toes-up position to get poised for the next downstroke part of the cycle.

This is a case where a half hour's practice is worth at least a thousand words and a dozen illustrations. When you feel the alternating push-and-lift, pulsing through each foot and each cycle, you've got it. But pick a place to practice where you don't have to watch traffic—you'll be watching your feet in some detail, and you simply can't do both safely.

Some people feel the trouble to learn ankling isn't worth the percentage of extra push it gives—somewhere around twenty percent, depending on how well you do it. They prefer the simple flat-foot-at-all-times approach. Some long distance cyclists alternate them, finding the change more restful than either one used full time. You can decide for yourself, now that you know what's involved. Maybe you'll only ankle up hills, where the extra push counts. Maybe you'll do it all the time. Try it and see for yourself.

Cadence is the next step to the professional use of your body to power your bike expertly, and here we have to consider the intricacies of the gearing system. We're only going to consider your gears slightly, however, because most gearing charts offend my sensitivities; they should be simpler, more informative and less formidable; you won't find one here. Gene Portuesi, of Cycle-Pedia (see Chapter 13, page 251) has made a science of them—if they interest you, write to him or consult your library; each probably has what you want. Their point, made extensively and quite confusingly, I think, is how much forward motion you get out of a single revolution of a gear with so-and-so-many teeth combined with a wheel of such-and-such a diameter. But you can discover it in practice, without bothering with formulas, and get the feel of the bike wisdom better, by the seat-of-the-pants method.

Cadence simply means the regularity with which you turn the pedals through their revolutions, and you can set any cadence that suits you. As it varies, your forward progress varies; the charts measure it down to the parts-of-an-inch you find meaningful; I don't think you need it measured, because I think it's more fun to *see* it.

Remember any army movie you ever saw, and any sergeant saying, *"Hup,* two, three, four, *Hup,* two, three, four . . ."? Well, you're the sergeant; the pace you set, and the size of your wheel's diameter, determine the amount of your progress; the *beat* of the progress should be as regular as possible, for ultimate professional expertise on a bike; and that's what your cadence is.

Some people call it "rhythm." Many bike people call it "spin"—as in "I was spinning sixty." Call it what you like, its regularity is more important than its total — which is hard to accept but true.

When you're beginning to cycle, your cadence will vary as things you meet seem difficult or easy to you. And that's natural, but a mistake. It should stay as even as possible, whatever you meet, whatever happens. When you meet a problem, *gear down;* then your cadence continues uninterrupted—which is good practice—and you come home a lot less tired. In fact, gearing down is the secret of most effective cycling—but it takes a while on a bike before you believe that, and aren't ashamed to be caught in your low gear. Using low gear properly is a sign of intelligent usage of the bike's capabilities. If you don't believe that, you will struggle needlessly, overtire your muscles and waste your strength, to show off—and to whom? Don't do it. Use your low gear whenever you need it, and be proud you know enough to save your energies for what's important.

High gears let your feet go around less for the same amount of forward progress, and when you're new to biking it feels like the discovery of the century—until you pull up to a stoplight, forget to gear down, and then try to start in high gear. Painful in the thighs, then and later, and highly educational. The resulting agony may be good for the thigh muscles (small comfort) but you'll feel it for days—and you don't need to put yourself through it.

If you learn to *gear down automatically* at a stop, or a difficulty, you'll suffer far less fatigue at the end of a ride; you'll have gone through more pedal revolutions, but you'll have pushed a great deal less, so each of the turns will have used less of your total energy. As you know, it's sudden, short-term overloads that burn out motors and tax generators, and make a muscle ache later. Under-gearing means you don't overload the muscle, you do learn a good cadence, and gradually, you increase it. Between sixty and eighty-five pedal strokes per minute is what the "average" experienced adult cyclist can do on a ten-speed bicycle. Racers do perhaps twice that much, but for short periods only, and they take literally years to work up to it. On a three-speed bike, the terrain would make a greater difference since you have fewer gear choices to help you up a hill. But don't listen to anything except your own comfort. And don't stop, in traffic, to count how you're doing—you'll lose more than your count.

Crouch vs. Non-Crouch Positions — Part of the Efficiency-of-Your-Riding Decision. This is one nobody will ever settle to everyone's satisfaction, so we can only give you some factors to weigh into your personal equation, as with bicycle choices.

Back where we told you how to fit a bicycle to you, we discussed saddle height and handlebar height, and gave some figures with which to measure yourself and your bike (page 103.) We didn't talk about the position you ride in, there, because it's a matter of choice, of experience, and, in the long run, of whether you're willing to put yourself out, to make yourself uncomfortable for a short time to learn a long-distance effective-riding technique, or whether you don't give a hoot about distance cycling. And that's a terribly personal decision.

Arguments for the Crouch Position: It has long been the preferred position for long-distance and racing cyclists in Europe; scientists who've studied the question agree that it's not only the most comfortable position for *long-distance riding* and the most efficient for hill-climbing, but that it is also beneficial to the slightly arched spinal column, and allows the cyclist to inhale and exhale more effectively as he works at his cycling movements. As a general rule, for top riding efficiency, they contend that proper adjustment of the saddle and handlebars (saddle slightly higher, bars somewhat lower than you or I would expect) makes a great deal of difference in comfort, fatigue, and energy output required to cover similar distances. Generally, they suggest handlebar height be lowered in proportion to the duration and energy-output of the ride; that's why expert racers and long distance riders prefer their dropped bars and hunch themselves over into the crouch position; it not only makes breathing easier, it gives the whole body less wind resistance to fight against—and that's a serious factor in racing. Did you know racers take turns, spurting ahead from the "pack," but dropping back after only a few minutes of the lead, because the lead rider breaks the wind — literally, cuts it down and away, like a boat breaking a wave—for those who follow behind—and therefore, being first all the time would take too much out of any one racer?

Arguments for the Sit-Up "Touring" Position: The first and best is that we're not all racers. Until you're fighting over half-of-a-second differences per lap, the crouch position requires a considerable amount of practice before it feels natural or comfortable; during that time, you're quite uncomfortable; and, if you plan to ride reasonably short distances, or any length, but on city and suburban streets where unexpected moves by cars and pedestrians offer considerable hazard, you jolly well *need* to sit up as tall as you can, see as much as you can, and in all directions. Eyes in the back of your head would be extremely useful. Crouching reduces what you can see peripherally, and what you can see *over,* unless you're truly expert at it; to the novice, it makes head-turning to see what's behind you a gymnastic exercise.

Your own wrists, shoulders, back, and neck will tell you more than any book can begin to convey; you can teach them, bend and school your muscles to your will, if you're bent on becoming a racer; you don't need to, and might not wish to, if you're not so inclined. Whatever you choose, do learn one thing from good racers: move your hands' position on the handlebars as you ride, occasionally or frequently, to rest them—all the experts do.

Teaching Someone Else

My first instinct was to suggest you go out of town instead, that weekend, since the someone else is usually a youngster. But then I learned about the Balancing Act Method described above, and took heart.

Basic principles stay the same: the learner must discover *for himself*, sitting on the saddle and pushing along with his feet, that he won't fall down, and that keeping the bike moving forward tends to keep it upright and in balance. Then he must gradually learn steering, pedaling, slowing, and stopping.

A person who is going to ride a coaster brake bike should learn on one—there's no point in anything else, since braking correctly should become an instant reflex when there's trouble. Lift the rear wheel off the ground, get it twirling with your hand on the pedal, then show how easily the coaster brake stops the wheel with a simple back-pedaling motion. (This is before your learner is on the bike, of course.) Back-pedal braking is easy to learn if you've seen how it works. Also prepare him for the fact that stopping will make the bike lean to one side or the other, and teach him to have a foot ready to put to one side, for balance. Otherwise, coming to a stop will cost him the balancing faith you've just been teaching him. Again, the bike should be enough smaller, or the saddle and handlebars set enough lower, so the feet of the learner reach the ground with ease. After that, it's clear sailing.

Teaching non-drivers (especially youngsters) the Rules of the Road

There is one responsibility in teaching bicycling that is all too often overlooked. Especially in the teaching of youngsters, it's often pushed off on overburdened schoolteachers, who may not even know when the bike lessons begin. So it's up to you, the youngster's parents, or both together.

Even if the youngster you're teaching is being taught he may only ride on the sidewalk, it's just a matter of time before he sort of leaks over and is riding in the streets. "The other kids do!" will be his defense, if you criticize—and he'll be right. Don't blame him. He thinks he's playing, and the street often looks empty. But you must prepare him for what he's going to meet in that street. *It is never going to occur to him that he is infringing on territory where cars expect to be alone—or where*

*they follow rules he too can follow, and must—unless
you tell him.*

Plan far enough ahead to get a copy of the vehicular
code of your city or state—usually a driver's training
manual is the clearest explanation of it there is—and
then make out a simple set of rules your learner must
know and obey, and ideas he must at least try to com-
prehend.

Method matters less than results, here. Make flash-
card games out of stop-sign and other sign shapes, if
your youngster would learn that way—point them out
as you drive, if that's better—or give him the driver-
training manual and ask questions, later, to be sure he's
used it, if he's old enough so its technical terms won't
confuse him. *Any means you use to make the concepts
clear are urgent and important to his safety and survival.*
Youngsters are pretty good about rules if they understand there are reasons for them; even young children
can ride quite safely if you make clear to them why it's
important to know the rules, if you keep the rules they
must learn simple, and if you obey them yourself.

Adults learning to ride, who haven't learned to drive,
usually find the whole process interesting, and have no
trouble.

*All bicycle riders, whatever their age or experience,
must obey street and highway signs and traffic signals,
just as motor traffic and pedestrian traffic must. It is
crucial that you, or the person you're teaching, be
thoroughly familiar with each of the rules and what they
mean.* It is also vital that you make clear that *just having
the green light doesn't always give one total safety—*
sometimes other people don't obey the rules—and *teach
your learner to look before leaping.*

There are three rules of first importance for bicyclists
not usually found in motor-vehicle booklets:

1) Bicyclists are alway safer when they ride in single
file.

2) Bicyclists are never safe when they "hitch" a ride on the back of a car or truck; its brakes and theirs don't work the same ways, and real danger lurks.

3) Never, ever, under any circumstances, ride two-on-a-bike unless it's a tandem.

Here's what Signals, Signs and Pavement Markings Mean You Must Do:

GREEN LIGHT means GO, but before you proceed, make sure it is safe. Check for turning cars, let pedestrians go first, and *never* turn in front of a moving car.

YELLOW LIGHT means WARNING, the signal is changing. SLOW DOWN, get ready to stop. Don't enter the intersection.

RED LIGHT means STOP. Don't enter the intersection, don't get in the way of cross-traffic. WAIT FOR THE GREEN LIGHT BEFORE YOU PROCEED, check for anyone else who's in motion—car or person—AND THEN GO WHEN IT'S SAFE FOR YOU.

FLASHING RED LIGHT means you must STOP, look in all directions, allow all cross-traffic to proceed first, then go when it is safe. Do not wait for a green light—there won't be one at such a corner.

FLASHING YELLOW LIGHT means caution, so ALWAYS SLOW DOWN. Sometimes they're up in the air, sometimes they mark a hole in the pavement.

A STOP SIGN means YOU MUST STOP. Slowing down is not enough. It is there to make a bad crossing safer, so WATCH FOR CROSS TRAFFIC, WAIT, and look carefully, so you're sure you're safe before you go.

A YIELD SIGN means faster vehicles are using the other road, and YOU MUST SLOW DOWN OR STOP UNTIL IT IS SAFE TO GO. You can only proceed when you won't interfere with the other traffic.

THIS ROUND SIGN ALWAYS MEANS A RAILROAD. SLOW DOWN. Listen for a train whistle, watch the crossing-gates if there are any—be ready to stop. Always dismount and *walk* your bike across if tracks are not perfectly level with their road bed.

THESE ARE DIRECTIONAL SIGNS. THEY TELL YOU WHICH WAY THE TRAFFIC FLOWS, WHICH WAY YOU MUST GO TOO. IT IS DANGEROUS NOT TO OBEY THEM since cars won't expect you to be coming from the other direction.

THESE ARE OTHER WARNING SIGNS TO TELL
YOU OF POSSIBLE DANGERS AHEAD.

**Pavement Markings are Just As Important As Lights
and Signs**

Sometimes signs are printed on the pavement. Then
bicycle riders and car drivers and pedestrians have to
learn to read the road.

MANY INTERSECTIONS HAVE WHITE LINES

WHITE LINES for pedestrian crosswalks mean you
must give them the right of way when they walk there
even if you have a green light and they don't.
The center line of a street is WHITE when there is
only 1 lane for traffic each way. ALWAYS STAY
ON THE RIGHT, ON ANY 2-WAY STREET.

DOUBLE YELLOW LINES mark the middle of a
street with more than 1 lane in each direction; neither
you nor the cars are supposed to cross over those
yellow lines, unless you're making a turn. Look both

ways carefully before you make your turn; 4 lanes of traffic usually move faster than 2 lanes do.

RIGHT OF WAY is a set of rules that say when one person goes and another waits. It is something you give, not something you take. Always wait for your turn. If anyone—a driver, a bicycle rider, or a person walking—doesn't seem to understand the rules, let him go first, or wait to see what he's going to do, so you can both move safely.

WHEN YOU COME TO AN INTERSECTION:

that's a 4-way stop: When more than one driver arrives at this kind of an intersection at about the same time, the first one to stop should be the first one to go. But no one really has the right of way at a 4-way stop, so be careful, and take your turn only when it is safe.

that's a 2-way stop: Many intersections have stop signs on only one of the roads that cross; the other one is a through street or highway. After stopping at the sign, you must yield the right of way to pedestrians and drivers on the through street before you go ahead. Check carefully; sometimes they can be coming pretty fast.

with no stop signs or signal lights, and you and someone else both arrive about the same time, the driver on the left must yield the right of way to the driver on his right. If you, on your bike, are the one on the right, pause just long enough to be sure the car understands the rules, and that he'll give you the right of way.

at any intersection, no matter what the rules do about giving you the right of way, be sure a car respects your right to it as a vehicle; some drivers don't remember to give a bicycle the same courtesies they'd give to another car. But don't sit there forever, either, as then you can both wind up moving at once, since he'll think you don't know the rules.

PEDESTRIANS HAVE THE RIGHT OF WAY
and bicycle riders *must* yield it under these conditions:

AT AN INTERSECTION OR A CROSS-WALK:
slow down or stop for people walking between the white cross-walk lines, or even outside them. When you want to turn a corner, you must give pedestrians in the cross-walk the right of way first.

AT STOP SIGNALS AND TRAFFIC SIGNALS:
after coming to a full stop, yield to pedestrians before proceeding, *even if you have the green light and they don't*. It can be maddening, but it's the law.

WHEN YOU MEET A BLIND PERSON: bicycle riders are required to come to a complete stop for a blind person who has a white cane or is being guided by a dog. If you and they are both on a sidewalk together, don't risk confusing them—dismount, walk past, and remount when you're out of their way.

IF YOU WANT TO TURN LEFT AT A CROWDED CORNER and you don't think cars or people will let you through easily, the best solution is to dismount, cross the first half of the intersection with the light, then turn and cross the street you were proceeding on with the next light-change. It's time-consuming but much safer.

TURN SIGNALS ARE VERY IMPORTANT, because they let other vehicles know what you plan to do. Inside a city or town, you must signal 100 feet before you turn (that's about 6 car-lengths); outside of cities the signal must be made 200 feet in advance (12 car-lengths).

STOP   LEFT   RIGHT

Pedal Your Way to Health and Happiness! Pedal Your Way to Work—in a Better Environment! Pedal Your Way into Such Shape That You, Too, Can Bicycle 50 Miles in One Day!

AFTER PROMISES like that, it's a shame to start negatively, but we need your answer to an important question: *How long since your muscles and your psyche had a daily chance to work together, instead of against each other?* Call the ailments what you will: "business tensions," "housewife's fatigue," "nerves," "alienation" — our present civilization seems bent on separating the physical self from the mental one, fractionating and/or polluting both, and then adding insult to injury by offering the shuddering body that houses all this confusion a series of palliatives, from mass-oriented TV to tranquilizers, which solve only the symptoms (if they do that) and utterly ignore the basic problem. Which is, *How long since you had any fun being yourself and doing something*? The old-fashioned name for that was re-creation, which I've broken up so you can see what it was meant to do for you. And that's where a bicycle in your daily life makes a world of difference; it gets you all together again, restores the wholeness missing in your life; nourishes your need to be *you*.

Listen to Dr. Paul Dudley White on the subject:

"Our soul is in our brain—a fact to which our clergy and psychiatrists should pay more attention. Our brain is nourished by our heart and our active muscles. Bicycles are an answer for both brain and body. If more of us rode them, we would have a sharp reduction in the use of tranquilizers and sleeping pills .

"As a physician, I have recommended cycling to many patients as a way of keeping fit, provided their condition is suitable and provided they can cycle safely. And I advise cycling for healthy people to help keep them healthy.

"In the first place, it is an aid to good muscle tone, much needed by the American people today. It aids the circulation, and thereby the heart and its work, by keeping the blood moving.

"It aids the lungs through good tone of the diaphragm and makes it easier to bring oxygen into the body and pump out carbon dioxide.

"It aids the nerves by improving sleep and maintaining equanimity and sanity.

"It aids our digestion and it may even protect against peptic ulcers provided we don't try to establish a new speed record every day.

"It aids our weight control if, at the same time, we keep the caloric and fat content of our diet where they belong.

"It probably aids our longevity (like any other healthful exercise) in reducing the amount of high blood pressure, coronary thrombosis, and diabetes which have engulfed us, although the certainty of this must be further determined by research.

"If cycling can be fully restored to the daily life

of all Americans, it can become a vital step toward rebuilding health and vigor in all of us . . . Let us bequeath our children more than the gadgets that surround us. The bicycle alone will not do this, but it can become a symbol of the red-blooded vigor, personal independence, and healthy mind in a healthy body that are so much needed in our beloved country today."

That was from a pamphlet Dr. White wrote with Curtis Mitchell to help celebrate American Bike Month in 1964—and it's getting truer every day that passes.

You Can Enjoy Better Health—At Any Age, No Matter What Condition You're In Now.

How *is* your muscle-tone? Your heart? Your wind? According to a surprising number of doctors, riding your bicycle regularly is one of the best possible ways to improve all three.

And all three are crucial to your overall health. Recently, doctors have taken a long, cold look at the kinds of exercise that simply build beautiful muscles. These exercises are okay for muscle-building—but the doctors concluded they don't do much for the rest of you. Many now believe that the kind of exercise that does the *whole* body the most good is one that pushes the cardio-vascular system just a little beyond its present capacity, to build, gradually, a far greater capacity. Little by little by little, you can change a lot. That's how you grew, after all. And that's how you can now decide to grow into the healthier, whole, happier *you* you want to be.

That's how the Air Force trains its men; that's where the now-famous Dr. Kenneth H. Cooper developed his widely admired conditioning system called *Aerobics.** Bicycling not only ranks high in Dr. Cooper's point-value exercise system, it is also specially suitable for those who

*Aerobics by Dr. Kenneth H. Cooper, M.D., published in 1968 by M. Evans & Co.

want to build a regular exercise program into their daily lives *enjoyable enough so they'll go on doing it.*

Best of all, it works—and not just for Air Force types. That's how a Dallas housewife dropped two dress sizes in three months—just by borrowing her daughter's bike and pedaling to and from the grocery store.

You Also Improve the Environment—Your Own and Others

Instead of driving or being driven, you pedal your own way, and everybody benefits. The air's cleaner for all of us, and you're out in it, enjoying it. Even when auto traffic must come to a halt from overcrowding, you can often pedal around the problem and go on your merry way.

Traffic pile-ups are surely a major unpleasantness we would all like to see eliminated from our environment. They foul the air with noise and air pollutants; they make driving a nightmare for all concerned, which, in turn, leads to spiraling accident and injury tolls—and they do this at great expense to us all.

City after city, town after town, from Washington D.C. to Davis, California, has discovered how greatly our transportation snarls can be unsnarled by providing safe bikeways for cyclists to use and safe parking places for bicycles.

Davis, California, put in bike lanes so good that now bicycles represent 40% of all rush-hour traffic there. They were installed in 1967, and to date there have been *no* bike-car accidents where the bike lanes are. Imagine —in a city of 24,000 people, who own 20,000 bikes!

And parking on ever-crowded Capitol Hill is easier today because more and more of the nation's top legislators are proving what a Chicago bicycle-commuter group discovered—you can park approximately 14 bicycles in the space *one* car needs, and you can often park bikes in places too small for cars.

Think of that same space-ratio on our overcrowded streets, too. The more times each of us rides a bike instead of a car, the more room there is for everybody—and the cleaner our air, the healthier our environment. Remember that great ecology slogan: "If you're not part of the solution, you're part of the problem."

You Can Beat Your Traffic Problems With Your Bike!

Don't take it from me—listen to others who've done it already. And I don't mean just youngsters. Who would expect anyone to commute 25 miles a day by bicycle—in windy Chicago? Yet that's exactly what 53-year-old Eugene Sloan does, pedaling the 12½ miles each way from his home in Evanston to his job directing communications, operations and public relations for the Chicago Midwest Stock Exchange—with energy left over for after-hours crusading to help bike commuters get better bike lanes and better bike-parking facilities in Chicago's busy Loop.

Or take it from Arthur Phillips, a 54-year-old professor at the University of Miami, who sold his car two years ago. His passionate view on the subject: "Bikes don't pollute, bankrupt, or kill you, and they keep you in shape."

These men are not only not alone, they're part of a widespread movement that's pushing for *and getting* money from state and local legislatures to create and safely mark bicycle commuting lanes, and establishing Bikeways for recreational uses.

How to Pedal Your Way Into Such Shape that You, Too, Can Bicycle 50 Miles in 1 Day!

Just about the worst mistake a novice or out-of-shape cyclist can make is to tackle a long trip before he's really up to it. It's no fun—for him or anyone else. But you can use daily rides, or even twice-a-week rides, to build your skills and get into condition to go on long trips with the best of cyclists. You only need to find the right bike for you (if you haven't already, after Chapter 2), then climb aboard and learn to be master of your craft without impatience or urgency. Postpone your yen to travel afield long enough to get into proper shape. Then you and everybody with you will have a better time.

A word of caution: Before you begin this, or any other exercise program, you should check with your doctor if you're under 35; you should *see* him if you're much over that, or have any suspicion that you're really out of shape.

The key to all effective conditioning programs is *gradualness.* Don't tamper with the plan; don't decide to do the one-month program in a crash three weeks by riding harder, longer, or oftener. That simply won't work, and you'll either harm your body, lose your spirit, fail utterly and probably give up the whole idea— which was a good one—or be a living nightmare to all who know you. If your doctor suggests you carry the same program out over a span of, say, six weeks instead of four, what does that matter? You'll still be at your goal in a surprisingly short time. Once you're back in better shape, continued regular use of your bicycle will *keep* you there, too.

This fifty-miles-a-day plan really works, and not only for the young adults it was designed for, but for youngsters well below adulthood, and people well past their youth. But if bicycling fifty miles in a day simply isn't your idea of fun, or isn't what you want as a goal—don't give up. You can still cycle yourself into better condition, good enough to do whatever you enjoy doing with your bike, and also enjoy all the health benefits that come with better circulation, better muscle-tone and a fully-responsive cardio-vascular system.

Yes, even if you have had a serious illness, there is a level of bicycling within your capabilities, if your doctor

CONDITIONING FOR A REALLY LONG TRIP: THE AMERICAN YOUTH HOSTEL'S 1-MONTH CONDITIONING PROGRAM WORKS YOU UP GRADUALLY TO BICYCLING 50 MILES A DAY— WITH PACK!

1st day: 5 miles — Get acquainted with your bicycle. Rest every mile or two. Take about an hour.

4th day: 5 miles — Repeat the first day. Practice riding in a straight line.

6th day: 5 miles — Ride without stopping. Aim for half an hour.

7th day: 5 miles — Same as 6th day, but carry a 10-pound load.

10th day: 10 miles — Rest halfway only. Take 90 minutes.

12th day: 10 miles — No rest periods. Take one hour.

14th day: 25 miles — Rest 5 minutes every 5 miles. Take 3 hours.

17th day: 25 miles — Repeat 14th day but carry a 20-pound load.

20th day: 40 miles — Take your lunch. Rest every hour. Take 5 hours.

27th day: 50 miles — Take your lunch. Rest every hour. Take 5 hours.

28th day: 50 miles — Take all day. Carry full pack.

Some judgment must be used in adapting this suggested program to local weather, terrain, and road conditions. Your present physical condition will also have an important bearing on how it goes. If you start to tire, listen to your body, not your mind, and rest. Then go on.

agrees to whatever you propose. But, until recently, neither you nor your doctor would have had any reliable way to estimate or check how good your present condition is in *exact medical terms,* in order to decide how much exercise would be of benefit to you, and exactly where to draw the line between that much and too much.

The same Dr. Kenneth Cooper who developed Aerobics has gone that necessary step further in *The New Aerobics,** he gives there a simple test you can take by yourself or in your doctor's office, which establishes *against some fixed medical norms* exactly what shape you're in; then, grouped according to these norms, suggest exercise levels that will help but not overtax your heart, your muscle tone, and your wind. Retesting yourself later lets you and your doctor know, again *in medical specifics,* how improved you have been by the cycling (and/or other exercise) you've done regularly, and let's you readjust the level of exercise you can handle happily.

For the elderly it's literally a Godsend and I can't recommend it strongly enough. Ask your doctor and he'll agree, I'm sure, that recommending "moderate exercise" means such different things to different people that it's almost no use at all as a prescription. The once-active man who's been seriously ill, and ought to walk once or maybe twice around the block, in good weather, holding the arm of a companion, may interpret the advice to mean 50 push-ups a day, do them, and suffer from over-strain; while his golf-cart-riding opposite, who sits whenever he does anything, may decide "moderate exercise" means stepping off the front porch and onto the walk to pick up the morning paper, instead of letting his teen-age son get it for him.

For the large majority of us who are neither elderly nor still-young, the same book offers equally useful norms. They're not written in insurance-style, either.

The New Aerobics by Dr. Kenneth H. Cooper, M.D., published in 1970 by M. Evans & Co.

They measure what your physical capabilities are; with no recriminations, no gnashing of guilts, they tell it like it is, then, tell you what you can do to improve from there. When you've been doing it a while, they let you measure yourself again to check on your improvement. (You'll feel it, but it's exhilarating to have it confirmed with statistics like pounds or inches lost, or blood-pressure levels down to where they should be.) As you're ready, you move on to each new level of physical competence. Step by step, with no agonies, no Charles Atlas techniques, you work your way out of flab, self-hate and inner despair into firmness and exuberance. That's what's so wonderful about bicycling as exercise; it turns out to be fun instead of a daily chore, so you don't give up just when it was about to do you some good. You go on, and the good starts to show, so you really go on, until you simply can't help but see and feel the happy differences.

Whatever system you undertake, good luck and God Speed to you.

When we're all healthier, we'll all have fewer other problems, and what we face won't seem so overwhelming. If each of us could take time to put each of our selves into good running order—eyes alert, step quick, self trim and muscles toned—think how great we'd each be. Don't you almost owe it to yourself? After all, whatever sort of body God gave you to start with, you're responsible for it now. Nobody's going to make it better for you but *you*. It's the only body you've got to live a lifetime in— why not enjoy it to the fullest?

CHAPTER 12

Are You up to a Long Trip? What's to See and Do?

Are you up to a long trip? is a serious question. In the past, the usual way to find out was to go. Which usually led to a varying series of disasters, near-misses, and some unexpected delights when things *didn't* go wrong. Planning what-to-take and how-to-pack it; looking up information on places you want to see—all the side issues were so occupying, many people forgot that pre-trip training and conditioning are at least as crucial to the enjoyment of the trip as any other single part, and often, more needed.

Even people who knew this had trouble arranging it. Training areas to build up your biking skills were few, far between, and often, dull. How many laps can you go around the same lake or reservoir or park, building your endurance though you be, without quitting from simple boredom?

Today's Boom in Bikeways Lets You Learn Distance Riding As You Ride

The remarkable boom in Bikeways has changed all that. Safe, well-marked, and planned to take you to interesting places, these new Bikeways invite you to explore and adventure as much *or as little* as you like. Two miles or five miles for starters and early-spring warm-ups; ten miles or twenty, as you gain mastery of your muscles and your machine again—and as the spirit moves you. As your explorations continue, you learn an ever-widening network of rides you know, and know you'll like—with variety to them. You're free to set the pace, rest often, and you're not too far from home if you tire before you expected to. Riding on your "second wind" is fine, shows spirit, and is good for the ego—but pushing yourself and your bike too far, too fast, too soon, is the surest way to come home with a totally sore set of muscles, robbed of the very thing you set out for—fun and enjoyment.

That's why Bikeways make such a great base for your conditioning program. You learn cycling by cycling, yet they offer fun, in and of themselves. There's more to see, more to do with your bike today than there ever was before; more ways to get to somewhere interesting, without too much hassle with motor traffic.

Bike paths and trails exist or are being built in nearly every state in the Union; some are short, some are state-wide, some cover areas in several states. Within the next decade, officials estimate there will be *two hundred thousand miles* of Bikeways, available for everyone's enjoyment, many near the heavily populated urban and suburban areas where people need them most.

And an ever-widening network of bicycle enthusiasts —some organized into clubs and hosteling groups, some casual, neighborly, informal groups—is growing right along with them.

Instead of spending two crucifying weeks on your bicycle after 50 weeks of waiting, you can now bike practically the year 'round, to get yourself into shape so that your two-week trip—or even a 10-week one—can be the glory it *should* be.

Where Can You Find A Bikeway Near You?

The list is ever-growing, thanks to much hard work on the part of bicycle enthusiasts all over the country, and the proven benefits in safe, healthy enjoyment of the great out-of-doors which Bikeways open up for both youngsters and adults. There are now over a hundred and forty in existence and more in the planning stages; for the Bikeways near you, check through the list at the end of this chapter.

What Can You Expect?

You'll ride on everything from covered bridges (Indiana and Ohio each have Covered Bridge Bikeway tours) to a towpath George Washington laid out along the old Chesapeake & Ohio Canal, to the Staten Island Ferry. You'll see everything from glacial terminal moraine (in Wisconsin and Illinois) to a palm-surrounded pool described as "the world's most beautiful swimming hole" in Coral Gables, Florida. You may meet anything from a Canadian Warbler (Wisconsin) to a flamingo (Florida) to a movie star (California or Manhattan); you'll be able to discover living pieces of the past in the Amish country in Ohio and Pennsylvania; country stores that still sell old-fashioned goods (Illinois, Ohio, Pennsylvania); and both buildings and places with big plans to influence the future (Author Louis Bromfield's Malabar Farm, in Ohio; the World Trade Center, in New York City). What you find all depends on which Bikeway you ride; and most towns that have one, have literature they'll send you if you send their Chamber of Commerce a stamped, self-addressed, legal-size envelope. Almost *all* Bikeways include a pleasant mix of enjoyments, so it's not all history, or geology, or all anything; you'll meet parks, playgrounds, arboretums, botanical gardens, and famous private gardens. Museums, zoos, battlefields, historic sites, and the homes of people who made history are all popular spots along the Bikeways, and well-marked. So are refreshment stops and comfort stations.

You will still have to watch for cars—as always—but at least the Bikeway designation means the cars will also be watching for you. There are three sorts of Bikeways: usually, Bikeway routes are planned along secondary streets that parallel main thoroughfares, to be as safe for everyone as possible; occasionally, they are traffic-free paths built or adapted just for bikers and hikers. Most rarely, Bikeways are given a special lane or lanes along one side of a street, and cars are not permitted inside the bike lane.

After Bikeways Come Bike Trails—As Your Reach Extends

Since both are so new, definitions are a little blurred. Generally a Bikeway is a route in or around a given smaller area. Two good examples are Staten Island, in New York, and Coral Gables, Florida, which each have Bikeways that offer over twenty miles of self-guided scenic touring. On each, cars share the route. A Bike Path or Bike Trail is usually a longer venture; the longest, at this writing, being Wisconsin's beautiful border-to-border one. Even that is soon to be expanded, with local loop trips hooking off to other points-of-interest; plans are in the works to connect it with the proposed Illinois Bikeway.

Here's where I suggest you invest in an absolutely fascinating book, the *North American Bicycle Atlas,* written by Warren Asa and published by the American Youth Hostels, Inc. For non-AYH members, the price is around $2 (depending on how you order; see page 248 for full information) and you couldn't imagine a more complete, more exciting, more useful book on how to get out into this country of ours on your bike and enjoy everything you see.

Mr. Asa, who is Western regional director of AYH,

knows what he is talking about, and if the maps alone didn't fascinate you, his brief, cogent, preliminary advice would. Here's a short sample:

"Conditioning . . . you should get in condition before a tour and the best way is by cycling, cycling and more cycling. Try to do some riding every day even if it's only a short ride, and cycle every weekend, working up to the distance per day you plan to cover on your trip.

"One mistake often made in training for a trip is to ride without your luggage. When you put on this added weight at the start of the trip, it slows you down and you become discouraged, so at least part of the time, practice with loaded saddlebags. . . .

"This is a good place to point out the importance of breaking in your leather bicycle saddle. The fastest method seems to be to rub neatsfoot oil into the underside and pound the top with a hefty stick. Repeat this several times over a period of a month or so. During this time ride only in old trousers as some of the leather dye may come off. A slower method is to rub in Vaseline or any other leather softening material and ride until the seat becomes soft. At any rate, you must 'break your saddle, before it breaks you.' There are those who say that bicycle saddles never actually get soft; it is just that your bottom gets tougher."

But Mr. Asa's advice is only the beginning. There are 100 mapped bike rides that criss-cross the country, coast-to-coast, or circle around in an area of it; they last from a week to a month or more; they cover forty-seven states, six Canadian provinces, Mexico and the Caribbean area. For those who aren't yet up to such long trips, there are sixty-two more one-day and weekend rides, all full of fascinating things to see and do, with routes, places to stay, sights to see, and further helpful information. Rides are carefully graded as to their difficulty; clear explanations tell what to look for, what to avoid, and what to expect in the way of navigational problems.

As an example of a long Bikeway where you can choose all or a part for your trip, here is an outline map and comments on one of the best bike rides anywhere along the Eastern seaboard—the Chesapeake & Ohio Canal Ride, as it appears in the *Atlas:*

**180 Miles   C & O CANAL RIDE
W. Virginia, Virginia, District of Columbia

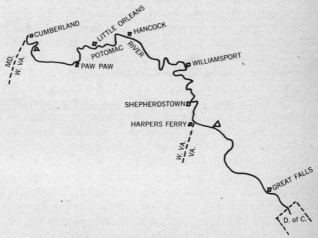

"Certainly one of the most unusual bicycle trips in the U.S. Not only do you cycle back into history, but you cycle on history as you actually ride on the towpath of the Chesapeake and Ohio Canal. In pre-Revolutionary days the frontier was moving west, but travel by land was slow. The Potomac River was accessible but rapids made it hazardous. In 1754 a

**(That's a difficulty rating; translates as fairly easy, some traffic, some hills, but longer distance per day than single-star easy trips.)

young surveyor named George Washington conceived a plan to dig channels so that boats could skirt the rapids. This system was used until 1828 when work started on the present more complex canal. Thousands of men labored on the canal for 22 years, many dying in cholera epidemics. The final cost was eleven million dollars or $60,000 per mile. The federal government purchased the canal in 1938, and it became a National Monument in 1961. A detailed set of 21 maps of this ride is available for $1.75 from the Potomac AYH Council, 1501 16th Street N.W., Washington, D.C. 20036. The trip is 180 miles and the terrain is as close to being flat as possible. There are two hostels in the area and more are planned. In addition to the many historic points, and the interesting rock formations and hardwood forests along the way, you will enjoy seeing the various canal features such as locks, dams, aqueducts and lock-houses. A good trip for novice cyclers. For article on canal see National Geographic Magazine, March 1960. Carry good light for use in long tunnels. Visit Antietam Battlefield."

Note, carefully, the advice about the light for the tunnels, the address where you can get detailed maps, and the general ease with which you can use this book to plan a successful trip. Note, also, what it does *not* do. On purpose. This *Atlas* is not planned to be something you pick up and dash out into Nature, clutching. Maps are purposely made without excessive detail, so you'll get up-to-date, detailed local ones *yourself,* mark them with your own information, your own special points-of-interest. If the *Atlas* had included close-up detail maps sufficient for every trip in the book, it would weigh too much, take up too much space, to travel well.

Are You the Hosteling Type?

No matter what you *think* your answer is, I suggest

you investigate. I guarantee you'll meet an exciting group of people. They're young, high-spirited and highly motivated, with remarkable abilities to enjoy life. Even confirmed non-joiners seem to thrive under their Thoreau-like rules that combine simplicity, self-reliance, and self-propulsion with mutual tolerance and consideration for the needs of others.

But a few definitions are in order.

Strictly defined, hosteling means traveling from place to place under your own motive power and using inexpensive, self-service, dormitory-style accommodations for overnight stays. Each hostel has a kitchen which is shared with others, a dining room and common room; except for families and sometimes even then, the sleeping areas are separate for the two sexes. Hostels are supervised by responsible adults, and in each, all hostelers are obligated to observe an international hosteling code of good conduct. Alcohol and drugs are both ruled off the premises. Since violation of rules means the hosteler loses his pass, keeping order isn't usually much of a problem.

American Youth Hostels, Inc. is a nonprofit, nonsectarian, nonpolitical corporation, a tax-exempt youth-service organization supported by voluntary contributions, membership, and program fees. Its goal is to help us all, the world over, gain a greater understanding of the world in its variety of people, and to help people develop into fit, self-reliant, well-informed citizens. Hiking is usually the least expensive mode of hosteling; cycling is usually the most popular since it enables you to cover a considerable amount of ground, and is physically demanding and exciting. Active sports and outdoor activities are encouraged, and places where you can enjoy them are likely sites for a hostel.

Since AYH is affiliated with the International Youth Hostel Foundation, membership for individuals in AYH gives one hosteling privileges in 47 countries. The combined international membership is almost 2 million, with 4,200 operating hostels; in 1969, all of them together registered 21 million overnight stays.

Emphasis has been on youth, from the beginning, and that will continue. But the upsurge in adult cycling is sure to bring a horde of adults beating a path to the AYH doors, and if the adults turn out to be able to carry their own weight, cope with unadorned, unvarnished realities, obey simple rules, and learn to pace themselves under and not over their own limitations, they'll find they've re-entered a world where sun on foliage, fresh air in your lungs, food when you're hungry, and sleep when exercise has healthily tired you give true, deep, "rain for your roots" refreshment. For additional information, AYH councils are listed in Chapter 13— get in touch with the one nearest you. Individual or family memberships are available for remarkably little money.

Want To See Europe On The Cheap?

AYH not only runs tours to Europe, chartering planes and all, and offering you then the choice of going with a group or going it alone, where and as you wish; they have several books that offer you the clues you need to seeing more of Europe on less money. Campsites and such are in one book; hostels, in another; all are listed in Chapter 13, under the AYH publications section. The trips you're invited to join, each year, are spectacular, and they'll have you all keyed up to condition yourself and *go!*

You can also See America First, as you condition yourself—jaunts are run not only by AYH but by many bicycle clubs (again, they're listed in Chapter 13, by state and by towns) that take a day, a weekend, or sometimes longer; they are run for cyclists at all levels of expertise. Many trips also combine either train or bus runs and then bike routes, so they greatly extend the amount you can see or do in a limited time.

Family Bike Trips—If You're That Sort of Family

Family and group trips can create memories you'll all cherish a whole lifetime long. Or they can create disasters, little and funny later, or, sadly, major and not funny at all. The difference usually lies in how well the plans you make suit you, as individuals and as a family; and in pre-trip planning. Anyone planning a family trip needs to be more honest about their own strengths and skills, more realistic about the scope of their plans, than individuals biking in age-clustered groups—particularly if the family trip plans involve one or more persons pedaling for two, with a child in a child carrier. If in doubt, plan to do less, leave more free time open, and if you've got the energy, do more *then*. Maybe you'll even feel like it. The simple lack-of-hurry-to-keep-to-a-grim-schedule can often make everything that happens more fun, more relaxed and enjoyable, and therefore easier.

Children who go along need to be taught what to expect, what to do, and what *not to do,* well in advance of the trip. That's true whether you're carrying them or they're biking under their own power. A few rules are in order here. Group riders are safer in single file where there's any chance of motor traffic, which you probably already know. You should have an established, understood group rule to cover the situation; the best, I believe, is the simplest. Whenever a car is heard approaching, whoever hears it first alerts the rest, loudly. If any two riders are then side-by-side, *the rider closer to the curb spurts forward, leaving room for the other rider, who always drops back*. This works even when you're on the left side of a one-way, and when a car comes close to the inside rider, it soon becomes clear why he or she should drop back and get out of the way.

Another good thing to plan out ahead of time is a group whistle—just a few notes, simple but personal to you—which means "Assemble" or "Come at once." Highly useful. If several members of the group are scattered over a park, a fair ground, or even a busy market, it'll save you hours of searching to find whoever doesn't know it's time to go on.

Your plans will vary greatly, of course, depending on your group's individual skills and ages. If you are bicycling with a child in a child-carrier, you should plan no more than four or five hours of cycling a day, in which time you'll probably be able to do thirty to thirty-five miles fairly easily. (After you've conditioned yourself, of course, to the double load of child and belongings.) Thirty miles is also the limit you should plan for a day's ride for young children who are cycling for themselves— say six- to seven-year-olds. But you'll be astonished at what distances youngsters over ten can cover, once they're conditioned to distance riding.

Whatever your mileage plans are, pause about every hour to let small children in the carriers get out and move around, especially if the weather's chilly. Their lack of movement will make them feel colder than you, who are exercising more. And a good long lunch break with some other interest besides cycling is a wise plan for most youngsters. The smallest children can usually be counted on to nap at their usual times, in your carrier; with larger ones, it all depends on the individual child. In planning, take advantage of the AYH Family Hosteling Guide, with some very real helps—see page 249.

Don't Let Your Trip Be A Bummer!

How to plan your route: Start by knowing approximately what you want to aim for, what things interest you and the people who'll travel with you, and the mileage the newest or most out-of-condition cyclists in your group can comfortably manage. Look into where the rest-overnight or stop-by-the-roadside opportunities match your group's interests, and you'll begin to be able to break your trip into manageable chunks. Then ask questions of everyone and anyone who can tell you more about (a) going there; (b) hills and road conditions on the way; (c) places to eat or *not* to eat; (d) weather conditions to expect; and (e) anything that happened to them that they didn't expect. Good or bad. "What was the most fun?" and "What was the awfulest thing that happened?" elicit surprising answers.

Whether you're a member or not, your nearest AYH council or local bicycle club would almost certainly answer questions, either by telephone or mail, if you limit them to a reasonable number and ask politely. They will *not* plan your itinerary for you or anyone else— nobody should really do that but you and your companions, anyhow. Auto-touring clubs and gasoline companies tend to be very helpful, but be sure to explain that you're going to be on bicycles, where you plan to be; many Freeways, Tollways, Turnpikes and Throughways—call them what you will, they mean express interstate routes for ultra-fast auto traffic—do not allow bicyclists or hikers, and it's important you know that in advance. Many good trips plan a combination of driving or riding by train or bus with cycling; perhaps that could be a factor in your plans, too.

Even if your group is as few as two people (and don't plan to go alone, for lots of reasons—you'll get lonely, you could need help, you'll have more fun with others along), *before* you set out you should establish several rules, or agreements in advance. Discuss and agree about: how monies are to be carried, handled, and spent; the *sort* of places you'll look for, to eat and sleep in, if they are not known and planned-in already; whether or not you'll stop, at will, for things like an unexpected parade, church bazaar, fish fry, or a predictable "Antiques—500 feet ahead." If possible, go on a shorter trip together first. You'll all know a lot more about each other's skills and characters afterward.

With large groups, it's wise to plan an eloquently named "sag wagon" that carries the weary and disabled, runs errands for parts if something should break, or, in major disaster conditions, transports an ill or injured member to doctor or hospital. If you're leading a large group, another wise thing is to go over the route, well ahead of time, alone or with help. One leader told me how he made a tour self-guided, and you can do just what he did: "We went out the weekend before, and we painted arrows, right on the pavement, every place where there was a turn in our route. We had police permission, of course, you can't just go paint up a town without asking. But then, everyone could move at their own speed, stop anywhere they wanted along the way, do what they liked. All they *really* had to do was wind up where the bus was before it was time to go home. Of course, we allowed more than ample time for that. Some kids took time out and went swimming. Some fast cyclists went on ahead, did a 25-mile loop around to see more of the country, and were back before all the others even got there for dinner."

If you're responsible for the trip, you're also responsible for seeing that someone carries such necessities as patch kits for innertubes, a spare-parts kit, a minimal tool-kit and a first-aid kit, plus some extra cash in case of unforeseen emergencies. But thirty people don't need to carry two tire irons each; divide the jobs and responsibilities up, be sure they're carried out, and everyone contributes to the good time you'll all have.

Highway rules are different: know them. Planning a long trip, or even a short trip outside your home state, means you have to know another state's traffic and safety rules. Write to the state highway department of the state or states involved, well in advance of your trip. If you can't get a better address, write to them in care of the state capital; in your letter, indicate the size of your group, the scope of your planned trip, and its approximate dates; ask them about do's and don'ts on their highways, especially in terms of roads where biking is not allowed. Allow plenty of time for them to answer your request—it may go through three or four departments before it reaches the desk of the man who knows the answers to what you ask. If your answer doesn't arrive in time—say a week before you plan to start out—ask someone in your local police or state highway department to find out anything urgent you might need to know; they may know just the man to call to ask.

Two More Sources of Good and Useful Information: First, the Chamber of Commerce of any towns where you expect to stop, think are big enough to represent a problem finding your way through on bicycles, or where you think something of interest to your group may be located but you don't know just how to get there. They're usually staffed by people set up exactly to answer those sorts of inquiries, and they often know about things that have been added recently that may also interest you, that you wouldn't hear of in time to plan into your trip, otherwise.

The second source is any bike club located in a town you find along the route where, again, you think local information will help you find how to get into or out of town on good bike routes; good places to see things of interest to your group, or perhaps even side trips to places nearby, off your direct route but worth planning in when you hear what's there. Again, stamped, self-addressed envelopes expedite everything, spare them the cost of being kind to you.

What to Take and What to Wear: Everything depends on where you're going, and what you'll be doing when you get there. If you're cycling from Chicago to New Salem to see the early-Lincoln country, for example, you want simple, relaxed clothes you can move around easily in, yet you want them clean enough, presentable enough, to get you into a decent restaurant at noon or night, should you decide to eat out. Simple shirts, blue jeans, and sneakers are frequently chosen—any easy, informal sports clothes. But sneakers don't give your foot much real support for long-distance cycling, and if anyone's jeans are the flare-leg type, they can catch badly in a chain, even if the bike has a chainguard, unless you wear a bicycle clip for each leg. (Clips usually cost about 25¢ to 50¢ apiece, and any bike shop has them.) Shorts are comfortable, and cool in the heat, but if you've not been in the sun much, you can wind up badly sunburnt and very uncomfortable. Or they can make you feel out-of-place on your arrival in an area where they're not every-day wear.

If you're riding from country to city, or including cities in your plan of places to see (as in the trip above, if you planned to see Lincoln's home, in Springfield; Springfield is a state capital, and you'd want to dress a little less casually, particularly to stay overnight), you almost certainly need two sets of clothes. The only alternative is to cycle in something that's appropriate to the city activities you plan on, carry gloves in your tool-kit so you don't get too filthy if you have emergency repairs, and pray for good weather. That can be risky; I suggest two sets, but choose lightweight, fold-small choices for your dress-up set; drip-dry fabrics like Ban-lon, Dacron and such, in weights appropriate to the weather, are musts; dark colors with a moderate amount of pattern, pack and arrive in better condition than light colors or solid colors. Many of the new knit fabrics really *don't* crush, as advertised; whatever you choose, *don't ever carry anything you have to iron*. Even in the summer, you'll need a sweater or jacket for cool nights, early mornings, or air-conditioned places. If you've room, dressy shoes for sightseeing are fine, much better than your sneakers—but they should be low-heeled, comfort-able for walking, and *well-broken-in ahead of time*. That's a good rule for anything you take—if it's new, wear it at least once first to be certain you're comfortable in it.

Rain protection is always a problem when you bike. Obviously, you can't ride along with an umbrella up (although ladies in the Eighties and Nineties rode with parasols, today we know that both hands on the handlebars are a must); but you might want a little fold-up umbrella in your saddlebag for when you're out sightseeing. All the other choices have one disadvantage or another; choose what gives you the most of what you want, the least of what you dislike: a rain cape works well as does a currently fashionable poncho (which is also useful for picnics and/or camping purposes), but both leave the feet exposed, both can flap about in the wind unless belted in. Belting them in, if they're really waterproof, can keep an uncomfortable amount of body heat and perspiration inside your protection, and get you wetter than the rain would. Many people choose ordinary raincoats, use them as housecoats or bathrobes at night, which may not be chic but is certainly space-saving. Some people go so far as to get rain suits, or have a regular suit rain-proofed with either a dry-cleaner's waterproofing (makes fabric stiffer but can usually be done to almost any kind of fiber) or a do-it-yourself spray. Problem here is simple: if it's really waterproof, it's got to be a non-breatheable (often rubberized or plastic-covered) kind of outfit—inside that, you're back to the body-heat-perspiration-trapped-inside problem; if it's only what they call rain-resistant (that means the fabric is more porous, to start with), where the air gets in and out the rain will too. In weather you can count on to stay warm, and rain you can count on to be light, some riders prefer no protective clothing at all, feeling that the sun and wind will dry them out after the rain has stopped. The risk here, of course, is lack-of-sun-after-rain, in which case you can get seriously chilled, even in supposedly hot-weather months.

In general, planning to dress in layers lets you adapt to changes in weather, and to your own metabolism's changes as you and the day warm up or cool down. And an extremely useful item in the layering process is a vest that buttons tightly across the chest, topped with a turtleneck or a scarf that tucks in, both of which offer very good wind protection; just remember Isadora, and don't let your scarf fly free to catch in chain or spokes.

Depending on weather and countryside, you'll need protection from sun (take sunglasses, un-blow-offable-hat, plus suntan lotion or sun-stop creams); from insects, particularly if you plan picnic lunches or any outdoor camping; from blisters (cycling gloves for hands are a must; so is moleskin adhesive in your first-aid kit for heels, toes, tender insteps); and, finally, from the unexpected (an extra pair of prescription glasses, if you wear them; anti-histamines, if you're a hay-fever or allergy victim, or the prescription your doctor recommends—both made up *and* written out). Add your personal toiletries kit, a minimal tool kit (that includes tube-patch kit, a small adjustable wrench, a screwdriver, tire irons, tire pressure gauge, and not too much else, except, for long trips, replacement parts that can give under stress, or that you think won't be available where you're going—an indicator spindle for three-speed hubs is a good extra, and it's little; a pair of brake shoes, ditto). European travelers should know that standard tires there are 28-inch or "700" size; neither will fit either 27-inch or smaller American wheels, so you'd better add both tires and extra inner tubes to your packing list, bar soap for washing both clothes and dishes, plus a change of underwear and socks, and you're practically packed. Arrange your packing so your maps and trip notebook, historical references, and guidebooks are easy to get at. Then consider whether you've room to add camera, film, writing paper, address book and stamps, sketch book or journal, a book to read yourself to sleep with—and consider each by the *ounce*.

In the famous hostelers' phrase, "He hostels best who travels lightest."

Because You Can't Possibly Carry Everything

Wherever you're heading, whatever you're going to do, whatever sort of unexpected event pops up—you're simply not able to carry more than a certain poundage with any real pleasure. Its total, of course, depends on your bike's weight and your strength, your gears and your packing skills, your condition and that of the roads you travel, the hills and winds you meet, and the hours you keep.

The less you have with you, the easier everything becomes. Going up a hill, getting up and out in the morning, finding what you need when you need it in a hurry. *Everything.* And of the two possibilities—taking too much or taking too little—you're infinitely more likely to try to take too much.

Different people have different systems for reducing the total volume. My husband's is that anything he takes anywhere has to do at least two, preferably three or more things, well. (Raincoat that becomes housecoat that also copes with cooler weather, perfect example.) If it won't, he won't take it. I'm not that stern, so I always carry too much, hate myself, and spend vast amounts of time looking for where I put something. The best system I know belongs to a friend, who always starts packing for a trip two to three weeks ahead. Totally. Then she starts taking things out. By the night before departure, she's removed about half of what she started with (she's incredibly disciplined); she's remembered the two things she did forget and would have missed; and she's got room to bring something home in. Also, she's rested next morning, while we who packed late are still wondering what we've forgotten.

Pursue any system that works for you, but aim at the same goal: *if you take about half what you think you'll want, you'll come out about right.* And as for the weight you can carry, or the volume, I suggest you pack your saddlebags and your handlebar bag as you would for your trip, at least two weekends ahead of time, dress as you plan to, and take a rehearsal ride, fully dressed and fully loaded. (Don't forget your tool kit and your snacks —you're testing your planning, as well as your energy levels.) Don't go too far from home, but go far enough to see what happens as the day heats up and the hills get taller.

Sailors call it a shakedown cruise. Call it whatever you like, but do it. I'll guarantee you'll come home more determined than ever to cut down your total, and every ounce you remove will add to your freedom, every inchfull you take out will leave room for what you may want that you meet along the roadside.

*For Practice, and For Local and Faraway Fun,
Here's the List of Bikeways:*

BIKEWAYS & TRAILS OPEN,
(as of December, 1971)

A
Phoenix, Arizona
Tempe, Arizona
Tucson, Arizona
Little Rock, Arkansas

C
Azusa, California
Berkeley, California
Catalina Island, California
Chula Vista, California
Corona Del Mar, California
Coronado Island, California
Davis, California
Goleta, California
Long Beach, California
Los Angeles, California
Manhattan Beach, California

Newport Beach, California
Palm Springs, California
Pasadena, California
Point Reyes, California
Pomona, California
Redondo Beach, California
Riverside, California
Sacramento, California
San Diego, California
San Francisco, California
San Mateo, California
Santa Barbara, California
Santa Monica, California
Santa Rosa, California
Sausalito, California
Boulder, Colorado
Colorado Springs, Colorado
Denver, Colorado

Littleton, Colorado
Pueblo, Colorado
Milford, Connecticut

D

Washington, D.C.

F

Clearwater, Florida
Coconut Grove, Florida
Coral Gables, Florida
Fort Lauderdale, Florida
Hollywood, Florida
Homestead, Florida
Miami, Florida
Ormond Beach, Florida
Palm Beach, Florida
Sarasota, Florida (state park)
Siesta Key, Florida
St. Petersburg, Florida
Tampa, Florida
Tomoka State Park, Florida

G

Savannah, Georgia

I

Boise, Idaho
Pocatello, Idaho
Aurora, Illinois
Chicago, Illinois
Elk Grove, Illinois
Geneva, Illinois
Palatine, Illinois
St. Charles, Illinois
Sterling, Illinois
Wayne, Illinois
West Chicago, Illinois
Wheaton, Illinois
Elkhart, Indiana
Fort Wayne, Indiana

Gary, Indiana
Hammond, Indiana
Hobart, Indiana
Lafayette, Indiana
Rockville, Indiana
Cedar Falls, Iowa
Des Moines, Iowa
Fort Madison, Iowa
Waukon, Iowa

K

Wichita, Kansas
Louisville, Kentucky

M

Baltimore, Maryland
Boston, Massachusetts
Cambridge, Massachusetts
Cape Cod National
    Seashore, Massachusetts
Holyoke, Massachusetts
Nantucket Island,
    Massachusetts
New Bedford,
    Massachusetts
Pittsfield, Massachusetts
Stockbridge, Massachusetts
East Detroit, Michigan
Mackinac Island, Michigan
Marquette, Michigan
Mt. Clemens, Michigan
Presque Island, Michigan
Excelsior, Minnesota
Minneapolis, Minnesota
Kansas City, Missouri
University City, Missouri

N

Lincoln, Nebraska
Omaha, Nebraska
Princeton, New Jersey

Buffalo, New York
Hamburg, New York
Nassau County, New York
New York City (Brooklyn,
    Manhattan, Staten Island,
    Bronx)
Poughkeepsie, New York
Syracuse, New York
Burlington, North Carolina
Chapel Hill, North Carolina

O

Cincinnati, Ohio
Cleveland, Ohio
Columbus, Ohio
Dayton, Ohio
Fairborn, Ohio
Fostoria, Ohio
Kettering, Ohio
Oakwood (Dayton), Ohio
Toledo, Ohio
Vandalia, Ohio
Yellow Springs, Ohio
Zenia, Ohio
Eugene, Oregon
Portland, Oregon

P

Bucks County, Pennsylvania
Mechanicsburg,
    Pennsylvania
Philadelphia, Pennsylvania

R

Providence, Rhode Island

T

Dallas, Texas
Fort Worth, Texas
Houston, Texas
Long View, Texas

V

Burlington, Vermont
Alexandria, Virginia
Arlington, Virginia

W

Mercer Island, Washington
Seattle, Washington
Spokane, Washington
Tacoma, Washington
Vancouver, Washington
Yakima, Washington
La Crosse, Wisconsin
Milwaukee, Wisconsin
Oshkosh, Wisconsin
Prairie du Chien, Wisconsin
Waukeshaw, Wisconsin
Wisconsin Dells, Wisconsin
Wisconsin State Bikeway

(The nation's longest, at
the present time. Begins
at La Crosse, covers 9
counties, terminates on
the shores of Lake
Michigan at Kenosha, a
distance of 320
spectacularly scenic
miles.)

BIKEWAYS HAVE BEEN DESIGNED FOR:

A

Scottsdale, Arizona

C

Bakersfield, California
Claremont, California
Eureka, California
Freemont, California
Glendora, California
Hemmet, California
Lakewood, California
Livermore, California
Lompoc, California
Long Beach, California
Los Gatos, California
Montebello, California
Newport Beach, California
Riverside, California
San Bernardino, California
San Jacinto, California
San Jose, California
Santa Ana, California
Santa Paula, California
Thousand Oaks, California
Ventura, California
Greeley, Colorado
Lakewood, Colorado
Loveland, Colorado
Wheat Ridge, Colorado
Danbury, Connecticut
New Haven, Connecticut
Wilton, Connecticut

F

Boca Raton, Florida
Cape Kennedy, Florida
Coco Beach, Florida

Jacksonville, Florida
Okefenokee Wildlife
    Refuge, Florida
St. Petersburg, Florida
Titusville, Florida

G

Atlanta, Georgia

I

Arlington Heights, Illinois
Champaign-Urbana, Illinois
Elmhurst, Illinois
Homewood, Illinois
Palos Park, Illinois
West Frankfurt, Illinois
Indianapolis, Indiana
Ames, Iowa
Cedar Falls, Iowa
Newton, Iowa
Sioux City, Iowa

K

Hutchinson, Kansas
Lawrence, Kansas
Mission, Kansas
Topeka, Kansas
Cleremont, Kentucky
Lexington, Kentucky
Winchester, Kentucky

L

Alexandria, Louisiana
Baton Rouge, Louisiana
New Orleans, Louisiana

M

Amherst, Massachusetts
Concord, Massachusetts
Falmouth, Massachusetts
Quincy, Massachussets
Springfield, Massachusetts
Woods Hole, Massachusetts
Wilmington, Massachusetts
Ann Arbor, Michigan
Battle Creek, Michigan
Birmingham, Michigan
Grand Rapids, Michigan
Kalamazoo, Michigan
Lansing, Michigan
Livonia, Michigan
Richmond, Michigan
Wayne, Michigan
Rochester, Minnesota
Jackson, Mississippi
Columbia, Missouri
Billings, Montana

N

Las Vegas, Nevada
Berkeley Heights,
  New Jersey
Linwood, New Jersey
Albuquerque, New Mexico
Cortland, New York
Ithaca, New York
Montauk, New York
Rochester, New York
Asheville, North Carolina
Greenville, North Carolina
Laurinberg, North Carolina
Raleigh, North Carolina

O

Centerville, Ohio
Delaware, Ohio
Mansfield, Ohio
Marion, Ohio
Middletown, Ohio
Sandusky, Ohio
Springfield, Ohio
Sylvania, Ohio
Upper Arlington, Ohio
Norman, Oklahoma
Oklahoma City, Oklahoma
Corvallis, Oregon
Salem, Oregon

P

Harrisburg, Pennsylvania
State College, Pennsylvania

T

Memphis, Tennessee
Austin, Texas
Houston, Texas

U

Ogden, Utah

V

Richmond, Virginia
Roanoke, Virginia

W

Vancouver, Washington
Parkersburg, West Virginia
Racine, Wisconsin

The Bikeways Explosion is Still Exploding!

In the planning or almost ready stages are several more very exciting Bikeways you'll want to know about and want to see when they're completed. Two are related to George Washington, although they're not very close together. One is a touring Bikeway that will start in the heart of metropolitan Washington, D.C. and go all the way (some forty scenic, history filled miles) to Washington's home at Mount Vernon, by way of equally historic and beautiful Alexandria, Virginia. The other, in fascinating Bucks County, Pennsylvania, takes you to the place where Washington made his famous crossing of the Delaware River.

Does whaling interest you? Ships? The romance of early New England? Then you'll be eager to see the one planned for New Bedford, Massachusetts, covering many of the places author Herman Melville made famous. And a bike path on Nantucket Island (more Melville country) in the Cape Cod National Seashore Park is already very popular and has careful maps prepared by the United States Department of the Interior to guide you, and a youth hostel. If early mining country interests you, perhaps you'd want to try the Mother Lode Bikeway in the California Sierras before they've even got it fully marked out.

And you can be sure, while the ink is drying on this page, many more Bikeways are being planned and developed.

CHAPTER 13

Where to Find Out More

Basic references: your owner's manual, your local library

When you buy a new bicycle, it's an exciting experience, and one of the better parts is often the owner's manual that comes with your bike. Style and format differ widely, but you can't listen to a better source. Not all makers have one available, and it's a pity; if it's well written, it's as though you were able to talk directly with the man who planned the bicycle, and it explains what and why, in words and pictures, with best adjustments indicated.

The "manual" that came with my husband's Raleigh bike (from England) is really a two-surface poster-size map of the bike and its parts, with careful illustrations of almost everything on it and tersely worded instructions on what to do, and *not* to do, to keep the bike in good shape.

The Schwinn and Columbia people, in America, each attach a booklet to every bicycle they sell, telling you all sorts of useful things, well beyond the simple "this is Part A, attach to Part B" sort of instructions that used to drive parents wild on Christmas Eve. The Huffman people have a book on bicycle racing—it's listed with the publications at the end of this chapter.

If you get such a manual with your bike, be careful of

it. Put it in a place where you'll know where it is, and as you use your bike, refer to it. Many things that seem complicated on a new bike get simpler as you begin riding, and you get used to them. But your questions tend to get more complicated as your knowledge increases, and that's where an owner's manual often supplies an answer you overlooked in your first reading.

If you don't get such a manual, you might learn a lot by writing to either The Columbia Manufacturing Co., Inc., Westfield, Massachusetts 01085, or to the Customer Service Department, Schwinn Bicycle Company, 1856 N. Kostner Avenue, Chicago, Illinois, 60639. (The Schwinn company also has some historical information and a collection of antique bicycles—write before you go, though, for an appointment.) While either company may not send you one of their manuals if too many people write in for them, they may have a catalog or other information to send, or the name of a dealer near you who'd let you read through a manual.

Your local public library is the other great source of information on bicycling—some of it is in books, some of it in magazine articles. Again, the look-before-you-buy technique works here; if there's a bike book that's expensive but you think you want it, look it over in the library first, and decide then. Maybe it's just what you want and need; maybe it's aimed at a different sort of bicycle enthusiast—only you can decide.

Bicycle Clubs, Local and National

It seems the more you know about bicycling, the more you want to know. If you spent a lifetime at it, there would still be things to learn. But one of the greatest things about bicycling is the people it attracts—they're literally young and old, rich and poor, dedicated urbanites and wouldn't-be-caught-dead-in-a-city country-dwelling nature lovers. Some of them have spent a lifetime learning about bikes and bicycling, and, almost without exception, all of them are enchanted to share what they know and answer your questions.

People in far places, who have never seen you, will often take the time to answer *courteous* inquiries about their town's Bikeways, or the best way to get to someplace local that interests you. People in bike clubs, for example; if you're planning a trip, they can be a better source of information than the local Chamber of Commerce or a national gasoline-company touring service, because they understand how to answer your questions *in bicyclists' terms*. Many local clubs have excellent maps showing the good ways to get into or through their town on a bike, the best places to stop, and things to see or do you might never otherwise suspect existed. Just remember, if you write to a bike club outside your neighborhood, they usually operate on tight budgets like everybody else; the courtesy of a stamped, self-addressed legal-size envelope will speed your reply without draining their treasury.

We are going to list here all the local and national bicycle clubs in the United States that are currently known to the Bicycle Institute of America. The list, not surprisingly, grows every week. Even the fact that it was up-to-date at press time won't keep it current forever, and the next local election of officers, or founding of a new club, changes things. Also, although many clubs listed are independent, many are affiliates of major national organizations. For your convenience, affiliations are indicated by initials in the listings, as keyed below to the national headquarters of each interest group. If you can't find a local branch near you, contact the national group for further information.

A B L of A indicates affiliation with the Amateur Bicycle League of America. National Headquarters, P.O. Box 2175, New York, N.Y. 10017; President Ernest Seubert, 137 Brunswick Road, Cedar Grove, N.J. 07009.

This is the governing body of competitive cycling in America; for further state and regional heads, see the end of this list. Many chapters of the ABL of A are included in our listings, but there are many more on college and university campuses not listed because no individual contacts were available. To learn who represents the ABL of A in your area, write

ABL of A Library, c/o William Lambart

3210 Byrd Place, Baldwin, New York 11510

AYH indicates affiliation with the American Youth Hostels, Inc. National Headquarters, 20 West 17th Street, New York, N.Y. 10011.

Regional AYH councils are given at the end of this list. Hostel accommodation sites are listed at the end of each state's list of clubs.

The AYH promotes low-cost activities for all age groups, many bicycling tours, charter flight trips, and bike hikes; local groups offer movies, instructional sessions on riding techniques and preventive maintenance, some social meetings, and, usually, both short and long bicycling trips.

National and regional AYH also offers publications which prepare you for bike touring and vacations, here and abroad (listed under publications.)

LAW indicates affiliation with the League of American Wheelmen; National Headquarters, P.O. Box 3928, Torrance, California, 90510.

The League promotes extended bicycle trips for experienced cyclists, and serves as coordinating agency for most American bicycle clubs. Organizes many long-distance bicycle tours in the nation. Membership directory is indexed by towns to offer an invaluable source of expert advice if you find yourself facing disaster in a locale that is strange to you.

TW indicates local chapters of The Wheelmen; Robert

E. McNair, Commander, 32 Dartmouth Circle, Swarthmore, Pennsylvania 19081.

The Wheelmen are a fascinating group of devotees dedicated to the enjoyment and preservation of historic bicycles and memorabilia. Members appear at centennials, ride in parades and attend local celebrations with their antique bikes (by previous arrangement, of course); they offer research assistance and issue bulletins on the restoration and safe ridership of antique machines, tell where you can get spare parts.

ALABAMA

Montgomery **Montgomery Bicycle Club,** c/o Recreation Department. Sponsored by Alabama Recreation & Park Society/Alabama Commission on Physical Fitness. Races, family rides, safety inspections. All ages.

ALASKA

Anchorage **Anchorage Bike Club,** c/o Ronald Crenshaw, 160 Jelinek, Anchorage 99504. Newly forming club, family oriented, bikeway program.

Fairbanks **Fairbanks Bicycle Club,** c/o J&R Bike Shop, 748 Airport Way, Fairbanks 99701. (LAW)

Juneau **Juneau Methodist Youth Hostel,** c/o M/M Don Kussart, 123 Fourth St., Juneau 99801. Accommodations for men and women, open June 1 to Labor Day. $1.

ARIZONA

Flagstaff **Ponderosa Pedalers AYH Club,** c/o Bruce Braley, 7 South Beaver St., #1, Flagstaff 86001.

Mesa **Mesa Bicycle Club,** newly-formed by AYH. Long distance tours, weekend rides, All ages. Meets Thursdays at Rendezvous Park. Call 964-3330.

Phoenix **Arizona State AYH Council,** 4634 E. Lewis St., Phoenix 85008. Information on state cycling activities, new clubs, overnight accommodations.

Phoenix **Central Arizona Hiking Club AYH,** c/o David Sundstrom, 4131 North 45th Place #4, Phoenix 85018.

Phoenix **Consumers Cycling Club,** c/o Barbieris' Schwinn Cyclery, 4112 N. 36th St., Phoenix 85018. (ABL of A). Races, competitive events. Long distance touring in winter. Fee: $5 per year.

Phoenix **Pera Bicycle Club,** c/o Millard Smith, P.O. Box 1980, Phoenix 85018.

Phoenix **Phoenix Wheelmen** (LAW), c/o James P. Beck, P.O. Box 7241, Phoenix 85011. Family and long distance rides. Membership fee.

Sun City **Pedal Pushers,** c/o Willard Lickfeldt, 10616 Sun City Boulevard, Sun City 85351.

Tempe **Senior Citizen's Bicycle Club** c/o Mesa's Travel Trailer Village Mobile Home Park. Open to all over 50. Weekly rides, physical fitness studies in connection with Arizona State University. No fee. Mon., Wed., Friday.

American Youth Hostels with overnight accommodations are found in Bisbee, Flagstaff, Holbrook, and Tucson.

ARKANSAS

Little Rock **Arkansas Bicycle Touring Club,** c/o James B. Conner, 5510 Edgewood Road, Little Rock 72207. (LAW). New club to promote family and long distance touring, development of scenic bike routes. Mr. Conner is a city planner who was instrumental in the designation of Little Rock Bikeways.

CALIFORNIA

Anderson **Shasta AYH Club,** c/o Tim Chamberlain, 5005 Cairns Drive, Anderson 96007.

Berkeley **Grizzly Pedal Pushers,** P.O. Box 9308, Berkeley 94709. (LAW, AYH) Extensive program of organized long and short-distance family touring, overnight bike hikes, social events. Open to all ages.

Ceres **Ceres Bicycle Touring Club,** c/o Ceres Recreation Commission, Ceres 95307. New, open to all ages, will sponsor long distance weekend rides, bike hikes, and safety demonstrations.

Concord **Diablo Wheelmen Bicycle Club,** 1788 Liveoak Ave., Concord, Calif. Long distance and short weekend tours, weekly Thursday morning "housewives special" for gals wishing to stay trim. Annual mid-June High Sierra Tour. Sunday evening family rides every week.

Daly City **Club Endspurt,** c/o Fritz Liedl, 757 Beachwood Drive, Daly City 94015. (LAW). Long-distance touring, family events.

Davis **Cal-Aggie Wheelmen,** c/o Dean of Students' Activities, Memorial Union, University of California, Davis. (LAW, AYH).

El Cerrito **"E.C." Riders,** c/o El Cerrito Recreation Center, 7007 Moeser Lane, El Cerrito 94530. New club.

Fresno **Fresno Cycling Club,** c/o Broadway Cycler, 829 Fulton Mall, Fresno 93721. (ABL of A). Long distance rides, family weekend activities, races, competitive events, social meetings first Wednesday of month. Dues: $6. Strong Bikeways program.

Granada Hills **Wheelmen of the Past Century,** c/o Earl LeMoine, 17167 Midwood Dr., Granada Hills 91344. Membership includes the grand old-timers of bicycle racing, and includes some who trained for 1932 Olympic Games. Holds one race a year.

Hayward **H.A.R.D. Hostel Club,** P.O. Box 698, Hayward Calif. Long and short-distance rides and family events, social events. Open to all over 13. Dues: 50¢.

Hollywood **North Hollywood Wheelmen,** (ABL of A), 5346 Laurel Canyon Blvd., N. Hollywood, Calif. 91607. Competitive events, long distance rides, races, social meetings. Dues: $10. sr., $5. jr. Racing oriented—"home of 4 Olympians."

Huntington Beach **OCC Orange County Cycling Club,** 10041 Theseus Dr., Huntington Beach (ABL of A). Long distance rides, competitive events, social meetings. Open to all ages. Dues: $10.

La Jolla **International Bicycle Touring Society,** 846 Prospect St., LaJolla 92037. A touring club for adults, accent on extended tours; one overseas tour every year. National in scope. Dues: $3. Illustrated brochure free.

La Palma **So. California Junior Wheelmen AYH Club,**

c/o Walker Jr. High School, 8132 Walker St., La Palma 90620. (AYH). Long distance rides, safety events.

Long Beach **Long Beach Sprockets,** c/o Will Decker, 182-1/2 Covina Ave., Long Beach 90803. Adult touring club with rides from 5 to 100 miles. Open to all ages over 16. One of the largest cycling programs in Southern California. Dues: $3-$5.

Los Alamitos **Lakewood Cyclers AYH Club,** 3801 "D" Howard Avenue, Los Alamitos 90720. Long distance rides, safety and social events. For youth 12-18.

Los Altos **Pedali Alpini, Inc.,** P.O. Box 28, Los Altos, Calif. 94022. (ABL of A). Long distance rides, races, social meeting last Friday of each month. Dues: $6 yr. Covers communities of Sunnyvale, Mt. View, Los Altos, Palo Alto, Stanford University and Central San Francisco Peninsula.

Los Angeles **Concerned Bicycle Riders for the Environment,** P.O. Box 24388, Los Angeles 90024. Nonprofit volunteer group working to educate the public and to implement measures which encourage bicycles as transportation. Politically oriented. Open to all.

Los Angeles **Earth Action Council** (activist group) University of California/Los Angeles, P.O. Box 24390, Los Angeles, California 90024.

Los Angeles **Los Angeles Wheelmen** (LAW), c/o John A. J. Wallis, 4334 Sunset Blvd., Los Angeles 90029. Long distance rides, family activities, social events, monthly meeting. Must be 14 or over. Over 150 tours each year through interesting, varied, historical terrain.

Menlo Park **Western Wheelers Bicycle Club.** P.O. Box 183, Menlo Park 94025. (LAW). Long-distance and family touring, many social activities. Heavy emphasis on bicycle legislation and development of bicycle transportation. Safety rallies, picnics, races, guided bike tours and maps. Many cooperative rides with families from neighboring clubs.

Modesto **Y Cyclist Club,** c/o YMCA Activities Office, Modesto, Calif. Many organized long distance bike tours for cyclists from 14 to 40. Family groups welcome. Summer tours to Carmel and San Francisco. Bike trip every Sunday.

Montebello **Montebello Bicycle Club,** c/o City of Montebello Parks and Recreation Department. Friday afternoons during summer. Open to youngsters 13 or entering 7th grade. Long and short trips. Call 721-3888. Meets at Youth Center.

Monterey **Cypress Cycling Club,** c/o Oliver Bradford, P.O. Box 391, Seaside, Calif. (LAW). Long distance and family weekend rides.

Napa **Napa Wheelmen,** 2267 Loma Heights, Napa Calif. (LAW). Organized weekend rides, family activities.

No. California National League of American Wheelmen, c/o Clifford L. Franz, No. Calif. Dir., 36 Grand Blvd., San Mateo 94401. Information on San Francisco and Northern California bike rides. Exchange info. Send him your favorite bike excursion data, he gives you routes and details of planned bike trips. Tel: 342-7863. Free.

N. Hollywood **Bicycle Touring Club,** c/o D. D. Hageman, 6518 Tujunga, North Hollywood, Calif. 91606. Newly organized to promote long distance bicycle touring. Must be adult. Club is sponsored by Classic Cycle Shop and members receive discounts. Dues: $10.

Oakland **Northern Calif. Assn. of Tandem Tourists** (NOCATS). c/o Ralph & Susi Heins, 6017 Margarido Drive, Oakland 94618. Designed to acquaint tandem owners with rides of approx. 40 miles at fast touring speeds. Both tandems and strong single riders are invited. Dues: $1 yr.

Orangevale **Orangevale Sidewinders,** c/o Dave Lawson, 9357 Nevins Way, Orangevale 95662. (AYH, LAW). Bicycle touring club.

Palo Alto **Skyline Cycling Club,** c/o Jim McCoy, P.O. Box 1016, Sunnyvale, Calif. 94306. (LAW). Long distance, weekend rides, social events. Must be 18 or over, and have 10-speed bike. Dues: $2.25. Fosters relaxed cycle touring and supports cycling organizations to improve area and state cycling conditions.

Paramount **Paramount Bicycle Touring Club,** c/o Parks and Recreation Department, Paramount, Calif. Long distance and local weekend rides, open to all ages, each tour led by experienced member of recreation staff.

Paramount **Paramount Peugeot Cycle Club,** 14924 S.

Paramount, Paramount, Calif. 90723. (ABL of A). Races, competitive events. Dues: $5. Meets every 3rd Monday, 8 PM.

Pasadena **Pasadena Athletic Association,** 391 S. Rosemead Blvd., Pasadena 91107. (ABL of A). Long distance rides, races.

Pasadena **Yankee Pedalers,** 1585 Pegfair Estates Drive, Pasadena, 91103. Long distance family weekend rides, safety instruction. Most members carry bikes on car racks to interesting destinations 35 miles from Pasadena. Evening rides made on Pasadena Bikeway near Rosebowl. Dues $5.

Placeville **Foothill Swiftwalkers,** 5131 Brookview Ct., Carmichael, Calif. 95608. Long distance rides, rallies, tours to Mother Lode countryside. Now for young bikers, may expand to include all ages.

Redding **Shasta Wheelmen,** 3540 Omega Lane, Redding 96001. Touring bicyclists may call 243-3090 for hostel accommodations while in Redding. (AYH-ABL of A). Long distance rides (Twin and Double Century), family rides, races, competitive events, social events, overnight bike camping. Adult oriented.

Redondo Beach **Junior Women's Club Bike Group,** Westloy Junior Women's Club, Marina District, Redondo Beach, Calif. Social events and bicycle-progressive dinner rides. Open to business and professional women.

Sacramento **Bike Hikers AYH Club,** 5270 Enrico Blvd., Sacramento 95820. Long distance and family rides, competitive and social events. Monthly meeting first Thurs. Must be under 50.

Sacramento **Capital City Wheelmen,** c/o David S. Wilson, 7379 Cranston Way, Sacramento 95822. (LAW).

Sacramento **Sacramento Bicycling and Outdoor Club,** c/o Harold Richey, 6019 4th Ave., Sacramento 95814. (LAW, AYH). Organized long distance and weekend rides.

Salinas **Salinas Wheelers,** 317 Margaret St., Salinas 93901. Open to all ages. Rides to points of interest, day-long trips, weekend tours, campouts, vacation tours, special events; some racing.

San Bernardino **Arrowhead Bicycle Club,** c/o Eli F. Lee, 1299 E. Highland Ave., San Bernardino 92404. (LAW).

San Bernardino **San Bernardino Cycling Club,** c/o Troy Foster, Pacific High School, Gilbert & Pacific Streets. (ABL of A) Competitive, racing events. Emphasis on youth.

San Diego **American Youth Hostels, San Diego Chapter,** 846 Prospect St., La Jolla 92037 (AYH). Long and short-distance family rides, races, competitive events, social events. Open to all. Dues depend on age.

San Diego **Convairiders,** c/o Richard W. Gilbert, 3694 Leland St., San Diego 92106. Employees of Convair Aircraft Corporation.

San Diego **San Diego Wheelmen,** c/o Myron Dickey, 4764 Mt. Harris, San Diego, California 92017.

San Francisco **Chronicle Cyclists,** 5th & Mission Sts., San Francisco 94119. Primarily for employees of the San Francisco CHRONICLE and their friends, but open to all. Family weekend rides. Dues $5.

San Francisco **Galileo AYH Club,** c/o David Mann, 1420-A Chestnut St., San Francisco 94123.

San Francisco **Golden Gate Council, AYH,** 625 Polk St., Rm. 201, San Francisco, 94102. (LAW, AYH). Long distance and overnight bike hikes, many family activities. Touring information in Bay Area.

San Francisco **San Francisco Bicycle Coalition,** 1405 7th Ave., San Francisco, 94122. Organized to promote the use of bicycles for transportation, and to sponsor and support legislation for bike facilities. Includes AYH, City College Bike Club, Ecology Center, LAW, San Francisco State Bicycle Action Committee. San Francisco Wheelmen, Sierra Club and San Francisco Tomorrow.

San Francisco **San Francisco Ecology Center,** 13 Columbus Avenue, San Francisco 94111. Talks on bicycling, bike paths, metropolitan bike transportation, repairs. Workshops and seminars. Bike parades, races, demonstrations. Open to all.

San Francisco **Sierra Club,** San Francisco Bay Chapter, c/o Paul DeWitt, 1082 Mills Tower, 220 Bush St., San Francisco 94104. Bike touring activities for families. (LAW,

AYH). Emphasis on development of interesting routes/ conservation.

San Francisco **The Spokesmen,** 504 Fawn Drive, Sleepy Hollow, San Anselmo, Calif. 94960. "A Touring Club for Elite San Franciscans." Membership open to adults.

San Francisco **Western Wanderers Bicycle Club of San Francisco,** c/o Mr. David Marshall, 439 Wellington Drive, San Carlos, Calif. 94070. Long distance rides, family weekend rides with camping, social meeting monthly. Rides every Sat. & Sun. at 1 PM at Bike Shop, 4621 Lincoln Way, San Francisco. Dues: $1.50 per year.

San Jose **East Valley Bicycle Club** c/o Tom Concannon, 1450 Mt. Palomar Dr., San Jose, Calif.

San Jose **Jolly Pumpers,** Dale Peape, 3489 Mauricia Ave., Santa Clara, Calif. Long distance tours and family activities.

San Jose **Santa Clara Valley Bicycling Association,** c/o Bruce M. Ball, President, 750 Stierling Rd. #149, Mountain View, California. Organized for express purpose of promoting bike routes in and around San Jose & Santa Clara County. Open to all ages.

San Jose **Santa Clara Valley Club of AYH, Inc.,** 532 Cinnamon Drive, San Jose 95150. Long distance, family rides, races, competitive and safety events. Dues: AYH membership. "A diversified group of young adults who enjoy the outdoors." All ages. Dedicated to promoting bike routes in and around the city of San Jose & Santa Clara County.

San Luis Obispo **San Luis Obispo Bicycle Club,** c/o Larry Souva, 1319 Kenwood Drive, San Luis Obispo 93401. Very active new group sponsoring long distance and short weekday and weekend tours, scenic rides. Adult oriented, but families welcome. Interesting newsletter. All rides include sag wagon. Special emphasis on designation of touring trails. Dues: 25¢ month per family.

San Rafael **Marin Cyclists, Inc.,** Box 2611, San Rafael, 94901. (ABL of A, LAW, AYH). Long distance (Century, double century, twin century), family weekday and weekend rides, morning rides, races, competitive events, social events 1st Thursday each month. Dues: $6.

Santa Barbara **Friends for Bikecology,** 1035 East De La Guerra St., Santa Barbara 93193. Promotes the ecological benefits of cycling for transportation. Organizes bicycle demonstrations throughout the country to focus attention on the need for cycling facilities. Sample publications upon request.

Santa Barbara **Santa Barbara Wheelmen,** c/o Roy Connell, Ortega by the Sea, P.O. Box 384, Sommerland 93067.

Santa Barbara **Senior Citizens Bicycle Club,** c/o Ingeborg S. Epperson, 180 Olive Mill Road, Santa Barbara. For older cyclists only, including those on adult tricycles. Easy rides to interesting places for picnics and sociability. Organized to reduce weight and encourage good health. Open to men and women.

Santa Rosa **Santa Rosa Cycling Club,** c/o 711 Coddington Center, Santa Rosa 95401. (LAW). New club for adults; call 539-1935, 542-9322, or 544-6910 during evening hours. Long distance weekend rides, socials at Alexander Valley Community Hall.

Seaside **Cypress Cycling Club,** P.O. Box 391, Seaside, Calif., 93955. (ABL of A). Long distance rides, racing events. 17-Mile Drive ride every Sunday 10:30 AM. Adults.

Soquel **Redwood Velocepedes,** 401 Old San Jose Road, Soquel, Calif., 95073. Promotes bike transport to schools and work, recommends school courses in bike riding and safety. Dues: $1. Sponsors long distance and family rides on weekends, monthly social and safety events.

Southern California Cycling Association, 4509 Briercrest Ave., Lakewood 90713. Information on competitive cycling activities in southern California.

Stockton **Stockton Bicycle Club,** c/o Howard Luyendyk, 251 E. Banbury Dr., Stockton, (LAW). Organized long distance and family rides, social events. Open to all ages.

Sun City **Sun City Bicycling Club,** c/o Town Hall, Sun City, Calif. For senior citizens, both singles and couples. Five to seven mile rides, ending in hot meals, picnics. Meets every Tuesday at 9 AM. Some riders use adult tricycles, several members observed golden wedding anniversaries. Open to all over 50. Color slide programs.

Sunnyvale **Pedalera Wheelmen,** Orgn. 00-93, Bld. 160, P.O. Box 504, Sunnyvale. For employees of Lockheed Missiles & Space Co., and their friends. (LAW). Long distance rides, family weekend rides, time trials, rodeos, safety demonstrations. Social events 3rd Wednesday. Dues: $4.

Susanville **Susanville AYH,** c/o Len Smith, 2115 River St., Susanville, Calif., 96130. (AYH, LAW). Many organized weekend activities for all ages, long distance tours.

Union City **Decoto Youth Center Bike Clubs,** c/o Decoto Youth Center, 2nd & E Sts., Union City. Races and competitive events for youngsters.

Ventura **Ventura Cyclers,** 4741 Rockford Court, or 157 Madera Ave., Ventura. Long Distance rides, family weekend and overnight excursions. Open to all. Dues: 15¢ teenagers, 45¢ family. Bikeway campaign.

Walnut Creek **Valley Spokesmen,** Valley Community Services District Recreation and Parks Dept. Organized family bicycle tours, safety seminars, active bicycle legislation and Bikeways promotion.

Woodland **Woodland AYH,** c/o Mr. and Mrs. Loren Smith, Rt. 1, Box 881 AM Woodland, Calif. 95695. (AYH).

Youth Hostels

AYH overnight accommodations are provided at **Calistoga** (Home Ranch Youth Hostel, c/o Duane Sands, 3400 Mt. Home Ranch Road, Calistoga 94515), **Hemet** (Meadowlark Farm Youth Hostel, c/o Peter Fisher, Rt. 2, Box 238, Hemet 92343, **Los Altos** (Hidden Villa Ranch Youth Hostel, 26870 Moody Road, Los Altos Hills 94022), **Los Angeles** (Weyburn Hall, 947 Tiverton Ave., Westwood Village 90024, Calif., **Sacramento** (Cal-Expo Youth Hostel, c/o John Curran, Cal-Expo Grounds, Sacramento. For res. write AYH, P.O. Box 15649, Sacramento 98513), **San Francisco** (YMCA Hotel 351 Turk St.,) **St. Helena** (Bar 49 Ranch Y.H. c/o Edward Keith & Jim Simpson, Bar 49 Ranch, 225 Kearney St., San Francisco).

COLORADO

Boulder **The Spoke Club,** 617 S. Broadway, Boulder 80302. Family rides, competitive events.

Denver **Colorado Mountain Club,** 1723 East 16th St., Denver, Colorado. Many summertime bicycling tours in this predominantly skiing and hiking club.

Denver **Bicycles Now!,** c/o Paul Thompson, 1005 S. Estes Ct., Lakewood 80226. Activist organization formed for the purpose of promoting bicycle commuting in the Denver Metropolitan area, with emphasis on bikers' rights, political action, publicity, safe routes, and legal help. All ages welcome. Newsletter. Chapter in Aurora, Englewood, Golden Lakewood, Littleton, Loveland, Wheatride.

Loveland **Pedal** c/o Arthur P. Minich, 3210 Butternut Drive, Loveland 80537. New club. Long distance and weekday rides. Social meetings. Open to all ages.

Pueblo **Velocipedes in Pueblo** c/o Mrs. Dorothy Urban, 3601 Azalea, Pueblo 81005. Long distance and family weekend rides, monthly social, safety activities. Aggressive bikeway program.

Colorado Youth Hostels, AYH Accommodations for overnight cyclists are provided at **Boulder** (1058 13th Street), **Divide** (Rocky Mt. Camp Youth Hostel, Box 6, Divide 80814), and at **Durango** (Ranch Youth Hostel, c/o Mr. & Mrs. Irwin A. Lechner, Silverton Start Rt., Box 60, Durango 81301). Colorado AYH headquarters are located at Boulder House, 1421 Broadway A, Boulder.

CONNECTICUT

Hartford **Poor People's Federation Youth Hostel Club** c/o Poor People's Federation, 1491 Main St., Hartford 06120.

Lakeville **Lakeville Cycle Club,** c/o Everett Britton, Director of Instruction, Housatonic Valley Region High School, Lakeville. Organized long distance and short weekend scenic tours for family groups and youths of high school age. Active program to develop bike paths. Safety inspections, competitive activities. Open to all ages.

Milford **Milford Bicycle Club,** c/o William Cannon, "Cycle Shop," Milford, Conn. (LAW).

Mystic **Mystic Seaport Velo Club,** c/o Lance Folworth, 162 Bayview Ave., Mystic 06355. (LAW).

New Haven **Yale Bicycle Club,** Room 215, Ray Tompkins House. Tower Parkway. Eastern Intercollegiate Cycling Assn. (ABL of A). Long distance rides, races, competitive events. Open to any Yale student. Non-Yale students invited to participate in long distance rides.

Southport **Fairfield Co. Council, AYH,** P.O. Box 173, Southport, Conn. 06490. (AYH). Long distance and family weekend rides, quarterly social events. Open to AYH-ers.

Stamford **Stamford Wheelmen.**

South Meriden **South Meriden Cycling Club,** c/o Carolyn Backus, 21 Sorries Court, So. Meriden 06450. Organized by H.S. students to encourage cycling for health and fitness. Membership: H.S. students.

Torrington **Torrington Bicycle Club,** c/o Gordon B. Whittaker, Jr., 173 Benham St., Torrington 06790. (LAW). Long distance touring and family events. Social meetings. Open to all over 18.

Westport **Westport Bicycle Club,** c/o Bike Barn, Westport, Conn. Long distance, weekend rides to scenic areas, shorter rides for family groups. Organized for fun; no dues, no organization. Open to all ages. Special emphasis on foliage tours.

Windsor Locks **Connecticut Valley Touring Club,** c/o Jack Boettger, 377 Reed Ave., Windsor Locks 06096. (LAW). Well-organized family activities, long distance scenic and foliage rides. Information on touring. Social events.

American Youth Hostels AYH overnight accommodations are provided in **Canton** (Sugar House Hostel, 11 Sugar Camp Road, Canton 06019), **Lakeside** (Bantam Lake Youth Hostel, c/o Mr. & Mrs. Alex Sobolewski, Lakeside 06758).

Hartford **Hartford Council, AYH,** c/o YWCA, 262 Ann St., Hartford 06103. Long distance and family weekend events. Open to AYH-ers. Dues according to age.

DELAWARE

Wilmington **Delaware Bicycle Club,** c/o Richard H. Jones, 233 Cheltenham Road, Newark, Del. 19711. Organized family bicycle rides every Saturday throughout the summer.

Services all riders in North Delaware and University at Newark. Source of touring information.

DISTRICT OF COLUMBIA

Washington **Potomac Pedalers Touring Club,** 2818 Pennsylvania Ave., NW, Washington, D.C. 20007. (AYH, LAW). Full schedule of long, medium and short rides, family tours, quarterly meetings and safety events. Must be over 16 or part of family. Dues: $5-7. Offers newsletter, derailleur clinics, library service, day tours of DC, Maryland and Virginia.

Washington **Summer in the Parks,** c/o District Parks & Recreation Department. Many summertime activities for youth, including long distance rides along C & O Canal, in park Bikeways, competitive events.

American Youth Hostel with overnight accommodations is found in Washington, D.C.

FLORIDA

Bradenton **K & K Mobile Park Bike Club,** c/o K & K Mobile Park, Bradenton, Fla. Organized for retirees and oldsters. Welcomes adult tricycles. Weekly outings end in breakfasts; many other social activities. Source of information on other senior citizen bike clubs in So. Florida. Open to all physically fit adults.

Clearwater **Clearwater Pedal Pushers,** c/o Alfred Pearsall, 2263 Habersham Dr., Clearwater 33516. Rides four times a week to interesting destinations. Adult oriented, but open to all. Special recognition for long distance mileage records.

Cocoa **Brevard Bikeway Association,** R. R. 2, Box 1190, Cocoa, Florida. Family weekend rides, safety events, and promotion of new, well-marked Bikeways. No dues.

Coral Gables **Coral Gables Bicycle Academy,** c/o Jack White, 2951 S. Bayshore Dr., Miami, Fla. 33133.

Deltona **Ardent Bicyclists Club,** c/o Jack H. Levinson, 1336 W. Hartley Circle, Deltona 32763. Organized but informal rides. Adult oriented.

Ft. Lauderdale **Broward Wheelmen,** c/o Fred Knoller, 2841 SW 9th St., Ft. Lauderdale 33312. (ABL of A). Long distance, family rides, races, competitive events. Dues: $3.

Ft. Lauderdale **Park City Bicycle Club,** c/o Walt Neal, Park City Mobile Park, Ft. Lauderdale, Fla. Almost exclusively for adult tricycling. Various leisurely rides to interesting places for senior citizens. No formal organization. Open to all.

Gainesville **Cyclists of Gainesville,** c/o Mrs. Mary Row, 114 SW 23rd Drive, Gainesville 32601.

Hollywood **The Dusters Bicycle Club,** c/o Hollywood Recreation Center, 2030 Polk St., Hollywood. Bike hikes and long distance touring for youngsters 11 to 14. Club participates in service projects throughout the city and assists in pollution control.

Homestead **Paul Dudley White Bicycle Club,** P.O. Box 1368, Homestead, Fla. 33030. Long distance and family rides, races, competitive events, business meetings 1st Thursday, Sunday afternoon rides third Sunday. Must be 18 or older. Dues: $3-4. Undertaking National Bicycle Center, hosts national tours. Good source of Florida touring information.

Miami **Sunshine Bicycle Club,** c/o North Miami Senior High School. Organized weekend rides for teenagers only. Prefer geared bicycles. Open to all of senior high age.

Nalcrest **Nalcrest Bicycle Club,** c/o Dora Snider, Town Center, Nalcrest, Florida. Leisurely short weekday and weekend scenic rides for senior citizens.

Naples **Hip Trimmers Bicycle Club,** c/o Arlene Boldt, Holiday Manor, Naples. For gals pedaling away the pounds. Call: 649-6550. Informal.

Pensacola **Pensacola Freewheelers,** c/o Dr. George M. Rapier, Jr., 400 W. Sunset Rd., Navy Pt., Warrington 32507. (LAW, ABL of A). Long distance rides, family activities, racing and competitive events. Organized according to age groups. Open to all ages.

Sarasota **Mr. and Mrs. Bicycle Club,** c/o City Mobile Home Park, Sarasota. Leisurely rides on safe streets, ending in social. For senior citizens. **Moonbeams Tricycle Club,** Venice Municipal Mobile Home Park. Open to men and women senior citizens. Weekly leisurely rides and many social events. Emphasis on fitness and activity.

St. Petersburg **St. Petersburg Bicycle Club.** 863 7th Avenue, No. St. Petersburg, 33701. Weekend long distance rides for families and other organized tours. Picnics and regular social meetings with movies, slides, and guest speakers. Open to all ages, but adult oriented.

West Palm Beach **West Palm Beach Recreation Bicycle Club,** c/o Robert Husky, 4138 Kirk Rd., West Palm Beach 33460. (ABL of A). Long distance and family rides, races, competitive events, social events. Stresses safety and instruction. Open to all. $1. for children, $3. for seniors.

Winter Park **Central Florida LAW,** c/o Bette or Ralph Boston, 2748 Cady Way, Winter Park 32789.

GEORGIA

Atlanta **Southern Bicycle Touring League,** c/o Beverly Hensley, 476 Seminole Ave., Apt. 3, Atlanta 30309. Long distance and overnight family and singles tours, weeknight events, picnics and social events. New racing program starting, directed by a doctor. Open to teens and up with reasonable riding skills. Accent on fun and fitness.

Gainesville **Huff & Puff Bicycle Club,** c/o Gainesville Park & Recreation Department. Organized for women who are interested in health and fitness. Rides during early evening hours.

Savannah **Chatham Cyclists,** c/o Fred Swanberg, 26 Noble Glen Drive, Savannah 31406. Organized long distance and weekend tours, tours of Savannah and surrounding historic areas. Monthly social meeting. Open to adults. Dues $3. Special emphasis on the development of city and county bikeways and touring routes.

Savannah **YMCA Bicycle Club.** Many special bicycle trips and safety events for youngsters through teens.

HAWAII

Island of Hawaii **Hilo Bicycle Club,** c/o The Bike Shop, P.O. Box 1103, Hilo, Hawaii 96720. New group works for the development of bike trails and organized events, bike safety. Open to all ages.

Island of Oahu **Hawaii Bicycle League,** c/o Jock Purinton, 2620 E. Manoa Road, Honolulu 96822. (LAW). Long distance rides, family events. Open to all over 16. Dues: $3. Special emphasis on development of bicycle trails and bike routes.

AYH overnight accommodations are privided at **Honolulu** (Hale Aloha YH, c/o John K. Akau, Jr., 2323 Seaview Ave., Honolulu 96822).

IDAHO

Boise **Highlands Bicycling Club,** c/o Mrs. Byron Erstadt, 1219 Highland View Drive, Boise. Weekend touring, other family activities. Open to all.

Idaho Falls **Idaho Falls Cycling Club,** c/o David Karpins, 576 N.E. Bonneville Drive, Idaho Falls. Long distance tours and family activities, with lectures on maintenance and safety. Open to all 13 or older. Special emphasis on development of interesting bike routes in Idaho.

ILLINOIS

Arlington Heights **Arlington Heights Park District Bicycle Club,** c/o Mary Ellen Spirek, Arlington Heights, Illinois.

Argonne **Argonne Bicycle Club,** P.O. Box 303, Argonne 60439. Planned weekend tours and evening rides. Some social meetings. Family and adult oriented. Membership is open to any interested bicyclist whether or not associated with the U.S. Atomic Energy Commission or the Argonne National Laboratory.

Aurora **Aurora Jaycee Bicycle Club,** Aurora Jaycees, 40 W. Downer Place, Aurora. Open to all over 15. Many weekday and weekend bicycle tours on Aurora Nature Trail during the summertime. Family activities, brown-bag picnics.

Champaign **Champaign Park District Bicycling Club** c/o Parks & Recreation Department. Varied program of long distance touring, weekend family activities and competitive events for all age groups and riders from Champaign-Urbana twin city area.

Champaign **Prairie Cycle Club,** 511-1/2 W. Vine, Champaign, Illinois. New student-community group dedicated to the improvement of bicycling conditions and promotion of bike events. Open to bikers with reasonable skills. Long distance tours, bikeway promotion, maps and info. on bike tours, lectures and clinics on bike maintenance and safety. Social meeting first Sunday of every month at 7 pm in Rm. 135, Animal Sciences Bldg., U. of Illinois.

Chicago **Association of Bicycle Commuters,** 1737 N. Park Ave., Chicago. Volunteer citizens' group formed to advocate the use of the bicycle as a basic means of urban transportation, using political means to improve the lot of cyclists.

Chicago **Bicycle Ecology,** P.O. Box 66498, Chicago 60666. Formed by interested citizens to achieve needed transportation reforms, and to encourage the use of bicycles for transportation. Emphasis on lobbying and legislation; ecology oriented. Open to all ages.

Chicago **Burnett Bike Bunch,** c/o Ron Elkins, Leo Burnett Advertising Co., Prudential Plaza, Chicago 60601. For members of Burnett Advertising, their families and friends. Special emphasis on encouragement of bicycle commuting in Chicago.

Chicago **Chicago Council, AYH,** 2210 North Clark St., Chicago 60614 c/o Cycle Chairman. (AYH, LAW). Long distance rides, family events, safety activities. Social events every weekend during summer. Open to all.

Chicago **Gladstone Park Bicycle Club,** c/o Gladstone Park, 5421 N. Menard, Chicago. For information, call RO 3-8338. Organized cycling activities in Gladstone Park for youth ages 10 through teens.

Chicago **Hyde Park Hostel Club,** c/o Paul Strauss, 2441 West 61st Street, Chicago 60629.

Chicago **Sauganash Cycle Club,** 6031 N. Cicero, Chicago 60646. (ABL of A.) Long distance rides.

Decatur **YMCA Bicycle Club,** c/o YMCA Cycling Director, Decatur. Family and youth activities. Rides of some distance being planned. Group cycles in wintertime. Open to all ages.

Elgin **Elgin Bicycle Touring Club,** c/o Richard Yahn, 432 South Street. Open to all ages, many organized summer weekend rides.

Elk Grove **Elk Grove Village Bicycle Club,** c/o Tom McCabe, 1317 East Cumberland Circle, Elk Grove.

Evanston **Evanston Bicycle Club,** 1601 Main Street, Evanston, Illinois. Long and short weekend rides. 3 rides every

Sunday during summer appealing to all ages. Social meetings and lectures on cycling and safety. Sponsored by Evanston Recreation Dept. Open to all 16 yrs. and older.

Franklin Park **Franklin Park Bicycle Club,** c/o Franklin Park Recreation Department, Franklin Park. Long and short rides during the summer. Open to all ages. Rides graduated according to skills of riders.

Galena **Galena Hostel Club AYH,** Galena 61036. Long distance tours for family and singles. Dues: $2. One of nation's best-equipped hostels. Club will assist cross-country cyclists and groups wishing to cycle or ski in area.

Geneva **St. Charles Bicycle Club,** c/o Paul Fitzgerald, 101 South 2nd St., St. Charles 60174, or the Park District. Family rides on weekdays, long distance tours every weekend. Open to all ages. Overnight bike hiking to Wisconsin State Bikeway.

Glenview **Glenview Hostel Club AYH,** c/o Glenview Park District, 2320 Glenview Road, Glenview.

Jacksonville **Easy Riders Bike Club,** c/o Mrs. William Chipman, 869 Edgehill Road, Jacksonville. Three division club for beginners to seasoned riders. Long distance touring, overnight hikes and camping trips.

Jacksonville **Jacksonville Easy Riders** c/o Sherwood Eddy YMCA, Jacksonville 62650. (YMCA). Regular Sunday rides of 10 to 100 miles; Wednesday evening rides during the season; Historical bicycle tour of Jacksonville. Open to adults and families. Dues: $1. for Y members, $5. others.

Macomb **Macomb YMCA Cycling Club,** c/o YMCA, Macomb. Organized weekday and weekend cycling, open to all from age 8.

Marquette (Chicago) **Marquette Park Bicycle Club,** c/o Mrs. Liz Ferguson, 4726 S. Leclaire, Chicago, Illinois. Various adult-oriented bicycle trips. Meets in Marquette Park fieldhouse, 67th & Kedzie.

Naperville **DuPage Valley Cycling & Cycle-Touring Club,** c/o Matt Prastein, 9S320 Barkdoll Road, Naperville. Weeknight & weekend "know Naperville" tours to scenic areas and on Illinois Prairie Path. Open to all ages. Future rides involve camping and long distance touring.

Northbrook **Northbrook Bicycle Club,** 111 Waukegan, Northbrook, Illinois 60062. c/o George Garner Cyclery. (ABL of A). Competitive and track events. Monthly social meetings. Located in suburb with velodrome.

Oak Park **Cross Roads Cycle Club,** c/o Edward Weiss, 523 Hachem, Oak Park 60304.

Palos Hills **Moraine College Bicycle Club,** Moraine Valley Community College, 10900 S. 88th St., Palos Hills. Offers bike riding for credit as part of physical education program; members encourage development of Bikeway routes.

Park Forest **Sauk Trail Hostel Club,** c/o Dept. of Recreation & Parks, Village of Park Forest, Illinois. (AYH). Long distance and family touring, competitive and safety events. Meets first Monday, third Wednesday.

Springfield **Lincolnland AYH,** 5001 Sand Hill Road, Springfield 62702. Organized long distance and family cycling events, overnight bike hikes. Closest hostel club to Lincoln Heritage Trail and loop Bikeways. Open to all over 18, and children when with parents. Dues: $5 and up.

Sterling **North Western Illinois Cyclers,** c/o Roger De Langhe, 1402 Howard Street, RR#3, Sterling 61081. Long distance and family weekend rides, races and competitive events. Open to all. No dues. Special emphasis on development of marked bike routes.

Wilmette **Wilmette Bicyclers Breakfast Club,** c/o Miss Patricia Dana, P.O. Box 398, Wilmette, Illinois. Weekday and weekend rides. Special groups for children, pre-teens, couples, singles, young adults, retired and senior citizens. Special emphasis on early morning activities. Meets at Michigan Shores Club, Wilmette.

American Youth Hostels with overnight accommodations are found in **Chicago, Carbondale, Galena, and Palos Park.**

INDIANA

Bloomington **Southern Indiana Bicycle Touring Association,** c/o Charles Eckert, P.O. Box 544, Bloomington 47401. Long distance tours, family bike activities, social events. Specialists in mapping scenic and historic bike routes in southern Indiana. Open to all ages, but riders should have geared bikes.

Corunna **Teenage Sportsmen's Club of Corunna,** c/o Mr. and Mrs. William Cook, Corunna. Organized bike rides and races for children from 6-16 throughout the summer. Emphasis on bicycle safety.

Elkhart **The Elkhart Chain Gang,** c/o Larry Metz, Physical Director, Bicycle Program, Elkhart YMCA, Elkhart, Ind. Sunday outings for anyone interested in good fun and fitness. Families especially invited but children under 15 must be accompanied.

Elkhart **Out-Spokin',** Box 370, Elkhart 46514. Sponsored by the Mennonite Church to encourage cross-country bicycling.

Elkhart **Elkhart Bicycle Club,** c/o Brantly Chappell, 301 South Main Street, Elkhart 46514. New club which will encourage family and adult bicycling activities. Strong Bikeways program.

Ft. Wayne **3 Rivers Velo-Sport,** 10580 Johnson Rd., Ft. Wayne 46808. Long distance rides, racing and competitive events. Youth oriented. Current project: development of banked bicycle racing track in Ft. Wayne.

Hammond **Calumet Wheelmen,** c/o William Gasper, 6415 Kennedy Avenue, Hammond.

Hartford City **deCycle Club,** non-denominational religious group of teenagers, who spend summer cycling across the U.S., staying at churches along the way, to offer young people the challenge of recreation and fulfillment. Membership limited to 60.

Indianapolis **Central Indiana Bicycling Association, Inc.,** c/o Mrs. Edward L. Dusing, 5304 Crown, Indianapolis 46208. (LAW). Long distance rides, family weekend rides, competitive events, safety activities. Socials held twice a year and during rides. Open to all. Dues: $2-3. Family touring every Sunday, 150-mile Sesquicentennial ride in June.

Indianapolis **Edgewood Wheelmen, Inc.,** 5506 Madison Ave., Indianapolis 46227. (LAW). Long distance rides, weekday evening rides for families, competitive events, safety activities. Dues: $2.50-$3.50. Founded 1933.

Indianapolis **Speedway Wheelmen, Inc.,** c/o James Andrew, 415 East 45th St., Indianapolis 46205. (ABL of A). Sponsors road and track races, now organizing long distance touring.

Club rides scheduled weekly throughout the summer. Open to all ages. Dues: $2-7.

Kokomo **Kokomo Wheelmen,** c/o Walt B. Farnsworth, 423 Forest Drive, Kokomo 46901. (LAW).

Lafayette **YWCA Bicycling Club,** c/o Mrs. Sam Flack, Y.W.C.A., Lafayette. Weekly rides for gals interested in good exercise, trimming up, and beautification of surrounding area. Ecology oriented. Gals only. Dues: YWCA membership.

Marion **Marion Y Wheelmen, YMCA,** 418 W. 3rd St., Marion, 46952. Local and long distance touring, family cycling, racing, safety activities. Monthly meetings. Dues: $1-3. Open to all age groups.

Mishawaka **Mishawaka Wheelmen,** c/o Jerry Woodruff, 3835 Lincoln Way East, Mishawaka, 46544. (LAW). Long distance touring, family events. Social meetings. Open to all ages.

Shelbyville **The Spokesmen Bicycling Club,** c/o Mike Beck, New Palestine, Indiana. Group of young men who spend summer holidays cycling across the U.S., covering more than 100 miles per day. For information, write Mr. Beck, tour leader.

Terre Haute **Wabash Wheelman,** c/o Bill Barber, 39 Doe Drive, Terre Haute. New club planning family weekend rides in the Terre Haute and Wabash Valley area, and the designation of interesting routes. Open to all ages and interests.

Upland **Wandering Wheels Bicycle Club,** c/o Taylor University, Upland, Ind. Group of 40 teenagers who each year cycle across the U.S. to demonstrate the "vitality of the Christian life and to provide a means of understanding Christ in a context of masculine adventure."

Valparaiso **Valparaiso Bicycle Club,** 105 McKinley, Valparaiso 46383. A family cycling organization devoted exclusively to touring. Sunday rides, monthly meetings. Dues: $3. Youth oriented.

Vincennes **Fort Sackville Bicycle Club,** c/o Hank Quinett, 416 So. 5th St., Vincennes. Organized weeknight and weekend tours for adults and families. Special social events for

wives. Children under 16 must be accompanied by an adult.
West Lafayette **State Farm Employees Activities Association
Bicycle Club,** c/o State Farm Insurance, 2550 Northwestern
Ave., W. Lafayette 47901. Membership limited to State
Farm Employees and their families. Long distance, family
weekend rides, competitive events, social and safety
activities.

IOWA

Cedar Rapids **The Hawkeye Bicycle Association, Inc.,** c/o
James Clifton, 4845 Kesler Rd., N.W. Cedar Rapids, 52405.
New club to encourage family bike riding and scenic bike
touring.

Council Bluffs **Council Bluffs Bicycle Club,** c/o Dennis E.
Butler, 1020 S. 36th St., Council Bluffs 51501. New club to
encourage bicycling for transportation and fitness, promote
legislation favorable to bikers.

Davenport **Quad City Bicycle Club,** c/o Fred K. Blessind,
2727 Grove St., Davenport 52804. Organized long distance
and weekend rides. Social meetings. Open to all ages.

Des Moines **Des Moines Bicycling Club,** c/o Tom Quick,
1900 Merklin Way, Des Moines. New club devoted to weekend family cycling activities and long distance touring. All
ages welcome. Call (515) 244-1030.

Des Moines **Des Moines YMCA Cycle Club,** c/o Edwin R.
Pugsley, 212 Americana Court, Apt. 45, Des Moines 50314.
Long distance and Century rides, time trials. Originally,
physical fitness club, now expanded to include touring from
May through October, with rides suitable for cyclists of all
abilities. Monthly socials and cycling films. Free bike available for trail rides. Newsletter and ride notices. Active
Bikeways program, rides for the blind. Dues: $4, YMCA
members; $10, non-members. (Sends brochure.)

Harvey **Knoxville Knee Knockers AYH Club,** c/o Knoxville
Kiwanis Club, Harvey RFD, Iowa 50119.

Mt. Pleasant **Mt. Pleasant Bicycle Club,** c/o The Rev.
Dennis Nicholson, 104 W. Saunders, Mt. Pleasant. Open to
families, youth and adults in the Mt. Pleasant area. Short
and long distance rides, social events.

Mt. Pleasant **Mt. Pleasant Pedal Pushers,** c/o Herbert E. Layson, 304 So. Cherry, Mt. Pleasant 52641.

Postville **Postville Hustlers' AYH Club,** P.O. Box 96, Postville 52162. (AYH). Long distance tours, bi-weekly social activities. Must be 13 or older. Dues: $2-$5 or AYH pass. Predominantly teenage. Year-round program of cycling, canoeing, skiing, community service.

Youth Hostels AYH overnight accommodations are provided in **Decorah** (Oneota Youth Hostel, c/o Dr. George Knudson, 616 Center St., Luther College, Decorah 52101), **Harper's Ferry** (R. W. Daubendiek, Harper's Ferry 52146.), **Iowa City** (Wesley House, David Schuldt, 120 N. Dubuque St., Iowa City 52240).

KANSAS

Ellis **Pedal Pushers,** c/o James Hall, 1209 Fauteaux St., Ellis. Weekday breakfast rides for adult women.

Salina **Salina Wheelmen, Inc.,** c/o Gerald Martin, 629 S. 9th Street, Salina, Kansas. A very active club.

Topeka **Topeka Wheelmen,** 1930 Webster Ave., Topeka 66604. Long distance and family rides, monthly meetings, June-Sept. Heavy emphasis on the development of bikeways and bike routes in Topeka and scenic bicycle touring routes in Kansas.

Wichita **Wichita Cycling Club,** c/o Emmett Carpenter, Hamilton's, 2106 East Central, Wichita 67214. (LAW). Organized cycling activities and long distance rides.

Wichita **Wichita Wheelmen,** c/o Ken Barnett, 5135 Fairfield, Wichita 67204. Weekend short and long distance rides, overnight bike camping. Open to all ages.

KENTUCKY

Henderson **Henderson Bicycle Club,** c/o Recreation Dept., Henderson. Organized and informal cycling activities, social events on weekends. Meetings held in Community and Youth Center. Adult oriented, but accompanied children welcome.

Lexington **Bluegrass Wheelmen Cycling Club,** c/o Don Burrell, 882 Maywick Dr., Lexington 40504. (LAW). Family weekend rides, social events. Dues: $4-6. Special events include annual fall tour to Red River Gorge. Special projects: establishment of network of bikeways for commuting and pleasure.

Louisville **Louisville Wheelmen,** 1737 Bardstown Road, Louisville 40520. (LAW). Long distance rides, family weekend events, races. Dues: $5-7.

Paducah **Women's Bicycle Club,** c/o Parks & Recreation Department, Paducah. Summer recreation program for women concerned with physical fitness and fellowship. Eight-weeks program ends with picnic. Safety instruction.

LOUISIANA

Alexandria **Cenla Bicycle Club,** c/o Marie D'Angelo, 850 Chester St., Alexandria 71301. (LAW). Long distance and weekend family rides, social events. Adult oriented. Special emphasis on bikeways and touring routes. Open to all ages.

Baton Rouge **Baton Rouge Cycle Club,** c/o H. H. Bradshaw, 2430 July St., Baton Rouge 70808. (LAW). Organized long distance scenic touring, family activities, social events. Famous for its Jambalaya rides which attract out-of-staters to well-planned long distance historical tours. Dues: $1.

Lafayette **Lafayette Bicycle Club,** c/o Bertrand DeBlanc, 260 Edgewoood Drive, Lafayette. Long distance and weekend touring, races, safety and social activities. The club has also incorporated to encourage bicycle legislation and development of Bikeways.

New Orleans **New Orleans Bicycle Club,** 1314 Joseph St., New Orleans. Racing, local and long range touring, social rides with other clubs. Dues: $1. Open to all.

MAINE

Camden **Penobscot Wheelmen,** c/o Dr. H. J. Bixler, 6 Sea Street, Camden 04843. (LAW). New club will feature long distance family and adult touring, development of scenic tours. Open to all over 16. Dues: $10.

American Youth Hostel with overnight accommodations is found in **South Waterford.**

MARYLAND

Baltimore **Baltimore Bicycling Club,** 304 Hilton Ave.,

Baltimore 21228. (LAW). Serves communities in wide area. Long distance and family rides. Special rides, picnics and yearly banquet. Graded for bikers of all degrees of skill. Rides all year and weeknights. Must be 16 unless member of family. Dues: $4-$6.

Columbia **Columbia Bicycle Club,** c/o Kenneth M. Jennings, Jr., 5250 Eliot's Oak Road, Columbia 21043.

Elkridge **The Wheelmen,** c/o Clyde Nitz, Rt. 4, Box 237, Elkridge 21227. (TW.) Devoted to the preservation and restoration of high wheeler bicycles, and participation in parades and centennial events.

Emmitsburg **The Dragoon Bicycle Club,** c/o Robert Obringer, Seminary, Mt. St. Mary's College, Emmitsburg 21727. Organized summer bike hike activities for youngsters from Frederick Co., Maryland and Adams Co., Pennsylvania. Restricted to boys.

Hyattsville **University of Maryland Bicycling Club,** c/o Tyler Folsom, 3423 Tulane Drive, Hyattsville.

Riverdale **Washington Vela Club,** c/o Robert Fisher, 4901 Tuckerman St., Riverdale 20804. (LAW).

Severna Park **Arundel Wheelers,** RD #1, Box 390X, Severna Park, Maryland. (LAW). Long distance and family rides, social meetings. Open to all over 16. Dues: $6-$15.

Silver Spring **The Beneficent and Impecunious Society of Sporadic and Convivial Cycle Tourers,** c/o Robert Peterson, 3005 Chapel View Drive, Beltsville, Md. 20705. C-level rides to local historical circuits with "adequate gustatory termini." Sponsors "crabs and beer" rides to Maryland's Eastern Shore, "beer and crabs tour of Southern Maryland," and the Virginia Velocipede Venture run through colonial tidewater Virginia. Membership composed mostly of NASA-Goddard Space Flight Center personnel.

The National 4-H Clubs of America, National Headquarters, 7100 Connecticut Ave., Chevy Chase, Maryland 20015, sponsors the organization of bicycle clubs throughout its chapters in every state. Write to them for information on how to organize a club, designate bike tours, and sponsor Bikeways.

American Youth Hostels with overnight accommodations are found in **Cumberland, Sandy Hook,** and **Seneca.**

MASSACHUSETTS

Ashland **Northeast Bicycle Club,** c/o William Driscoll, 18 Oak Tree Lane, Ashland 01721. (ABL of A). Emphasis on racing, and competitive events. Occasional social events. Membership on basis of 2/3 vote of members. Dues: $5.

Boston **Great Boston AYH,** 251 Harvard Street, Brookline, Mass. 02146. (AYH, LAW). Many bike-hike events for all age groups, long distance tours and overnight trips to interesting places. Good source of touring information.

Boston **Marblehead Touring Club,** c/o Jeri Theriault, 17 State Street, Marblehead 10945. (AYH).

Cambridge **Charles River Wheelmen,** c/o President, 131 Mt. Auburn St., Cambridge 02138. (AYH, LAW). Long distance rides, leisure, intermediate and Road Runner rides. Meets 3rd Thursday of the Month Oct. thru April. Open to all ages. Dues: $10. Special emphasis on the development of Bikeways.

Fall River **Freewheeler Bicycle Club,** c/o Henry J. Levesque, 292 Durfee Street, Fall River 02720. New club sponsoring informal weekend tours for family groups and cyclists of all ages.

Marion **People Powered Bicycle Club,** c/o Chick Mead, 137 County Road, Marion 02738. Long distance touring, local rides and safety information. Informal.

New Bedford **Derailleur Club of New Bedford, Mass.,** c/o William J. McIlmail, Prospect Road, Mattapoisett 02739. Long distance and local scenic rides.

Springfield **Cyclonauts Bicycling Club,** c/o Dr. Leo Rademacher, 111 Meadowbrook Road, Springfield 01128. Local and long-range touring, family cycling, racing, instruction, social events, camping, regional rallies, Century, Double Century, fund-raising, guest speakers, field trips, promoting bike legislation. Biweekly events, monthly meeting. Dues: $5-$11.

Worcester **Worcester County Bicycle Club,** c/o Joseph Cote, 103 Fitchburg Road, Townsend, Mass. Many organized trips for all ages. Source of information on mapped scenic routes.

American Youth Hostels with overnight accommodations are found in **Boston, Gloucester, Granville, Hyannis, Littleton, Nantucket, Orleans, Pittsfield, Sheffield, Springfield, Sunderland, Truro, and West Tisbury.**

MICHIGAN

Ann Arbor **Ann Arbor Bicycle League,** 417 Detroit St., Ann Arbor, 48104. Family rides and safety demonstrations. Open to all ages. $1 contribution. Major emphasis on development of commuter bikeways as alternative to automobile, with steering committee of volunteers of all ages.

Ann Arbor **Maize Bicycle Club,** c/o Daryl Barton, 1324 Broadway, Apt. 2, Ann Arbor. Seasonal bicycle tours of various lengths, campouts and overnight tours, information on bicycle touring in area. Sponsored by the University of Michigan and composed mostly of students, but open to others.

Bay City **Bay City Bicycle Club,** c/o John Peltier, 805 Columbus Ave. Frequent long distance family rides during summer. Information on local bicycle touring.

Dearborn **Dearborn Cycling Saddlemen,** 3807 Monroe, Dearborn 48124. Organized activities for family groups and singles. Racing and safety events. Well-planned long distance tours. Open to all over 12.

Dearborn **Dearborn Wheelmen,** 6411 Orchard, Dearborn 48126. Family rides and races. Dues: $5.

Dearborn **Fordson Hostel Club AYH,** c/o Mary Beth Wysocki, 1762 North Gulley, Dearborn 48128.

Detroit **AYH Metropolitan Detroit Council,** 14335 W. McNichols Road, Detroit 48235. (AYH). Many long distance weekend rides for all age groups. Bike-hikes, social meetings.

Detroit **Cass Tech AYH Club,** c/o Janet Rapkin, 2421 Second Ave., Detroit 48221.

Detroit **Cody High Hostel Club,** c/o John O. Hanesian, Cody High School, 7719 Beaverland, Detroit 48228.

Detroit **Henry Ford AYH Group,** c/o Miss June Crocker, 6110 West Outer Drive, Detroit 48235.

Detroit **Lessenger Youth Hostel Club,** c/o Carol Pistolesi, 8401 Trinity, Detroit.

Detroit **Redford High School AYH Club,** c/o Jess Helwig, 16759 Fielding, Detroit, Michigan.

Detroit **Twinn Tenna Bicycle Club,** c/o Douglas Rowland, 16915 Normandy. Organized by group of young men on Detroit's West Side. Call 862-3116.

Detroit **Wolverine Sports Club,** c/o Mike Walden, 26545 John R. Madison Heights 48071. Long distance family cycling; information about local cycling conditions. Open to all ages capable of long distance touring.

East Lansing **Michigan State Cycling Club,** c/o Michael J. McCarty, 127 Whitehills, East Lansing 48823. (LAW). Long distance weekend touring, information on area bicycle trails. Racing team, instruction.

East Lansing **Michigan State U. Cycling Club,** 201 Men's IM Building, East Lansing 48823. (ABL of A). Long distance rides, races, and competitive events, social meetings, bi-weekly tours or picnics. Meetings Wednesdays. Open to all students at MSU. Dues: $5. Michigan State has elaborate system of campus bikeways.

Farmington **North Farmington Youth Hostel Club,** c/o Darrell Younger, 13 Mile Road, Farmington 48024.

Grand Rapids **Grand Rapids Hostel Club,** c/o West YMCA, 902 Leonard NW, Grand Rapids 49504.

Grand Rapids **Rapid Wheelmen,** c/o Dale Sonke, 6208 Blythefield, NE, Rockford 49341. (LAW). Organized adult bicycle rides and long distance tours. Info. on local bicycle trails.

Hart **Hart Bicycle Club,** c/o William F. Hanna, 19 Courtland St., Hart. Information on local bicycle touring.

Jackson **Jackson Joy Riders Bicycle Club,** 1150 Fairfax Ave., Jackson 49203. Family oriented touring club. Full schedule of summer activities. Open to all ages.

Kalamazoo **Kalamazoo Bicycle Club,** c/o J. Brian Chappel,

5112 S. Westnedge. Long distance and weekend rides for all ages, with special emphasis on scenic tours.

Lathrup Village **Square Wheels,** c/o Tom Hart, 1575 Roselawn, Lathrup Village. Open to all riders in Oakland County. Information on bike touring.

Lincoln Park **Downriver Bicycle Club,** c/o Doug McCormick, 2084 Paris Ave., Lincoln Park. Organized bicycle rides and family events. Information on local touring conditions.

Livonia **Bentley AYH Club,** c/o William G. Conger, Bentley High School, 15100 Hubbard Ave., Livonia 48154.

Livonia **Franklin High School AYH Club,** c/o Roger Miller, 31000 Joy Road, Livonia.

Madison Heights **Michigan State Bicycle Federation,** c/o Mike Walden, 26545 John R., Madison Heights. (ABL of A, LAW). Information about bicycle racing in Michigan, and touring by bike; represents all bike clubs in state; good news letter.

Mt. Clemens **Macomb County Bicycle Club,** c/o Robert A. Clubb, Sr., 39682 Twenlow, Mt. Clemens 48043.

Northville **Northville Youth Hostel Club,** c/o Stephen Knapp, P.O. Box A, Northville 48167.

Northville **Northville Youth Hostels Club,** 108 W. Main St., Northville 48167. New AYH group whose bicycle program is planning long distance weekend tours for family and youth groups.

Petersburg **The Wheelmen,** c/o Keith Larzelere, P.O. Box 38, Petersburg 49270. (TW). Devoted to the riding, preservation, and restoration of antique bicycles, and participation in parades and centennial events.

Port Huron **YMCA Ladies Bike Fitness Club,** c/o G. Dale Packer, YMCA Physical Director, YMCA, Port Huron. Frequent rides weekdays during the summer for women interested in keeping physically fit.

Royal Oak **Bicycle to Brunch Bunch,** c/o Chuck Harrington, 910 Donald, Royal Oak. Sunday morning rides and other family events. Information on local bicycle touring.

Saginaw **Old Towne Bicycle Club,** c/o Courtney King 306

S. Hamilton. Family weekend tours and information on local cycling events.

Southfield **Southfield-Lathrup Hostel Club,** c/o Lenore Goldman, 27714 Shagbark, Southfield.

Traverse City **Bikeways Committee,** c/o Wes Nelson, 3515 Jefferson, Traverse City. Special emphasis on development of Bikeways in Traverse City. Frequent family urban rides. All ages welcome.

Warren **Edelweiss AYH Ski Club,** c/o Barbara Lillie, 30052 Holly Court, Warren 48092.

Warren **Slow Spokes of Macomb Co.,** c/o Fred Hamann, 14640 Bade, Warren 48089. Long-distance touring, weekend family rides. Source of information on regional bicycle routes.

Westland **Whittier American Youth Hostels Club,** 28550 Ann Arbor Trail, Westland 48185. Various cycling and hiking activities for Jr. High ages only. Bimonthly social meeting, and safety inspections. $2 yearly.

Ypsilanti **Young Independent Pedal Pushers of Ypsilanti** (YIPPI), c/o Ruben Marshall, 510 Emerick, East Junior High, Ypsilanti. (AYH). Long and short distance rides, social events. Open to all ages. Dues: $2.25 and AYH membership.

American Youth Hostels with overnight accommodations are located in **Bessemer, Cassopolis, Cedar, Detroit, Kalkaska,** and **Milford.**

MINNESOTA

Minneapolis **Gopher Wheelmen, Inc.,** c/o Maurice Battin, 21 Circle West, Minneapolis 55436. (LAW). Local touring, racing, social events. Weekly events. Monthly meetings. Dues: $1-3. Youth oriented.

Minneapolis **Minnesota Council AYH,** P.O. Box 9511, Minneapolis 55440.

Minneapolis **The Wheelmen,** c/o Russ Gotfredson, R&F Bike Shop, 1109 W. Oakland, Austin 55912. (TW). Devoted to preservation and restoration of old high wheel bicycles, participation in parades and centennial events.

Richfield **West Richfield AYH Club,** c/o Chris Cage, 6708 Morgan South, Richfield 55423.

Rochester **Rochester AYH Club,** 1546 4th Ave., SW, Rochester 55901. (AYH). Long distance and family rides, competitive events. Social meeting, 3rd Wed. Open to all who meet AYH requirements. Sponsors annual "Centurion Ride" over beautiful countryside last Sunday in July.

St. Paul **Midway Speedskating Club,** 2451 No. Albert, St. Paul, Minn. 55113. (AYH). Long distance rides, family outings, social events. Wintertime devoted to ice skating, with several Olympic skaters as members. Bicycle, rowing, and running competitions. Dues: $3-5.

American Youth Hostels with overnight accommodations are located in **Grand Marias** and **Sebeka.**

MISSISSIPPI

Indianola **Indianola Bike Club,** c/o Kiwanis Club, 203 Fashion Ave., Indianola (ABL of A.) Organized to provide full summer activities program for youngsters and teenagers, including overnight rides. All rides accompanied by adults. Dues: $2. Open to all area youngsters.

Greenville **Dixie Wheels,** 739-741 Washington Ave., Greenville, Miss.

Jackson **Jackson Wheelmen,** c/o Buddy Coury, 291 South Prentiss, Jackson, Miss. 39203. A new club.

Morehead **Black Wheelmen,** Morehead, Miss. A new club.

Starkville **M-S-U Starkville Bike Club,** c/o Boyd Gatlin, Route 1, Box 14A, Starkville, Miss. 39762.

Tupelo **House of Wheels Bike Club,** P.O. Box 1282, Tupelo, Miss. 38801.

MISSOURI

Columbia **Boone's Lick Hostel Club,** c/o Ozark Council AYH, 1203 Rogers Street, Columbia 65201.

Kansas City **Ecobike,** c/o Jack Ashmore, 5531 Locust, Kansas City 64110. Organized to develop local bike trails and to help set up national standards for licensing and safety. Activists, this is the one for you. Mostly composed of students at the University of Missouri at Kansas City.

Kansas City **Kansas City Bicycle Club,** c/o Frank Hutchison, 7118 Highland, Kansas City 64131. (LAW). Informal bicycle rides and social events. Touring enthusiasts.

Kansas City **Lewis & Clark Council AYH,** 12201 Blue River Road, Kansas City 64146. (AYH). Organized long distance and family rides, social meetings. Touring information. Open to all ages. Regular AYH membership dues.

Springfield **Cycledelics,** c/o Jack Allen, 1019 South Barnes. (AYH). Short and long-distance touring. Cross-U.S. tours using chartered bus and bikes to Cape Cod. Open to adults. Social events.

St. Louis **Ozark Area Council AYH,** 2605 S. Big Bend, St. Louis, Missouri. (AYH). Long distance and family organized rides, social events. Open to all. Dues: AYH membership.

St. Louis **St. Louis Cycling Club,** c/o Chester Nelsen, Sr., 4701 Natural Bridge St., St. Louis 63115. (ABL of A). Long distance and family rides, races, competitive events. Meets second Thursday of month. Dues: $5. Oldest bike club in the United States (1887).

American Youth Hostels with overnight accommodations are located in **Kansas City** and **Lexington.**

MONTANA

Missoula **Missoula Bicycle Club,** c/o Dan Burden, 602-1/2 So. 6th St., W. Missoula 59801. Newly organized group sponsoring **Tour of the Swan River Valley,** long distance tour through beautiful country. Organized similar to the Tour of the Scioto River Valley.

NEBRASKA

Grand Island **Grand Island Bicycling Club,** c/o Rolland Hancock, Parks & Recreation Department, City Hall, Grand Island. Organized family weeknight and weekend cycling activities during season May-November. Active Bikeways program. Open to all ages.

Lincoln **Lincoln South East High School Ecology Club,** c/o Mary Henderson, 2438 Lake Street, Lincoln 68502. Ecology oriented group of students who are encouraging the development of local Bikeways, and promotion of biking to fight pollution.

Lincoln **Nebraskaland Youth Hostel Club,** c/o Carol Peterson, Parks & Recreation Department, City of Lincoln, 2740 "A" St., Lincoln 68502. Many organized tours for cyclists of all ages, interesting out-of-city rides on weekends. Safety instruction.

Omaha **Omaha Peddlers,** c/o Fred Hess, 3137 Farnam St., Omaha. If there's an organized ride, it will be organized through this group. Check them for current information (345-1424). (LAW).

Ord **Ord Bicycle Club,** c/o Clarence Pierson, 1330 "L" St., Ord. Weekday evening rides, weekend, long distance rides. Limited to adults.

NEVADA

Reno **Students to Oppose Pollution** (STOP), activist group to encourage Bikeways in Reno. c/o David J. Borought, 208 Vassar St., Reno 89502.

NEW HAMPSHIRE

Concord **Northwood Bicycling Club,** c/o Mrs. Maurice Caverly, Northwood Ridge. Organized activities for all ages, long distance scenic and foliage rides.

Gilmanton **Winnipesaukee Bicycle Society,** c/o James Farnsworth, Gilmanton Iron Works 03837. (LAW). Organized long and short distance tours, family activities. Touring information.

Nashua **Big Wheelers,** 16 Woodland Drive, Nashua 03060. Local touring and family cycling. Rides are unscheduled. Meetings every two weeks in summer. New club.

Salem **Granite State Wheelmen,** c/o Joanne Schottler, 12 Palomino Road, Salem 03079. Long distance rides, shorter leisurely rides for family groups. Overnight bike hikes and social events. Open to all ages with reasonable cycling skills.

American Youth Hostels with overnight accommodations are found in **Alton, Claremont, Danbury, North Conway, North Haverhill,** and **Warren.**

NEW JERSEY

Boy Scouts Of America, Bicycle Department. National headquarters, North Brunswick 08902.

Bogota **North Jersey Bicycle Club,** 97 Queen Anne Road, Bogota 07603. (LAW, ABL of A). Family rides, races, competitive events, social meetings first Monday during racing season, first Tuesday other times. Much emphasis on road & track racing. Dues: $5. Youth oriented.

Elizabeth **Union County Hiking Club,** c/o Union County Park Commission, Warinanco Park, Elizabeth. A chapter of the New York-New Jersey Trail Conference, this club sponsors summer bike trips over bike trails in both states, usually on weekends.

Fair Lawn **Fair Lawn Bicycle Club,** c/o Paul M. Rosenberg, 2-01 17th St., Fair Lawn 07410. (AYH). Long distance weekend rides, family rides. Must be 14 or over. Small charge for each trip.

Flemington **Jaerer Wheelmen,** c/o Robert Yard, RD #4, Flemington. (ABL of A). Long distance rides, races and competitive events. Open to all ages.

Freehold **The Wheelmen,** co David Metz, 25 Broadway, Freehold 07728. (LAW, TW). Devoted to the preservation and restoration of antique bicycles; interesting newsletter. Open to those interested in bicycle memorabilia.

Glen Rock **Glen Rock High School Bicycle Club,** c/o Glen Rock H.S., 600 Harristown Road, Glen Rock 07452. (AYH).

Metuchen **Metuchen Bicycle Touring Society,** c/o Metuchen Bicycle, 457 Main St., Metuchen 08840. (LAW). Long distance rides, family rides, competitive events. Socials last Friday of month. Rides every Saturday & Sunday. Open to all. Dues: $4.

Middletown **Middletown Bike Club,** and **Middletown Adult Bike Club,** c/o Ted Ratkus, Middletown Community Center, Middletown. Two organizations for youngsters and adults. Long and short distance weekday and weekend trips, lectures, proficiency tests. Overnight trips for both groups. Special emphasis on designation of Bikeways and bike routes. Dues: $2-$4.

Middletown **Middletown Bike & Hosteling Club,** c/o Middletown Recreation Commission, Township Hall, Middletown 07748. Open to all age groups, with emphasis on family rides, weekend and long distance touring. Active Bikeways and bike train programs. Dues $2.-$4.

Morristown **Morristown Bicycle Club,** c/o Ken Chavious, Physical Director, YMCA. New club holding organized family weekend long distance and local touring. Open to cyclists of all ages and ability levels. Current information: 539-1115.

Newark **Alpine Wheelmen,** c/o Ed Holle, 64 Norwood St., Newark. (ABL of A). Races and competitive events.

Plainfield **Tri-Boro Bicycle Club,** c/o James B. Currier, 1706 Oxford Ave., So. Plainfield. (LAW). Long distance rides, family weekend events, safety inspections. Open to all.

Princeton **Princeton University Bicycle Club,** c/o Dick Swann, "Elm Field," Cherry Valley Rd., Princeton 08540. A very active club, which includes local youngsters and adults as well as students.

Somerdale **So. Jersey Bicycling Club,** 600 So. White Horse Pike, Somerdale 02083. Organized weekend and weekday rides for all groups, some racing and social activities.

Somerville **Somerset Wheelmen,** c/o Saling, 91 Duval St., Somerville. (ABL of A). Races and competitive events. Open to all ages. Dues: $2-$4. Operates nationally famous Somerville bike races.

Teaneck **Teaneck Hostel Club,** c/o Dept. of Recreation, Town House, Teaneck 07666. (AYH).

Tenafly **Tenafly High School AYH Club,** c/o Miss Nancy H. Land, Tenafly High School, Sunset Lane, Tenafly 07670.
Willingboro **Outdoor Club of South Jersey,** 260 Club House Drive, Willingboro 08046. (AYH). Family weekday and weekend rides, safety inspections. Open to all ages. Dues: $1.25. Emphasis on long tours of 25 miles and up six times yearly.

American Youth Hostels with overnight accommodations are found in **West Cape May.**

NEW MEXICO

Albuquerque **Highland High Cycling Club,** c/o Activities Dept., Highland High School, Albuquerque Public Schools, S.E., Albuquerque 87108. Weekend bike touring club for students. Participation in parades, etc.

Albuquerque **Velo Cycling Club,** 816 San Mateo Ave., S.W., Albuquerque 87108. (ABL of A, LAW). New club divided into two interest groups: touring and racing. Many long distance and weekend events for family groups, social meetings. Time trials and racing events. Safety activities.

Portales **Portales Bicycle Club,** c/o Galen Farrington, Box 3036, Portales 88130. New organization consisting of students at the Eastern New Mexico University. Weekend long distance touring during school season. Open to all interested adults.

Santa Fe **Old Santa Fe Bicycle Touring Society,** c/o Dr. Raphiel Benjamin, 3869 Old Santa Fe Trail, Santa Fe 87501. New club to promote family and weekend bike hikes and long distance rides. Open to all adults with reasonable skills, and youngsters. Will specialize in scenic and historic touring.

American Youth Hostel with overnight accommodations is found in **Taos.**

NEW YORK

Amherst **Bikeways for Amherst,** c/o Mrs. John Beach, 2630 N. French Road, E. Amherst 14051. Organized primarily to develop bike lanes in the town of Amherst, this group holds supervised short and long distance rides throughout the summer. Open to all ages.

Binghamton **South Tier Bicycle Club,** c/o Dr. A. P. Mueller, 109 Carol Ave., Vestal 13760.Long distance, family weekend rides, races, social events. Must be 12 yrs. or older. Active Bikeways program.

Bronx **Bronx High School of Science Bicycle Club,** c/o Peter Melzer, 75 West 205th St., Bronx 10468. (AYH). Seasonal organized bike activities. For high school students.

Buffalo **Niagara Frontier Bicycle Club,** c/o Michael Sullivan, 737 Parkside Ave., Buffalo 14216. Long distance and family rides, time trials, picnics at most rides, and winter social events. Open to all over 18 if not part of family. Dues: $3.

Kenmore **Kenmore Bicycle Club,** c/o Gary R. Moorhouse, 144 Euclid Ave., Kenmore. Long distance and family weekend rides, usually scheduled by telephone. Must be 18 or over.

Long Island **German Bicycle Club,** c/o William Lambert, 3210 Byrd Place, Baldwin 11510. An organization devoted to bicycle racing and competitive events. (ABL of A).

Mamaroneck **Mamaroneck High School Youth Hostel Club,** c/o Mamaroneck High School, Mamaroneck 10534. (AYH). Club holds 2 or 3 outings per school year, raises own funds by rummage sales, etc. Open to high school students in the area. Regular AYH membership (student.)

Manhattan **Bicycle Institute of America,** 122 East 42nd St., New York City 10017. Represents American bicycle industry. Source of information on bicycle safety, development of Bikeways and bike paths, legislation, films. Will provide names of cyclists interested in development of Bikeways in your area. Many free publications, including Newsletter.

Manhattan **Bike for a Better City,** c/o Barry Fishman, 39 W. 71st St., NYC 10023. Organized to make biking safe and feasible as a means of transportation. Political action and Bike-to-work Thursdays. Social events, scenic and cultural tours to concerts, etc. Dues: $1 non-New Yorkers, $2 residents. Newsletter, bumper stickers, buttons, etc., to members.

Manhattan **Chase Bicycle Club,** c/o Mike Rothberg, Data Communications Dept., Chase Manhattan Bank, #1 N.Y. Plaza, N.Y. 10004. Open to employees of Chase Manhattan Bank and its branches. Long distance touring, picnics, safety clinics, Bike-to-work program. Encourage bicycle parking in the city.

Manhattan **Girl Scouts of America,** Bicycling Dept., National Headquarters, 830 Third Ave., New York 10017. Information on bicycle hiking and touring, and Girl Scout bike clubs.

Manhattan **Metropolitan New York AYH,** 535 West End Ave., N.Y.C. 10024. (AYH). Long distance weekend rides, competitive events. Programs of interest to almost every age group. Overseas bike tours, charters. Regular AYH regulations. Fun and fact-filled newsletter. Store at same address, good source for useful, low-cost biking, hiking and camping equipment; catalog free.

Manhattan **New York Cycle Club,** c/o Vic Magrabi, 143 Grand Ave., Apt. 1D, Englewood, N.J. (LAW). Very active organization with many long distance and family rides throughout the season; ski activities in winter. Meetings 2nd Tuesday of month. Open to all adults. Dues: $3.

Manhattan Pedal Pushers, c/o James P. Seepes, 95 West 95th St., Apt. 20H, New York 10025. Independent club which promotes biking for fun and transportation. Holds annual treasure hunt, many weekend tours from April to November. Provides guide-led bike tours for visitors.

Manhattan **The Wheelmen,** c/o Allan Blair, 107 East 2nd St., Apt. 11, New York 10009, (TW). Devoted to the preservation and restoration of antique bicycles, and bicycle memorabilia.

Massena **Massena Bicycle Club,** c/o Salvation Army, Salvation Army Building, Victory Road, Massena. Summertime long-distance rides for youngsters and young adults.

Mount Marion **Hike-A-Bike Club,** Box 79, Mt. Marion 12456.

American Youth Hostels, Inc., National Headquarters, 20 West 17th St., N.Y.C. Source of "Hostel Guide and Handbook," "International Youth Hostel Handbook," "North American Bike Atlas," and "Family Hosteling Manual." The National AYH also provides help on establishing youth hostels, medical advice for the traveler, how to select the right bike for hosteling, and how to condition for the long ride, plus other helps.

New Baltimore **New Baltimore Hikers and Bikers Club,** c/o Dick Hartmann, New Baltimore. Summer scenic rides for teenagers.

New York City **ABLA Amateur Bicycle League of America,** National Headquarters, P.O. Box 2175, N.Y.C. 10017.

Sponsors a national program of amateur bicycle racing events. Write for information on establishing local chapters, and for rules and regulations for racing events.

New York City **Antique Bicycle Club of America,** c/o Dr. Roland Geist, 260 West 260th St., N.Y.C. 10471. Composed of former cyclists, interested in antique bicycles, swapping, selling, participation in parades; visit bicycle museums, and collect memorabilia. Good source of information on bicycle history (enclose stamped, self-addressed envelope). Group sponsors the American Bicycle Hall of Fame, Richmondtown, Staten Island, New York.

New York City **Century Road Club Association, Inc.,** c/o Louis Maltese, 78-12 269th St., New Hyde Park 11040. (ABL of A). Racing, competitive events. Meets twice monthly, 1st and 3rd Fridays. Dues: $3. Major emphasis on the encouragement of bicycle racing.

New York City **College Cycle Club,** 260 West 260th St., New York 10471. (LAW). Touring, safety, and social events. Adults only.

Poughkeepsie **Mid-Hudson Bicycle Club,** c/o Mrs. John Gurtz, 12 Westview Terrace, Poughkeepsie 12603. (LAW). Long distance and family rides, social events during the year; holds Century Runs, annual 3-day bike camping tour. Open to all, children must be accompanied. Dues: $2-$3.

Rochester **Rochester Bicycling Club,** 46 W. Cheltenham Rd., Rochester 14612. Long distance and family weekend rides, time trials, two yearly business meetings and winter party. Open to all ages. Dues: $3-$5. Famous for tours and touring information.

Rochester **Rochester Institute of Technology Bicycle Club,** c/o One Lomb Memorial Drive, Rochester 14623. (AYH). Long distance rides. Open to students of RIT.

Rochester **Silver Crank S.E.T. Bicycle Club,** c/o Stanley E. Trick, 46 Cottage St., Rochester 14608. (LAW). Long distance weekend and weekday rides of historic and scenic interest. Emphasis on enjoying, not racing. Open to families and singles. Monthly social events. Dues: $5-$8.

Schenectady **Mohawk-Hudson Wheelmen** (Schenectady Div.), c/o Charles Siple, 2104 Dean St., Schenectady 12309.

(AYH, LAW). Long distance rides, family weekend tours, something every week. Open to all good riders in Troy, Albany, Schenectady, and nearby communities. Cooperates with other clubs in developing statewide bike routes, Bikeways. Source of information on N.Y. state touring. Dues: $4.

Staten Island **Staten Island Bicycle Club,** c/o Dr. Fred W. Schmitt, 118 Central Ave., St. George, S.I., N.Y. 10301.

Syracuse **AYH Syracuse Council,** 735 S. Beech St., Syracuse 13210. (AYH). Organized bike and hike activities. Youth oriented.

Syracuse **Onondaga Cycling Club,** 113 East Onondaga St., Syracuse 13202. (AYH, LAW, ABL of A). Long distance and family rides, weeknight rides, races and competitive events, socials, safety instruction. Open to all, 18 years or older, 12-17 by qualifications. Dues: $3. Famous for organized seasonal tours. Newsletter.

Tonawanda **Big Wheels Bicycle Club,** c/o Recreation Dept., John Silsby, Town of Tonawanda. Long distance and short scenic rides on weekends during the summer, bike picnics and historic tours. Open to all ages, but require good bike.

Westbury **American Unicycling Society,** c/o William Jenack, Jenack Cycles, 67 Lion Lane, Westbury. Organization of unicycling enthusiasts who share correspondence, research, and club activities. Local organization appears at celebrations and festivals.

Westbury **Nassau Wheelmen Assn.,** c/o Vito Perrucci, 165 Post Ave., Westbury 11590. (AYH). Long distance rides, races, competitive events, safety inspections. Open to all. Dues: 50¢ a month. Long distance fall tour a special event.

Williamsville **Multi-Speed Bike Club,** c/o Nicholas Ledger, 5 Ponderosa Drive, Williamsville 14221.

AYH overnight accommodations are provided at **New York City** (N.Y. University, University Heights, Silver Residence Hall, University Heights, 181st St., Bronx 10453), **Niagara Falls** (YMCA, Portage Road & Pierce Ave. 14301), **Niagara Falls,** Canadian side (Schirrmann International Hall, 4699 Zimmerman St., Ontario, Canada), **Nunda** (Hillcrest Genesee Valley YH, c/o Maj. Lyman F. Barry, 9297 Town Line Rd., Nunda 14517, **Stamford** (Scotch Mist Inn,

Stamford 12167), **Syracuse** (Downing YH, 735 So. Beech St., Syracuse 13210.)

NORTH CAROLINA

Chapel Hill **Chapel Hill Bicycle Club,** c/o Phillip Gray, 700 D, Hibbard Drive, Chapel Hill. Weekend family touring both long and short distance. Open to all ages. Ecology oriented.

Charlotte **Charlotte Bicycle Touring Club,** c/o Gerald A. Gruber, 1527 Briarfield Drive, Charlotte 28205. New club which will promote scenic bike tours on weekends and other family oriented activities, development of scenic routes.

Durham **Duke University Bicycle Club,** c/o Association of Student Governments, Duke University, Durham. Frequent bicycling events during the school year.

Greensboro **Greensboro Cycling Association,** 4412 Cornell Ave., Greensboro. (ABL of A). Sponsoring organization for bicycle racing and competitive events. Open to all ages. Some long distance road events.

Greensboro **Greensboro Cycling Club,** c/o Higgins Bicycle Shop, 1214 Spring Garden, Greensboro. Weekend, family bicycling activities, some long distance rides. Source of information for central North Carolina touring.

Pembroke **Pembroke Bicycle Club,** c/o J. G. Locklear, Chief of Police, Pembroke. Summer bike activities for youngsters.

Raleigh **North Carolina State University Bicycle Club,** c/o Robert Ramsey, Dept. of Mathematics, N.C. State University, Raleigh. Long distance tours, but emphasis is on bicycle racing and training.

Statesville **Grace Park Bicycle Club,** c/o Bill Gill, Grace Park Recreation Center, Grace Park. Outings to designated areas, safety lectures, care of the bicycle. New club.

NORTH DAKOTA

Fargo **Great Plains Bike Club & Bison Wheelmen of N.D. State University,** c/o Dr. Earl Alan Scholz, 1128 7th St., Fargo 58102. Organized bicycle tours for university students, some family activities, social events. Strong emphasis on development of Bikeways and long distance bike routes. Good touring information.

OHIO

Akron **Akron Bicycle Club,** 400 Kenilworth Dr., Akron 44313. (LAW, AYH). Long distance and family weekend rides. Over 18, or with parents' consent. Request geared bicycles. Adult oriented. Dues: $1.50-$3.

Berkey **Naturalist Scouts,** Secor Park Nature Center, Berkey 43504. Long distance bicycle tours for youngsters and young adults. Public service activities in Toledo Metropolitan Parks, many other outdoor activities for children. Dues: $2.

Bowling Green **Bowling Green Youth Hostel,** City Bldg., 175 W. Wooster, Bowling Green 43402. (AYH, LAW). Long distance and family weekend rides, racing and competitive events. Monthly meetings. Open to all. Dues: AYH membership. Special project: designation of Wood County Historical Bikeway. Sponsors **Wintergarden Youth Hostel.** Contact Mrs. Dorothy Joyce, 11 Darlyn Drive, Bowling Green 43402.

Canton **Stark County Bicycle Club,** c/o Richard Kelly, 628 Smith Avenue, S.W. Canton 44706. Long distance weekend and overnight bike hikes, appealing to all age groups. Train Charters. Rides on Ohio's many designated bike routes, and seasonal rides through spectacular scenery.

Chesterland **The Geauga Y-Cyclists,** c/o the Geauga YMCA, Box 265, Chesterland 44026. Club is youth oriented (12 & up) but welcomes adult and family participation. Monthly tours, Century runs, two long distance bike hike trips during summer, safety, maintenance presentations, local races and hill climbs. Dues: $7, YMCA members; others $7-14, depending on age.

Cleveland **Cleveland Wheelmen Bicycle Club,** c/o Vernon Barnes, 6110 Brookside Drive, Cleveland 44109. (ABL of A). Short and long distance rides, races. Dues: $5. Primarily a racing organization.

Cleveland **Lake Erie Council AYH,** 2000 Terminal Tower, Cleveland 44113. Long distance and overnight bike hikes, weekday rides. Wide variety of activities for all age groups.

Columbus **Columbus Council AYH,** c/o TOSRV Communications, P.O. Box 23111, Columbus. (AYH). Long distance rides, family rides, races, competitive events, monthly social meeting. Open to all ages.

Columbus **Franklin Bicycle Club, Inc.,** 632 East Beaumont Road, Columbus 43214. (ABL of A). Founded in 1934. Sponsors of 2-day bike races, Buckeye OSU Auterium club, road and track point championships with trophies. Rides every Sat. & Sunday when not racing. Thursday nite criterium series May to September. Dues: $3-$5. Excellent newsletter.

Columbus **Tour of the Scioto River Valley Club,** TOSRV (AYH) Communications, P.O. Box 23111, Columbus 43223. Each year sponsors long distance tour, attracting thousands from nearly every state. Brochures and information from above address.

Dayton **Dayton Cycling Club,** c/o Ansel John, 741 East Dixie Drive, West Carrollton 45449. (LAW).

Dayton **Miami Valley AYH Bicycle Club,** 3811 Corkwood Drive, Dayton 45424. (AYH). Long distance rides, family bicycling events, social meeting 1st Wednesday.

Dayton **The Wheelmen,** c/o Fred Fisk, 2815 Moraine Ave., Dayton 45406 (TW). Dedicated to the restoration and preservation of antique bicycles, bicycle memorabilia.

Findlay **Hancock Handlebars AYH Club,** 543 Cherry St., Findlay 45840. (AYH). Long distance rides, family weekend rides. Social every 3rd Wednesday. New but very active club.

Fredericksburg **Fredericksburg Bicycle Club,** c/o Bill and Ray's Bicycle Sales, Fredericksburg. Organized for youngsters 6 and up to provide summer recreation. Overnight bike hikes, camping, safety meetings, bike races and rodeos.

Harrison **The Harrison Cycle Club,** c/o Mrs. D. E. Kraus, 121 Westfield Drive, Harrison 45030. New club to encourage long distance and weekend family touring; development of interesting bike routes.

Huron **Firelands Wheels,** c/o William A. French, 525 Wilbor Avenue, Huron 44839.

Lima **Lima Council, American Youth Hostels,** P.O. Box

173, Lima 45802. (AYH, ABL of A). Long distance rides, family rides, races, competitive events, monthly social meeting. Open to everyone. Dues: $5-$12.

Mentor **Mentor Cycle Club,** c/o Edward Kramer, 7512 Mentor Avenue, Mentor 44060. (LAW, ABL of A). Long distance touring, weekend rides, racing and competitive events.

Springfield **Clark County Bicycle Association,** c/o 224 South Clairmont, Springfield, Ohio. New Club.

Streetsboro **Boy's Bike Club,** c/o Richard Grove, Streetsboro Junior High School. Long distance, cross-country summer bike tours. By invitation. Write to Coach Richard Grove.

Toledo **Toledo Area Council AYH,** 5320 Fern Drive, Toledo 43613. Long distance and overnight bike hikes. Open to all age groups. Dues: Regular AYH membership.

Wooster **Wooster Bicycle Club,** c/o Parks and Recreation Department, Wooster. Many summertime bike hikes and long distance tours for youngsters.

American Youth Hostels with overnight accommodations are located in **Bellefontaine, Bowling Green, Lima, New Plymouth, Toledo,** and **Yellow Springs.**

OKLAHOMA

Norman **Norman Bicycle Touring Society,** c/o Robert D. McMinn, 1602 Avondale, Norman 73069. New club to encourage family and long distance bicycle touring and other weekend events, Bikeways and trail route programs, strong membership expected from University of Oklahoma.

OREGON

Beaverton **Beaverton Bicycle Club,** c/o Bill & Betty Clifton, P.O. Box 957, Beaverton 97005.

Corvallis **Corvallis Bicycle Club,** c/o Park & Recreation Department, City Hall, Corvallis. New club to sponsor Bikeways and touring routes of city, branching into recreational tours.

Eugene **Emerald Valley Cycling Club,** c/o Ernest Drapela, Parks & Recreation Dept., 105 City Hall, Eugene 97410. Very active organization promotes Bikeways and commuter cycling. Many long distance touring events and family outings. Open to all ages who share interest in biking.

Eugene **PEBU,** or **Physicians to Encourage Bicycle Use,** (committee of the Lane County Medical Society) aims to promote the use of cycling in Lane County out of a concern for three areas of public health: reduction of air pollution; physical fitness; and traffic safety and prevention of injury, working with and through the City Bicycle Committee of Eugene.

Klamath Falls **Klamath Falls Bicycle Activities,** c/o Klamath Falls Recreation Department. Moore Park, Klamath Falls. Summer racing activities for young adults. Developing program of bicycle touring activities.

Pendleton **The Red Beret Bicycle Club,** c/o Mary Nelson, 235 SW 5th, Pendleton 97801. (LAW). Organization of senior retired citizens who enjoy riding adult tricycles and bicycles. Average age: 70. Leisurely weekday and weekend bike rides, many social activities during rides. Open to all oldsters with youthful spirit.

Portland **Alpenrose Cycling Club,** c/o Alpenrose Dairy, 6144 SW Shattuck Road, Portland 97221. (ABL of A). Strictly for racers.

Portland **The Bicycle Lobby,** Room 405, South Park Hall, Portland State University, Portland. Organized to promote the increased use of bikes for transportation, and the development of facilities and trail systems. Open to all ages.

Portland **Oregon Cycling Association,** P.O. Box 1141, Portland 97207. (ABL of A, LAW, AYH). The governing group for bicycling in the state; regulates all track events. Most clubs are represented on the board, which meets once a month. Olympic training program available for new and younger riders under expert guidance. Track racing throughout the summer.

Portland **Portland Wheelmen Touring Club,** c/o Dottie Heard, 7850 S.E. Stark, Portland 97215. Organized long distance and weekend family rides. Current information, phone 253-1191.

Portland **Rose City Wheelmen,** c/o Mike Ackley, 2807 N.E. Glisan, Apt. 304, Portland 97323. (ABL of A, LAW).

Emphasis on bicycle racing and road and track events. Open to all ages.

Salem **Salem Bike Club,** c/o Carroll Quimby, 685 Court St., N.E., Salem 97301. Organized weekend long distance tours and leisurely rides. Open to all ages with reasonable riding skills. Social events. Special emphasis on Bikeways and designated bike trails. Sponsors overseas bike charter tours.

PENNSYLVANIA

Dallas **Wyoming Valley Bicycle Club,** c/o Aaron "Bill" Skinner, R.D. #1, Box 135, Dallas 18612. (LAW). Long distance touring, family events. Social meetings.

Doylestown **Gotham Cyclists,** c/o Ernest H. McAdams, Doylestonian Apts., 200A, Rt. 611, 403 S. Main St., Doylestown 18901. (LAW). Family cycling tours.

Gibsonia **Western Penna. Wheelmen, Ltd.,** c/o William J. Coester, 5482 Gibson Road, Gibsonia 15044. (LAW). Organized weekend touring and family activities. Adult oriented.

Harrisburg **Harrisburg Bicycle Club,** c/o James G. Kehew, 413 Appletree Road, Camp Hill 17011. (LAW). Long distance touring to scenic and historic places in Pennsylvania, local weekday and weekend rides, many social activities, meetings with other bike groups. Overnight bike-hikes for families. Dues: $2-$5.

Hazleton **East End Bicycle Brigade,** c/o Byron Evert, 401 E. Cranberry Ave., Hazleton. Leisurely rides, group trips on weekdays and weekends, field excursions and social activities. Open to adult bicyclists.

Lancaster **Lancaster Bicycle Touring Club,** c/o Robert Carvell, 929 McGrann Boulevard, Lancaster. New club. Long distance and shorter weekend rides for family groups and singles with reasonable riding skill.

Media **Penncrest Youth Hostel Club,** c/o Bob Puphal, 134 Barren Road, Media 19063. (AYH).

Newtown **Newtown Hosteling Club,** c/o Jack Scott, Council Rock Youth & Community Center, 28 North State Street, Newtown 18940. (AYH). Long distance rides, meetings first and third Tuesdays. Some week-long and 3-day bike hikes.

Philadelphia **Buck Ridge Ski Club,** Cycling Committee, c/o Joan Strachota, 508 S. 22nd St., Philadelphia 19146. Summer weekend bike hikes for winter ski buffs.

Philadelphia **Center City Bicycle Club,** 1119 West Pine St., Philadelphia 19107. (LAW). Long distance weekend rides and family events. Social meetings. Open to all ages. Dues: $1-$2. Rides leave every Sunday from above address.

Philadelphia **Cycling Enthusiasts of Greater Philadelphia,** c/o John Bockman, 301 Boyer Rd., Cheltenham. Devoted to serious, long distance touring of 60-100 miles. Must be 16 or over. Dues: $1. Rides every Saturday and Sunday, year round.

Philadelphia **Delaware Valley Council, AYH,** 4714 Old York Road, Philadelphia 19141. Long distance rides, family bike hikes, safety events. Open to all ages. Dues: $2-$15.

Philadelphia **Doctor's Bicycle Club,** sponsored by the Dept. of Recreation, 15th & Arch St., Philadelphia 19107. Informal rides organized by medical doctors and medical technicians. Open to all interested in physical fitness.

Philadelphia **Gratz Hosteling Club,** c/o Joan Horowitz, Gratz High School, 17th & Luzerne, Philadelphia 19140.

Philadelphia **Outdoorsmen Club of Central & Girls High,** Broad and Olney Ave., or c/o Sharon Lee, 315 N. 33rd St., Philadelphia 19104. (AYH). Long distance rides and social events every weekend during school year.

Philadelphia **Pennsylvania Bicycle Club,** c/o John G. Braden, 4611 Newhall St., Philadelphia 19144. (LAW).

Philadelphia **Philadelphia Bicycling Club,** c/o Earl C. Williams, Athletic Specialist, Philadelphia Dept. of Recreation, 15th & Arch, Philadelphia 19107. Long distance and family rides, races, safety inspections and rodeos. City-sponsored rides each Sunday of the year with special rides on Saturdays 8 months during year. Open to all ages.

Philadelphia **South Philadelphia High Hosteling Club,** c/o Deborah DiBallista, So. Philadelphia High School, Motivation Office, Broad & Snyder Streets, Philadelphia 19148.

Philadelphia **Upside Youth Hostel Club,** c/o Denise Carter, West Colonial, Philadelphia 19126.

Philadelphia **Valley Forge Cycling Club,** c/o Burt Cohen,

729 Charette Road, Philadelphia 19115. Organized long distance and weekend rural tours. (LAW).

Pittsburgh **Pittsburgh Bicycle Club,** c/o Allen Sher, Vince Widmer or Michael Hurwitz, 6300 Fifth Ave., Pittsburgh 15206. (LAW). Long distance and weekend events. Open to all ages who have reasonable skills.

Pittsburgh **Pittsburgh Council AYH,** 6300 Fifth Ave., Pittsburgh 15232. (AYH). Organized family and long distance touring. Social meetings. Open to all ages.

Roslyn **Bux-Mont Bicycle Club,** 1446 Birchwood Ave., Roslyn 19001. Open to all ages. Sunday afternoon ride once a month and dinner-social meeting in January. Dues: $2.

Scranton **Scranton Bicycle Club,** c/o Peter J. Muchisky, RD #3, Box 424-A, Moscow 18444. (LAW).

Southampton **Bucks Hostelers Club,** c/o Matthew Cohen, 1240 Woods Road, Southampton. (AYH). Youth oriented. Rides in Bucks Co., Delaware Valley.

State College **Centre Region Hike-Bike Association,** 341 East Waring, State College 16801. Major emphasis on the establishment of bicycle touring trails and Bikeways. Dues range from $1 individual to $25 institutional.

Swarthmore **The Wheelmen,** c/o Robert E. McNair, Commander, 32 Dartmouth Circle, Swarthmore 19081. Dedicated to the enjoyment and preservation of historic bicycles and bicycle memorabilia. Provides research assistance and offers interesting publication. Membership: national. Issues bulletins on restoration, available parts, safe riding, identification, proper attire, etc. $1 brings sample publication/ membership info.

York **York Bicycle Club,** c/o Dr. Paul H. Douglass, Apt. A1, Country Club Manor, York 17403. New club. Many long distance and family weekend tours. Co-op meetings with neighboring clubs. Open to all age groups. Newsletter.

American Youth Hostels with overnight accommodations are found in **Bowmansville, Brickerville, Bushkill, Denver, Geigertown, La Anna, Philadelphia,** and **Weisel.**

RHODE ISLAND

Ashton **The Wheelmen,** c/o Charles Mateo, 9 Scott Road,

Ashton 20864. (TW). Devoted to antique bicycles, bicycle memorabilia, and bicycling history.

Providence **Narragansett Bay Wheelmen,** c/o Mrs. Dotty Snyder, 51 Woodbury St., Providence 02906. (LAW). Weekend and long distance touring, shorter rides for families.

SOUTH CAROLINA

Camden **Carolina Cyclers,** c/o Edward D. Western, 1703 Kennedy Drive, Camden 29020. (ABL of A). Long distance rides, races and competitive events. Open to all ages. 25-mile time trial events. Emphasis on speed riding.

Clemson **Clemson University Bicycling Club,** c/o Robert Gray, Box 4965, Clemson University, Clemson 29631. New club will plan long distance tours and family events, some competitive rides.

Rock Hill-Greenville **Piedmont Peddlers,** c/o Dr. William Wilson, 350 Shurley St., Rock Hill 29730. (LAW). Long distance weekend touring along scenic routes, Carolina coast as far as N.C. line and as far south as Pawley's Island. Holds 100-mile Century Run. Open to all ages, but adult oriented.

Sumter **Federation of Carolina Cycling, Hiking and Jogging Clubs,** c/o Ray Guest, 1994 Forrest Drive, Sumter 29150. New club to promote physical fitness. Source of information on cycling activities. Membership open to all ages.

SOUTH DAKOTA

Sioux Falls **Dakota Hostelers,** c/o Bill Carlson, 2500 Maryknoll Drive, Sioux Falls 57105. (AYH). Sponsored by Sioux Falls Park & Recreation Dept., rides are held frequently throughout the summer. Open to all ages.

TENNESSEE

Chattanooga **Chattanooga Bicycle Club,** 713 East 11th St., Chattanooga 37402. (LAW). Specializes in family touring and weekend activities throughout a long cycling season. Limited to age 16 and over. Dues: $2. Strong Bikeways program.

Memphis **Memphis Hightailers,** c/o Charles Finney, 1181 Inman Cove, Memphis 38111. (LAW). Long distance and family weekend rides. Emphasis on good camaraderie and recreation.

Murfreesboro **Middle Tennessee State University Bicycle Club,** c/o K. Kallenberger, Box 183, Murfreesboro 37130. Weekend rides and long distance touring, during school season. (LAW).

Nashville **Nashville Wheelmen Bicycle Club,** c/o Richard Greer, 323 Lawndale Drive, Nashville 37217, or David T. Irvine, 2008 Riverwood Drive, Nashville 37216. (LAW).

TEXAS

College Station **Texas A&M Wheelmen Bicycle Club,** Student Activities Department, Texas A&M University, College Park 77840. Organized to promote cycling as healthful and non-polluting sport for the young and not-so-young. Intercollegiate bike races, campus Bikeway program, encourage good citizenship. Cycling films, speakers and maintenance clinics. Open to all university students and others. Dues: $1. Meets 7:30 p.m. each Wednesday at Sbisa Hall. Info.: 845-4641.

Dallas-Richardson **Richardson Bicycle Touring Club,** c/o Roland Forgy, 14050 Rolling Hills, Dallas 75240. Long distance and family weekend rides throughout the summer. Qualification rides up to 25 miles. Many social events during cycling season. Strong Bikeways program.

Dallas **S.M.U. Chapter of Zero Population Growth,** Box 1733, SMU, Dallas 75222. Environmental group that sponsors "Ride for Cleaner Air" in which participants find people to pledge money for each mile they ride on a designated route; funds are then applied by ZPG for ecology action.

Ft. Worth **Fort Worth Bicycling Association,** 4440 Harlanwood Drive, Ft. Worth 76109. Weekend and long distance family rides.

Galveston **St. Louis Cycling Club,** c/o Robert C. Vierling, 5108 Ave. R, Galveston 77550. (LAW). Organized weekend "ride and eat" events. Strong Bikeways program.

Houston **Houston AYH Bicycle Club,** 1408 Richmond, 343, Houston 77006. (AYH). Long distance rides and extended bike hikes, family cycling events, social meetings second

Tuesday of month. Several safety events during year. Open to all over 17. Dues: $4.

Houston **Houston Bicycle Club,** c/o Don Wing, 285 Bryn Mawr, Houston 77001. (LAW). Long distance and family weekend rides. Social meetings. Open to all ages.

Lake Jackson **Lake Jackson Bicycle Club,** c/o Jess Bain, 114 Tulip Trail, Lake Jackson. New club scheduling long distance and family weekend bike hikes and tours. Picnics and social events. Open to all ages.

Lubbock **Lubbock Adult Bicycle Clubs,** c/o Mrs. Bonnie Cain, 3606 47th St., Lubbock 74913. Club divided into groups according to riding skills. Weekend long distance touring and short rides. Dues: $5. Sponsors Santa Fe-Los Angeles Fiesta Weekend on Labor Day. Newsletter. Many ride and eat events. Strong Bikeways program.

Lubbock **The Conspiracy,** c/o John Baird, 2613 29th St., Lubbock. Sponsored by Texas Tech University. Operates year round. Open to all students at Texas Tech and their friends. Very social. Many long distance and weekend rides.

Orange **Orange Bicycle Club,** 1413 N. 20th St., Orange 77630, or c/o David C. Harrison, 1500 Link Ave., Apt. 66, Orange 77630. (LAW).

Plano **Plano Bicycle Club,** c/o Park & Recreation Dept., Plano. Summer bike hikes for youngsters of all ages. Call 995-6531.

Richardson **Richardson Bicycle Touring Club,** c/o John Spencer, 745 Greenhaven, Richardson 75080. (LAW). Long distance tours and family weekend events. Open to all ages. Sponsors yearly three-day tour of Mexico. Source of local bike trail and map information. Monthly socials and rides. Adult and family oriented.

San Antonio **San Antonio Bicycle Touring Club,** c/o Elliot Weser, M.D., 301 Lamont, San Antonio 78209. New club of bike enthusiasts will plan weekend scenic tours and other family events. Strong Bikeways and bike trails program. Open to all ages.

UTAH

Ogden **Wasatch Wheelmen,** c/o Al Miller, 2435 Kiesel Ave.,

Ogden 84401. (ABL of A, LAW). Organized as racing club, but expanding to weekend adult cycle touring. Good source of information on regional bike tours. Dues: $2-$5.

Provo **Utah Bicycle Touring Society,** c/o Keith M. Cottam, 513 East 4380 North, Provo 84601. Organized long distance and weekend cycling events. Source of information on Utah bike touring. (LAW).

Salt Lake City **Bicycle West, Salt Lake,** and **Bicycle Awareness Committee,** c/o Warwick Craig Hansell, 2312 Walker Lane, Salt Lake City 84117. Long tours, family rides, races, social events and safety inspections. Dues: $3.50. Strong Bikeways and legislative support program. Club divided into two interest groups.

Salt Lake City **Salt Lake Wheelmen,** c/o Rodney J. Golsan, 1080 Euclid Ave., Salt Lake City. (ABL of A). Organized primarily to encourage bicycle racing, now expanding to cover organized weekend cycling tours for family groups and adults. Call 364-9347.

American Youth Hostels with overnight accommodations are found in **Park City, Alta** and **Venice.**

VERMONT

Bennington **Pedal People,** c/o Rev. Thomas D. Steffen, 201 Crescent Boulevard, Bennington 05201.

Brattleboro **Brattleboro Bicycle Club,** c/o Dave Mroczek, Red Circle, Inc., 60 Elliott Street, Brattleboro. New club will organize family weekend and weekday tours according to interests. Cooperates with Putney Bicycle Club in group activities.

Burlington **Green Mountain Bicycle Club,** c/o Keith Gardiner, Mills Ave., S. Burlington. Long distance tours, summer family rides, racing and cross-country events. Open to all ages. Recreation and fun oriented. Dues: $3.

Hanover **Connecticut River Athletic Club,** c/o Marty Hall, Box 25, Hartford 05047. Bicycle tours and family events, racing and competitive meetings during summer, cross-country skiing during winter. Open to all ages.

Johnson **Johnson State College Bicycle Club,** c/o Mike

238 • THE BIKE BOOK

Gallagher, Physical Education Department, Johnson. Summer family rides, cross-country cycling, racing. New club.

Putney **Putney Bicycle Touring & Ski Club,** c/o Robert H. Gray, West Hill Road, Putney. Family tour oriented, some competitive events.

American Youth Hostels with overnight accommodations are found in **Guilford, Lowell, Putney, Richford, Rochester, Warren** and **Waterbury Center.**

VIRGINIA

McLean **McLean TRAILS,** c/o Langley High School, 6520 Georgetown Pike, McLean 22101. Organization of youngsters and adult advisors who are interested in establishing Bikeways. Hold demonstration rides, etc. Strong emphasis on developing bike trails.

Newport News **Yorktown Riders,** c/o Frederick C. Grant, 399 Stanton Road, Newport News 23606. New club. Original interest was distance, but organized scenic and historic weekend tours for family groups are being set up. Call 595-1023. Open to all ages with reasonable skills.

Norfolk **Norfolk Bicycling Club,** c/o Martin Teeuwen, 1814 Hardwood Lane, Norfolk 23518. New club sponsoring family weekend rides to scenic areas. Accent on fun and physical fitness. Open to all ages. Holds combo rides with Newport News club.

Richmond **Richmond Area Bicycling Association,** c/o Mr. Bernard C. LaRoy, Rt. 2, Box 284, Midlothian 23113. Long distance rides, family tours, social meetings monthly, Oct.-March. Special emphasis on designation of Bikeways and bike routes. Dues: $2-$3. Broad range of activities for all ages and interests.

Roanoke **Roanoke Valley Bicycling Club,** c/o Gene Dixon, Dixon's Bicycling Center, 10003 Tazewell Ave., Roanoke. New club with schedule of adult and family weekend bike rides, long distance tours. Social meetings 1st Tuesday of month at above address.

American Youth Hostel with overnight accommodations is found in **Sperryville.**

WASHINGTON

Bellevue **Wheelsport Cycling Team,** 12020 Bellevue-Redmond Road, Bellevue 98004. (ABL of A). Races and competitive events only. Open to all ages. Dues: $3.

Edmonds **Olympic Cycling Club,** c/o Mountlake Terrace Parks & Recreation Pavillion, Edmonds. Or call Michele Church, 776-1927. Long distance and weekend touring, endurance rides, lectures and evening classes on cycling and bike touring. Racing and safety events.

Everett **Everett Bicycle Club,** c/o Joe Richer, Instructor, Everett High School, 24th & Colby, Everett. New club holding organized family bike rides on weekends. Open to all cyclists with reasonable skill.

Mercer Island **University of Washington Bicycle Club,** c/o Intermurals Athletic Department, U. of Washington, Mercer Island. Open to students and faculty of the University. Long distance and weekend and weekday rides. Emphasis on fun and fitness. Call Greg Rubstello, LA 2-2625.

Mercer Island **Cascade Cycling Club,** c/o Michael S. Quam, 3403 77th Ave., SE, Mercer Island 98040. (LAW). Organized long distance weekend rides, overnight bike hikes, social events, safety activities. Strong Bikeways program. Club involved in lobbying for bicycle facilities. Open to all ages with reasonable bike skills.

Mercer Island **Cyclemates,** c/o Miss Frances Call, English Dept., North Mercer Jr. High School, Mercer Island. This club, led by Miss Call, annually cycles from Washington State to Washington, D.C. to encourage physical fitness, good citizenship and "determination." Composed entirely of Jr. High and High School students. Group limited to about 15.

Mercer Island **Mountaineer Club Bicyclists,** c/o Mrs. Harry S. Slater, 2835 60th Ave., SE, Mercer Island 98040. (LAW).

Seattle **Boeing Employees Bicycle Club,** c/o Boeing Co. Recreation Unit. P.O. Box 3707, Seattle 98124. Organized weekend and long distance bike tours for employees, their families and friends.

Seattle **Seattle Bicycle Touring Society,** 1031 116th NE,

Bellevue, Seattle. Long distance (30-100 mile) rides, two weekend rides monthly, overnight bike hikes. Must be 16 or over. Dues: 50¢. Phone EA 2-1677.

American Youth Hostels with overnight accommodations are found in **Ashford** and **Spokane.**

WEST VIRGINIA

Charleston **Wonderful West Virginia Wheelmen,** c/o Bill Currey, P.O. Box 6368, 1105 West Washington St., Charleston 25302. New club, family and adult oriented. New season of organized rides. Open to all ages with reasonable skills.

Huntington **YMCA Bicycle Club,** c/o Youth Activities Director, YMCA, 935 10th Ave., Huntington 25701. Holds marathons and yearly long distance racing events. Open to all age groups.

St. Albans **St. Albans Bicycle Touring Club,** c/o John Turner, 309 MacCorkle Ave., SW, St. Albans 25177. New group with several organized family bicycle tours during the long cycling season. Phone: 727-2180.

Wheeling **Wheeling Park Bicycle Club,** c/o Earl Gaylor, General Manager, Wheeling Park Commission, Oglebay Park, Wheeling 26003. Full season of rides and family cycle tours in the planning stages over the area's numerous bicycle trails. Open to all ages.

American Youth Hostels with overnight accommodations are found in **Harper's Ferry** and **Morgantown.**

WISCONSIN

Fond du Lac **Junior Optimist Boy's Bicycle Club,** c/o Frederick Krueger, Juvenile Officer, Fond du Lac Police Department, City Hall, Fond du Lac. Organized for boys 10 to 14, the club teaches proper handling and repair of bikes, with several bicycle hikes and outings for youngsters, sponsored by the Noon Optimist Club.

Kenosha **Kenosha Road Runners,** 5006 7th Ave., Kenosha 53140. (LAW). Long distance rides, family weekend rides, social meetings. Open to all ages.

La Crosse **Tri-State Bicycle Touring Society,** 1025 Green

Bay, La Crosse, Wisconsin, (LAW). Long distance rides, family outings, races and other competitive events, overnight bike hikes. Safety instruction. Open to all over 18. Dues: $3.

Madison **The Two Tyred Wheelmen Hostel Club,** c/o Richard Ball, 1054 Sherman Ave., Madison 53703.

Manitowoc **Manitowoc Bicycling Club,** c/o Manitowoc Recreation Dept., City Hall Manitowoc, Wisc. Summer cycling activities for all ages. Phone 684-3331.

Milwaukee **Milwaukee Wheelmen, Inc.** 3926 W. Burleigh St., Milwaukee 53210. (AYH, ABL of A). Long distance rides, family rides, races and competitive events, social meetings, dances and picnics. Open to all ages.

Oshkosh **Oshkosh Bicycling Club,** c/o Neil Koeneman, Recreation Program Supervisor, Oshkosh Recreation Department, 215 S. Eagle St., Oshkosh. Summer bike tours and short rides for all ages, sponsored in cooperation with the police, City Hall, and the Breakfast Optimist Club.

Rice Lake **North Road Bicycle Club,** c/o W. R. Pearson, 307 W. Newton, Rice Lake 54868. (LAW, AYH). Open to all ages. Long distance and local touring (75%) and racing events (25%). "Only bicycle club in northern half of Wisconsin." Dues: $1 Monthly newsletter. Social meetings on the 1st of each month.

West Bend **West Bend Cyclists,** c/o Kent Eriksen. Long and short rides, all ages. Call 334-4487.

American Youth Hostels with overnight accommodations are found in **Cable, Colfax, Greendale, Kansasville, Tomah,** and **Two Rivers.**

WYOMING

American Youth Hostel with overnight accommodations is found in **Jackson Hole.**

CANADA

Windsor, Ontario **Windsor Bicycle Club,** 4776 Wyandotte St. E. Windsor 15, Ontario. Organized health and fitness rides for all age groups. Sponsored by the Canadian Institute of Better Health & Learning.

For information on Canadian bicycle clubs and touring information, write Kenneth V. Smith, Executive Director, Canadian Cycling Association, 333 Rover Road, Vanier, Ontario, Canada.

BICYCLE RACING ORGANIZATIONS

AMATEUR BICYCLE LEAGUE OF AMERICA
Pres.: Ernest Seubert
137 Brunswick Road
Cedar Grove, New Jersey 07009
Governing body of competitive cycling in America

ASSOCIATION CYCLISTE CANADIENNE
Mr. Kenneth V. Smith
BP. 2020 succursale D.
Ottawa, Canada (Ontario)
The governing body of competitive cycling in Canada

EASTERN CYCLING FEDERATION
Ernest McAdams
Doylestonian Apartments
403 So. Main Street
Doylestown, Pennsylvania 18901

EASTERN INTERCOLLEGIATE CYCLING
ASSOCIATION
William Lambart
3210 Byrd Place
Baldwin, New York 11510

FEDERACION MEXICANA DE CICLISMO
Co Confederation Sportive Mexicaine
Av. Juarez 64-311
Mexico DF, Mexique
The governing body of competitive cycling in Mexico

OLYMPIC CYCLING COMMITTEE/U.S. OLYMPIC
ASSOCIATION
Alfred E. Toefield
87-66 256 Street
Floral Park, L.I., New York

PROFESSIONAL RACING ORGANIZATION OF
      AMERICA
Pres.: Chris Van Zent
      340 Holly Street
      Denver, Colorado 80220
Affiliate of the Union Cycliste Internationale

STATE AND REGIONAL RACING ORGANIZATIONS WITHIN THE A.B.L. of A.

ILLINOIS CYCLING ASSOCIATION
      Mr. Nick Steder
      43 No. Illinois
      Villa Park, Illinois 60181

NO. CALIFORNIA CYCLING ASSOCIATION
      Mr. Joe Shaw
      P.O. Box 57
      Santa Rosa, California 95402

OHIO CYCLING ASSOCIATION
      Mr. Tim Silbereis
      2101 Schroyer Road
      Dayton, Ohio 45419

NEW ENGLAND CYCLING ASSOCIATION
      Mr. Bill Driscoll
      18 Oak Tree Lane
      Ashland, Mass. 01721

OREGON CYCLING ASSOCIATION
      Mr. Donald Curey
      5445 S.W. Childs Road
      Lake Grove, Oregon 97035

SOUTHERN CALIFORNIA CYCLING ASSOCIATION
      Robert Stinton
      4509 Briercrest Avenue
      Lakewood, California 90713

UNIONE CYCLISTE INTERNATIONALE
      Alfred Toefield
      87-66 256th Street
      Floral Park, L.I., New York

BIKE POLO

U.S. BICYCLE POLO ASSOCIATION

Carlos F. Concheso
P.O. Box 565
FDR Station
New York, New York 10022

Affiliate of U.S. Polo Association. Governs and regulates bicycle polo tournaments, helps organize chapters. Organized 1942, now has 18 chapters. For information, write to national headquarters listed above.

CHAPTERS IN:

Aiken, S. C.; Ardmore, Oklahoma; Harvard University (Cambridge, Mass.); U. of Pennsylvania, Philadelphia; Concord, N. H.; Waterville Valley, N. H.; Pebble Beach, Calif.; Newport Beach, Calif.; Venice Beach, Calif.; Locust Valley, L.I., New York; Westbury, L.I., New York; Cold Spring Harbor, New York; Southampton, L.I., New York; New York City, N. Y.; Wichita Falls, Texas; Pittsburgh, Pennsylvania; Chicago, Illinois.

CLUBS RELATED TO CYCLING

Antique Bicycle Club of America
Secretary, Roland C. Geist
260 West 260th Street
New York, New York

Bicycle Stamp Collectors
Section of Sports Philatelists International
Secretary, Robert M. Bruce
1457 Cleveland Road
Wooster, Ohio

Canadian Bicycle Hall of Fame
Exposition Grounds
Canadian National Exposition
Toronto, Ontario, CANADA

National Center to Honor Dr. Paul Dudley White
George S. Fichter
P.O. Box 1368
Homestead, Florida 33030

Veteran Wheelmens Association
Franklin Institute
Philadelphia, Pennsylvania

The Wheelmen (High Wheel Riders)
Robert McNair
32 Dartmouth Circle
Swarthmore, Pennsylvania 19081

Unicyclists Association of America
William Jenack
Jenack Cycles
67 Lion Lane
Westbury, New York

NOTE: If you have a question about whether a specific make of antique bicycle is part of a museum or private collection, contact: Don Adams, The Wheelmen Antique Bicycle Club, 214 Maywinn Road, Defiance, Ohio. For a list of old bicycle catalog reprints available, contact Clyde Nitz, R.F.D. #4, Box 237, Baltimore, Maryland 21227. If you wish to sell, trade or purchase an antique bicycle, The Wheelmen Newsletter, c/o Keith Larzelere, P.O. Box 38, Petersburg, Michigan 49270, has an antique bicycle "want ad" page.

AYH LOCAL COUNCIL OFFICES

ARIZONA:

Arizona State Council
4634 E. Lewis
Phoenix 85008

CALIFORNIA:

Golden Gate Council
625 Polk St.
San Francisco 94102

Los Angeles Council
318 N. La Brea Avenue
Los Angeles 90036

Northern California Council
P.O. Box 15649
Sacramento 95813

San Diego Council
7850 Eads Avenue
La Jolla 92037

San Gabriel Valley Council
215 West 1st St.
Claremont 91711

CONNECTICUT:
Fairfield County Council
P.O. Box 173
Southport 06490

Hartford Area Council
YMCA, 315 Pearl St.
Hartford 06103
New Haven Council
48 Howe St.
New Haven 06511

DISTRICT OF COLUMBIA:
Potomac Area Council
1501 16th St., N.W.
Washington, D.C. 20036

ILLINOIS:
Metropolitan Chicago Council
2210 N. Clark Street
Chicago 60614

MASSACHUSETTS:
Greater Boston Council
251 Harvard St.
Brookline 02146

MICHIGAN:
Metropolitan Detroit Council
14335 West McNichols Rd.
Detroit 48235

MINNESOTA:
Minnesota Council
P.O. Box 9511
Minneapolis 55440

MISSOURI:
Lewis & Clark Council
12201 Blue River Rd.
Kansas City 64146
Ozark Area Council AYH
2605 Big Bend
St. Louis 63143

NEBRASKA:
Nebraskaland Council
2740 A St.
Lincoln 65802

NEW YORK:
Metropolitan New York Council
535 West End Avenue
New York, N. Y. 10024
Syracuse Council
735 S. Beech St.
Syracuse 13210

OHIO:
Columbus Council
P.O. Box 3165
Columbus, Ohio 43210
Lake Erie Council
2000 Terminal Tower
Cleveland 44113
Lima Council
Box 173, Lima 45802
Toledo Area Council
5320 Fern Drive
Toledo 43613

PENNSYLVANIA:
Delaware Valley Council, AYH Inc.
4714 Old York Rd.
Philadelphia 19141
Pittsburgh Council
6300 Fifth Avenue
Pittsburgh 15232

WISCONSIN:
Wisconsin Council
P.O. Box 233
Hales Corners, 53130

SPECIAL INFORMATION SOURCES

The Bicycle Institute of America helps bicycling and bicyclists in an astonishing variety of ways. Supported by the manufacturers of American-made bicycles, they're admirably equipped to help anyone with almost any bicycle problem, from teachers who want safety films to show their classes to individuals who write in and ask, "How can I start a club (or a Bikeway) in my town?"

Among their regular publishing activities are the following:

Bikeways Newsletter, a free periodical covering nationwide developments as they happen, establishment of Bikeways and Bike Paths, new cycling legislation being proposed or enacted, and how-to-get-it-in-your-town information.

Safety publications are one of their biggest items; they range from how to teach safety on a bike, through safety tests (to be administered by a town's schools, police, or community groups like church, PTA, Scouts, etc.) for bicycles *and their riders*. A list of currently available materials will be sent free to anyone requesting it on an organizational letterhead.

Do-it-yourself-plans for building your own car-top bike carrying rack (free).

Bicycle movies: Some on safety, some on where to go and what to see; catalog of audio-visual materials sent free if requested on a letterhead by a teacher, or an organization or club leader.

List of all the American bike clubs—all the way from the 1-member one (he's really something) to the ones that have (literally) 30,000 members, listed by state and town, with clear information about how to get in touch, what amount of bicycle experience you need to feel at home with the rest of the group, plus affiliations, if any, with national groups.

To request any of the above, write to Bicycle Institute

of America, Department P, 122 East 42nd Street, New York, New York 10017.

They are also very versatile at problem-solving. If you have a question not covered by one of the publications or services listed, a letter to them will probably produce an answer you wouldn't have thought of by yourself, or a reference to a source (a person, a library of specialized facts, or a bike club) near you who might have the information you need or want.

* * *

American Youth Hostel publications cover a lot of territory. You do not need to be a member to order; however, membership does get you a discount on the *Atlas* and a free yearly copy of the *AYH Hostel Guide & Handbook*. To order the books you want, write to AYH National Headquarters, Dept. P., 20 W. 17th Street, New York, N.Y. 10011; indicate if you're an AYH member (give your pass number, if you are) enclose check or money order, including appropriate tax if you're a New York resident. *None of these books can be mailed abroad.*

AYH Hostel Guide & Handbook lists all the youth hostels in the U.S.; covers hosteling equipment, how to choose and care for your bike, how to get in condition for long trips, map sources, etc. Contains 135 down-to-earth pages about the basics of bicycling. Price: $1.20 to non-members, free with annual AYH memberships which run from $5 to $12.

AYH North American Bicycle Atlas by Warren Asa; 100 mapped rides that take from a week to a month, go coast-to-coast or circle a given special area, plus 62 shorter one-day or weekend rides. Covers the U.S., Mexico, Caribbean area, plus 6 Canadian provinces. It's recently published, but so good it's already in it's second edition. Costs $1.50 to AYH members, $1.95 to non-members, plus 50c to either if sent by mail, for postage and handling. (You can pick it up, as with

other AYH books and pamphlets, from your local
council, save the postage and the wait.)

Family Hosteling Manual costs only 70¢ postpaid, is
worth its weight in good suggestions about places to go,
how to carry a child *safely* on your bike, what to get
when the child is ready to bike under his own steam—
even a full Family Packing List suggesting what you may
all need on a typical trip. Also good for canoeing, skiing,
or hiking family trips.

Canada Handbook: Hostel locations and information,
70¢ postpaid.

European Camping & Caravaning International Guide
lists more than 3,000 campsites, bungalows, and motels;
describes facilities, suggests tour routes, advises best-
bets on equipment. Price: $4 plus $1.25 for postage west
of the Mississippi, 75¢ for postage east of Mississippi.

International Youth Hostels Handbooks: rules and
customs governing hostels in each country, listing of
hostels by city, map showing locations and access routes:

Volume I, Europe, $2.45 ($2.70 by air mail);

Volume II, Asia, Australasia, Africa, and the Ameri-
cas, $2.30 ($2.50 air mail).

Care and Use of the Derailleur Bicycle (free).

Other Bicycle Camping and Touring Information Services:

Bibliography of Bicycling and Bike Trails, compiled
by the United States Department of the Interior; lists all
references to bikes and bike trails from 1900 to 1970.
$3 from National Technical Information Service, Spring-
field, Virginia 22151.

Bicycle Touring Information on a swap basis. Clifford
L. Franz, Northern California Director of the League of
American Wheelmen, 36 Grand Avenue, San Mateo,
California 94401, offers free touring service in exchange
for *your* favorite local bicycle tour (mapped). You send
your excursion data, he sends you: (1) recommended

route on detailed section or state maps, (2) a list of campgrounds and/or motels along the route, (3) check-lists on what to take along for men or women, (4) a handy guide for camping from the bike, and (5) for added protection, a list of the names and addresses of LAW officers along the route you'll take who can be called upon for up-to-the-minute trail information. Specializing in cross-country routes, California tours, the Pacific coast and/or any part of the U.S. or Canada.

Potomac Trail Book by Robert Shosteck, foreword by Justice William O. Douglas; fine paperback with fold-out map of Potomac Valley Trails, descriptions and maps of 45 hikes, 8 circuit bicycle trips, 30 weekend camping areas, plus information on natural history, geology and local history of this famous area. $1.95 cover price; Potomac Books, 1518 K Street, N. W., Washington D.C. 20005.

Mail Order Dealers for Bicycling Equipment, Hiking and Camping Equipment Cyclists Might Be Interested in Owning:

AYH Equipment Catalog (free)
Metropolitan New York Council
American Youth Hostels, Inc.
535 West End Avenue, Dept. P
New York, New York 10024

L. L. Bean, Inc.
Freeport, Maine 04032

Big Wheel Ltd. Handbook of Cycling ($2.10)
Dept. P, 310 Holly Street, Denver, Colorado 80220

Blacks
930A Ford Street
Ogdensburg, New York 13669

Bruskin's Bicycle Center
1144 Chapel Street
New Haven, Connecticut 06511

Camp & Trail Outfitters
21 Park Place
New York, New York 10007

Gene Portuesi's CYCLE-PEDIA ($1)
311 N. Mitchell, Cadillac, Michigan 49601

Gerry, Inc.
Box 910, Boulder, Colorado 80302

Himalayan Pack Co.
807 Cannery Row
P.O. Box 950, Monterey, California 93940

Moor & Mountain
67 Main Street,
Concord, Massachusetts 01742

Montrose Bike Shop
2501 Honolulu Avenue
Montrose, California 91020

Ben Olken
Bicycle Exchange
3 Bow Street, Cambridge, Massachusetts 02138

Stuyvesant Bicycle—(Direct importers of many European specialties made to order for them exclusively—write explaining what you want and they'll send information.)
10 East 13th Street, Dept. P
New York, New York 10003

Wheel Goods (Bike Handbook & Catalog)
2737 Hennepin Street, Dept. P
Minneapolis, Minnesota 55408
(A handbook which covers many aspects of cycling,
    and includes a catalog; $2 postpaid)

BOOKS ON BICYCLE REPAIRING

Anybody's Bike Book by Tom Cuthbertson,
available by mail (paperback) for $3.25
from the Ten Speed Press, 2510 Bancroft Way,
Berkeley, California 94704.
It's the best written, so clear that literally anybody can
understand it, a delight to anyone at any level of bicycling
skill. Part by part, it explains your bike, how to cope
with its ills, predictable and unpredictable; separates
three-speed people from ten-speed people effortlessly,
tells each what to look for in language that makes you
understand and chuckle at the same time. (Many book-
stores and bike shops have it at $3, since no postage
needed.) So good it's going to come out in hard cover,
too.

The Bicycle Book (50¢)
Earth Action Council,
P.O. Box 24390
Los Angeles, California 90024

Written by students at the University of California;
covers buying, maintenance, theft prevention, and
reasons for the bike as transportation. Strictly for ten-
speed owners.

SPECIALIZED BIKE-RELATED INFORMATION
Rainwear for Cyclists
    Shaker Velo-Sport, 18734 Chagrin Boulevard,
    Cleveland, Ohio 44122
    Catalog of capes, leggings, spatees, hats, mudguards,
    over-trousers, and repair kits for these items.

Bike Racks for Cars
    Gerard Metal Craftsmen, Inc.
    151 West Rosencrans
    Gardena, California 90247

    JC-I Industries
    904 Nogales Street
    Industry, California 91744
    (Several models, including one for tandems)

    Plans for make-it-yourself racks, also from
    Bicycle Institute of America—see earlier listing.

Bike Racks for Parking
    Free list of current manufacturers,
    Bicycle Institute of America—see earlier listing.

    also

    J. E. Burk Co., U.S. #1, College Bridge,
    New Brunswick, N.J. 08901
    (Heavy duty racks)

    Everwear Park Equipment, Inc.,
    36535 W. Highway 16,
    P.O. Box 291, Oconomowoc, Wisconsin 53066
    (Heavy-duty racks)

Bicycle Racing Handbook
    A Handbook on Bicycle Tracks & Cycle Racing (free)
    Huffman Manufacturing Company
    P.O. Box 1036, Dept. P, Dayton, Ohio 45401

Bicycle Route Signs (Manufacturers)
    Vinyl Corporation of America, Department P
    600 N. Irwin Street, Dayton, Ohio 45403, or
    1921 N. Harlem Avenue, Chicago, Illinois 60635, or
    98-69 Queens Boulevard, New York, N.Y. 11374

Official Bike Route and Bike Crossing Signs, directional arrows, or made-to-order signs. Only U.S. commercial manufacturer. Specification catalog if requested on letterhead, or from individual working on behalf of organized group.

Bicycle Ecology Buttons
Hewig-Marvic Company, Dept. P
861 Manhattan Avenue, Brooklyn, New York 1122

Design your own or order ones you've seen and liked, with help of catalog "Buttons Say It Best." (Free)

Bicycling in the School Fitness Program
School Physical Ed. instructor, or accredited group leaders, write for the book *Cycling in the School Fitness Program,* American Association for Health, Physical Education & Recreation, Dept. P., 1201 16th Street, N.W., Washington, D.C.

General Cycling Magazines and other Publications
BICYCLING! Magazine
H.M. Leete & Co., Publishing
Dept. P, 256 Sutter Street
San Francisco, California, 94108

Published 12 times a year, subscription $6 in U.S., $7 elsewhere. Articles, pictures, features and columns of interest to the sport or recreational cyclist. America's only exclusive bicycling magazine. Even their ads are informative.

Cycling Touring, put out by the
Cyclists' Touring Club
Cotterell House
69 Meadrow, Dept. P
Godalming, Surrey, England

6 yearly issues, for the current equivalent of 12 shillings, sixpence (probably around $2 at the end of 1971); highly useful if you plan to cycle abroad.

Illinois Rules of the Road, 80 page booklet that uses both language and color to fullest advantage to make the rules of the road clear to youngsters, or anyone with no driving experience, and thus to teach safe bicycling in traffic situations. Illinois residents only, write to the Office of the Secretary of State, Springfield, Illinois 62706. (This booklet cannot by statute, be offered either free or for sale to anyone else, but Illinois urges other states and cities to publish one like it covering their own local rules, and can offer officials some aid in doing so. Write on letterhead to William H. Colvin, Supervisor, Research & Development Division, Office of the Secretary of State, Springfield, Illinois 62706.)

And, Finally, A Bicyclist's Bookstore

You reach them by mail, and their name is *Books About Bicycling.* Write Post Office Box 208, Nevada City, California, for their free folder. Their list fascinated me, and I think it will fascinate you too; it includes categories like racing, history, maintenance, fiction, and children's books, all related to bicycling or about it directly. But that doesn't explain the really incredible range. They offer for example, the drawings of Edward Gorey in a book I'm sure would be useless but delicious, *The Epiplectic Bicycle* ("It can be read anywhere from a minute and a half to five hours and is delightful, instructive and peculiar. #1-23, $3.00") or a book I'm told is marvelous and hard-to-come-by, *The Bicycle In Love, Life, War, and Literature,* by Seamus McGonagle (#1-18, $4.95). Surely they could get you the Aerobics books by Dr. Cooper, too, and things like that, if you wish.

THE THANK-YOU PAGE

Bike people really are a special breed—enthusiasts almost to a man, but alert to potential dangers arising from innocence or mistaken ideas, quick to answer an honest question with an honest, unforgettable "No, if you did it that way you'd break something—either your bike or your leg." It is a privilege to be thanking such wise and helpful people as:

Judah Apsell	Jim McIntyre
Francis Bollag	Bill Parish
Sal Corso, of	Sam Shayon
Stuyvesant Bicycle Shop	Dr. Paul Dudley White (and
Eric Hodgins	Mrs. Thayer, his secretary)
Earle Ludgin	Elliot Winick
(and his horse, of course)	

Without them, this book would have been infinitely less use to you and less fun for me. Special three-star thanks go to Jim Hayes and Ralph Hanneman of the Bicycle Institute of America, and Bill Nelson of the National Board of American Youth Hostels (he's not only Travel Director, he conducts their leadership courses), who read the manuscript, red-pencil poised for inaccuracies. My goofs and wrong-headed opinions are my own, of course — but some of the best "dope" here came from these three patient gentlemen.

Since I hate long lists of thank-yous at the front of other books, we've put this here, where we both have a better idea what I'm thanking these people for; the lovely thing about biking is that the people you meet and ask will probably be as helpful to you, too.

BIBS MCINTYRE

INDEX

(Page numbers italicized indicate illustrations)